D1422445

The Pocket Guide to
MILITARY
AIRCRAFT
and THE WORLD'S AIRFORCES

First published in Great Britain in 2001
by Hamlyn, a division of Octopus Publishing Group Ltd

This edition published in 2003 by Bounty Books,
a division of Octopus Publishing Group Ltd
2-4 Heron Quays, London E14 4JP

ISBN 0 7537 0821 3

A CIP catalogue record for this book is available from the British Library

Printed and bound in China

PICTURE ACKNOWLEDGEMENTS

All artwork and photographs © copyright Aerospace Publishing
Limited, except the following:
page 14: Paul Eden; 19: BAE Systems; 25: McDonnell Douglas
Helicopters; 28: Boeing; 32: Boeing; 35: McDonnell Douglas;
36: Boeing; 38: Boeing; 43: Boeing; 44: Boeing; 47: British
Aerospace; 55: Peter Steinemann (via Aerospace Publishing);
57: François Robineau/Dassault/Aviaplans; 59: François
Robineau/Dassault/Aviaplans; 61: François Robineau/
Dassault/Aviaplans; 65: Eurocopter/MP Guillot, Marine
Nationale; 69: Eurocopter/Gérôme Deulin; 71: British
Aerospace; 77: Airshots; 87: Luca la Cavera; 89: USAF;
95: Lockheed Martin; 97: Anton Roels; 99: Lockheed Martin;
100: Lockheed Martin; 101: Lockheed Martin; 103: USAF;
107: Gert Kromhout; 109: Boeing; 111: McDonnell Douglas
Helicopters; 117: via Yefim Gordon; 119: Yefim Gordon;
121: Yefim Gordon; 122: Gerard Keysper (via Soph Moeng);
126: Sergei Skrynnikov; 130 Katsuhiko Tokunaga/NH
Industries; 133: Northrop Grumman; 137: Daimler Benz
Aerospace; 147: Sikorsky; 150: Sergei Sergeyev;
153: Khian Noush; 155: Vaclac Semecek; 157: via Yefim
Gordon; 159: Soph Moeng; 161: Yefim Gordon; 163: Matra
BAe Dynamics (via Soph Moeng); 165: Jelle Sjoerdsma

The Pocket Guide to
MILITARY
AIRCRAFT
and THE WORLD'S AIRFORCES

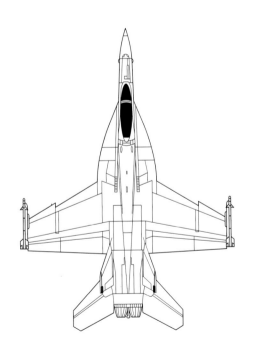

CONTENTS:

Air forces section 166

AERMACCHI MB-339

Following prolonged studies Aermacchi flew the prototype MB-339 trainer on 12 August 1976. The type was developed from the company's previous successful MB-326 design; the chief modification compared with the MB-326 was the redesign of the tandem cockpits to give the instructor a good view ahead over the helmet of the pupil. Directional stability was maintained by a larger fin and canted ventral fins, and standard equipment included the Viper Mk 632 engine and Mk 10F zero/zero seat. The first of 100 MB-339A trainers for the Italian air force (AMI) was handed over on 8 August 1979. Other AMI variants include the MB-339PAN of the *Frecce Tricolori* aerobatic team and the MB-339RM calibration aircraft. In addition, aircraft generally similar to MB-339A standard have been widely exported to customers which include Argentina, Dubai, Ghana, Malaysia, Nigeria, Peru and the UAE. Aermacchi also produced the MB-339B, with upgraded attack capabilities, but this was dropped in favour of the even more advanced MB-339C. Variants of the MB-339C include the MB-339CD for advanced/fighter lead-in training and its MB-339FD export equivalent, with a fully digital cockpit, and the MB-339CB which has been delivered to New Zealand. Eritrea received six MB-339E non-digital variants of the MB-339C. Developed in 1995 from an MB-339A, the MB-339AM is a variant specialised for anti-ship attack and armed with two Marte Mk 2A missiles. On 30 May 1980 the prototype MB-339K Veltro 2 entered flight testing. The forward fuselage was broadly similar to that of the MB-326K with a single-seat cockpit and two 30-mm guns below. Advanced avionics, comprehensive weapons compatibility and a rugged airframe failed to tempt customers, however, and the variant was quietly dropped.

Specification: Aermacchi MB-339C
Origin: Italy
Type: basic and advanced trainer with weapons training and light attack capabilities
Armament: up to 4,000 lb (1814 kg) of external stores, including Mk 80 series bombs up to 1,000 lb (454 kg), cannon or machine-gun pods, pods containing rockets of various calibre, MATRA R550 Magic 2 or AIM-9L/P AAMs
Powerplant: one Piaggio-built Rolls-Royce (Bristol Siddeley) Viper Mk 680-43 turbojet rated at 4,400 lb st (19.57 kN)
Performance: maximum level speed 508 mph (817 km/h); combat radius 311 miles (500 km) on a hi-lo-hi attack mission with four Mk 82 bombs and two drop tanks
Weights: empty equipped 7,562 lb (3430 kg), maximum take-off 14,000 lb (6350 kg)
Dimensions: wing span 36 ft 9¾ in (10.86 m) over tip tanks; length 36 ft 10½ in (11.24 m); height 13 ft 1¾ in (3.99 m); wing area 207.74 sq ft (19.30 m²)

Aermacchi MB-339C

AERO L-39 ALBATROS

Following its great success with the L-29 Delfin, the Aero team at Vodochody worked closely with the Soviet Union in planning the L-39 second-generation trainer, which first flew on 4 November 1968. Entering service in 1974, the L-39 is especially noted for its robust and fuel-efficient Soviet turbofan engine. The cockpits are slightly staggered and contain zero height/93 mph (150 km/h) rocket-assisted ejection seats. Fuel is housed in five rubber cells in the fuselage and small non-jettisonable tiptanks. Double-slotted flaps are fitted, and the levered-suspension main gears are stressed for impact at high rates of descent. By 2000, in excess of 2,800 L-39s of all versions had been built. Variants include the L-39V target tug, L-39ZA ground-attack/reconnaissance, L-39ZO weapons trainer and L-39MS versions. This latter was developed as the L-59, a far more capable machine with a more powerful engine, strengthened airframe and upgraded avionics. As well as the Czech and Slovak air forces, the L-59 has also been delivered to the Egyptian and Tunisian air arms. The L-59 in turn was further developed into the even more capable L-159. This machine, flown as a single-seater from the front cockpit in the same manner as the L-39ZA, is a dedicated fighter lead-in trainer and light-attack platform. Its 6,300-lb st (28.02-kN) AlliedSignal ITEC F124-GA-100 turbofan bestows a performance between 30 and 100 per cent better than that of the L-39C. Avionics include an EFIS cockpit and HOTAS controls and HUD, while the pilot sits on a zero/zero ejection seat and the aircraft carries additional internal fuel. A comprehensive weapons compatibility is included. The 72 aircraft on order for the Czech air force are set to be key warplanes within that country's inventory.

Specification: Aero L-39 Albatros
Origin: Czech Republic
Type: armed trainer and light attack/reconnaissance aircraft
Armament: underfuselage centreline point for podded 23-mm GSh-23 twin-barrelled cannon with 180 rounds, plus up to 2,204 lb (1000 kg) of weapons on four underwing pylons including 1,102 lb (500–kg) bombs, 57-mm and 130-mm rocket pods, gun pods and two drop tanks
Powerplant: one ZMDB Progress DV-2 turbofan rated at 4,850 lb st (21.57 kN)
Performance: maximum level speed 'clean' at 16,405 ft (5000 m) 544 mph (876 km/h); ferry range at 29,530 ft (9000 m) 932 miles (1500 km) with drop tanks
Weights: empty equipped 9,149 lb (4150 kg); maximum take-off 12,566 lb (5700 kg) with external stores from a grass strip
Dimensions: wing span 31 ft 3½ in (9.54 m); length 40 ft 0¼ in (12.20 m); height 15 ft 7¾ in (4.77 m); wing area 202.37 sq ft (18.8 m²)

Aero L-39C Albatros

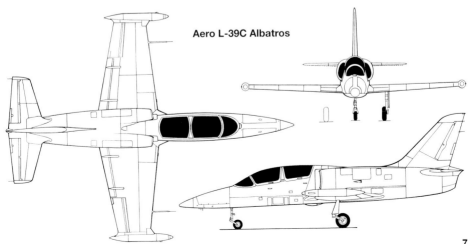

AGUSTA A 129 MANGUSTA

Conceived in response to an Italian army requirement of the mid-1970s, the A 129 Mangusta (Mongoose) was the first dedicated attack helicopter to be designed, built and deployed by a European country. It was also the first in the world to be built around an advanced MIL-STD 1553B digital databus, which allows a high degree of automation, considerably reducing the crew workload. The first A 129 prototype made its official maiden flight on 15 September 1983 at Cascina Costa (although it had already taken to the air twice before on 11 and 13 September). The original Italian requirement had been for 100 Mangustas in distinct anti-tank and scout versions, but as the threat of all-out war in Europe receded, the final order was cut back to 60 A 129s. In the event, a total of 45 A 129s was delivered to AVES (*Aviazione Escercito* – Italian army aviation) between October 1990 and 1992, when production was stopped. Funding problems, and changing operational needs, forced the Italian army to re-evaluate its requirement for dedicated anti-tank helicopters. The need for a more multi-role helicopter was reinforced when Mangustas were deployed on UN peacekeeping duties to Somalia between 1992 and 1994. The Mangusta's primary TOW missile armament left it inflexible where combat against tanks was not a priority mission. Hence, Agusta has developed the Mangusta International, which features an undernose 20-mm cannon, uprated 1,362-shp (1016-kW) AlliedSignal LHTEC CTS800-2 engines and a five-bladed main rotor system. This aircraft also retains the HeliTOW target acquisition system, making it a highly versatile combat helicopter. The Italian army is looking to receive the balance of its Mangusta order in International form, albeit with Rolls-Royce engines, and the International is being actively marketed for export.

Specification: Agusta A 129 Mangusta
Origin: Italy
Type: two-seat lightweight anti-tank and scout helicopter
Armament: maximum weapon load of 2,646 lb (1200 kg), including up to eight TOW-2A anti-tank missiles, 52 2.75-in (70–mm) rockets or larger 3.19-in (81-mm) SNIA-BPD Medusa rockets or underwing 0.5-in (12.7-mm) gun pods
Powerplant: two Piaggio (Rolls-Royce) Gem 2-2 Mk 1004D turboshaft engines, each rated at 825 shp (615 kW)
Performance: maximum speed 161 mph (259 km/h) at sea level; maximum rate of climb at sea level 2000 ft (610 m) per minute; radius 62 miles (100 km) for a 90–minute patrol
Weights: empty 5,575 lb (2529 kg); maximum take-off 9,039 lb (4100 kg)
Dimensions: main rotor diameter 39 ft 0½ in (11.90 m); wingspan 10 ft 6 in (3.20 m); length overall 46 ft 10½ in (14.29 m) with rotors turning; main rotor disc area 1,197.20 sq ft (111.22 m²)

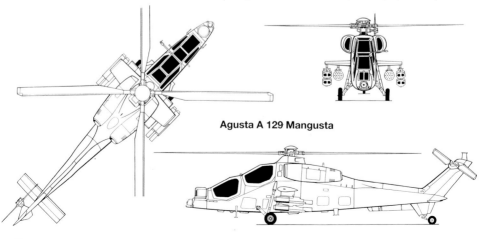

Agusta A 129 Mangusta

AIDC F-CK-1 CHING-KUO

Taiwan's ambitious programme to develop an advanced fighter to replace its fleet of F-5s and F-104s began in 1982, after the US government placed an embargo on the sale of the Northrop F-20 and any comparable fighter. The same restrictions were not placed on technical assistance, however, and US aerospace companies have collaborated closely with AIDC to develop an indigenous fighter and weapons system. Assistance has been provided by General Dynamics (airframe), Garrett (propulsion), Westinghouse (radar) and a Smiths Industries-led team (avionics). The aircraft is equipped with a Golden Dragon GD-53 multi-mode pulse-Doppler radar based on the AN/APG-67(V) developed for the F-20, but incorporating some technology from the Westinghouse AN/APG-66 unit used by the F-16A. Of mostly conventional all-metal construction, the Ching-Kuo is of conventional configuration, albeit with wing/fuselage blending. The pilot sits on a Martin-Baker Mk 12 ejection seat and the pressurised cockpit is fitted with a sidestick controller, a wide-angle HUD, and three multi-function look-down displays. The first prototype made its maiden flight on 28 May 1989, and on 10 February 1994, the Republic of China Air Force's No7 Squadron publicly unveiled its aircraft, which included two production single-seaters (designated F-CK-1A) and two production two-seater conversion trainers (F-CK-1B). In March 1993, the country's legislature announced that procurement would be limited to only 130 aircraft, to equip two, instead of the planned four, wings. The final two aircraft were delivered in 2000. AIDC seeks government approval to offer a downgraded version of the two-seater Ching Kuo for export as a lead-in/advanced fighter trainer. This would not retain radar, internal gun or ECM systems.

Specification: AIDC F-CK-1A Ching-Kuo
Origin: Taiwan
Type: single-seat multi-role fighter
Armament: one internal 20-mm M61A1 cannon; weapons include Mk 80-series bombs, LGBs, cluster munitions, AIM-9P AAMs and indigenous IR-homing Tien Chien I (Sky Sword), radar-homing Sky Sword II AAMs or three Hsiung Feng II (Male Bee II) anti-ship missiles
Powerplant: two ITEC (Garrett/ AIDC) TFE-1042-70 (F125) turbofans each rated at 6,060 lb st (26.80 kN) dry and 9,460 lb st (42.08 kN) with afterburning
Performance: maximum level speed 'clean' at 36,000 ft (10975 m) more than 792 mph (1275 km/h); maximum rate of climb at sea level 50,000 ft (15240 m) per minute
Weights: empty operating 14,300 lb (6486 kg); maximum take-off 27,000 lb (12247 kg)
Dimensions: wing span over wingtip missile rails 28 ft 0 in (8.53 m); length including probe 46 ft 7½ in (14.21 m); height 15 ft 3 in (4.65 m); wing area 261.1 sq ft (24.26 m²)

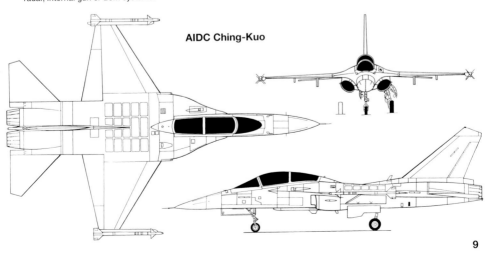

AIDC Ching-Kuo

AIRTECH CN.235

Following the success of their C.212 Aviocar, CASA of Spain and IPTN of Indonesia joined forces on a 50/50 basis to create Airtech specifically for the design and development of a larger and more efficient pressurised transport for both civil and military use. Work on the resulting CN.235 began in 1980, and prototypes were simultaneously constructed in the partner countries. The Spanish prototype made its maiden flight on 11 November 1983; the Indonesian prototype followed suit on 30 December 1983. Deliveries from both production lines began in December 1986 and February 1987 respectively. In January 1990 a licence was signed with TAI for assembly and later construction of 50 aircraft in Turkey. The main variants have been the CN.235 Series 10 initial model with two 1,700-shp (1268-kW) CT7-7As; the Spanish-built CN.235 Series 100 and Indonesian-built CN.235 Series 110 improved model with CT7-9Cs; the CN.235 Series 200 and CN.235 Series 220 with structural strengthening and aerodynamic refinements; the Indonesian-developed CN.235 Series 330 Phoenix aimed at an RAAF requirement; the CN.235 M military transport; the Spanish-built CN.235 MP Persuader and the Indonesian-built CN.235 MPA maritime patrol types with advanced avionics and six underwing hardpoints; and the CN.235 QC quick-change cargo/passenger transport. Military sales have been brisk, and the type currently serves with air forces in some 20 countries. In 1997, CASA began development of the stretched CN.295. Powered by 2,645-hp (1972-kW) Pratt & Whitney Canada PW127G turboprops and fitted with a full EFIS cockpit, this has a payload some 50 per cent greater than that of the CN.235, with the capacity to carry 78 troops. The first CN.295 flew on 28 November 1997, and the first of nine production machines for the Spanish air force will enter service in 2004.

Specification: Airtech CN.235 M Series 100

Origin: Indonesia/Spain

Type: short-range medium utility transport

Payload: maximum payload 13,227 lb (6600 kg); up to 48 troops, or 24 litters plus four attendants for casevac role

Armament: maritime patrol variant armed with two AM 39 Exocet anti-ship missiles

Powerplant: two General Electric CT7-9C turboprops each flat-rated at 1,750 shp (1305 kW) without automatic power reserve or 1,870 shp (1394.5 kW) with automatic power reserve

Performance: maximum speed 276 mph (445 km/h) at sea level; range 2,706 miles (4355 km) with a payload of 7,936 lb (3600 kg) or 932 miles (1501 km) with maximum payload

Weights: operating empty 19,400 lb (8800 kg); maximum take-off 36,376 lb (16500 kg)

Dimensions: wing span 84 ft 8 in (25.81 m); length 70 ft 2½ in (21.35 m); height 26 ft 10 in (8.18 m); wing area 636.17 sq ft (59.10 m²)

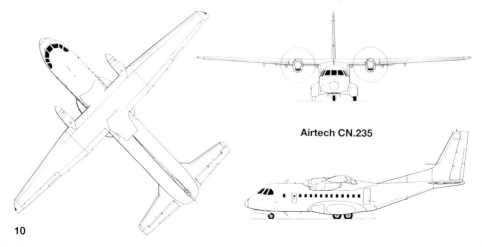

Airtech CN.235

AMX INTERNATIONAL AMX

In April 1978, Aeritalia and Aermacchi combined their resources to meet requirements from the Italian air force (AMI) for an advanced multi-purpose strike/reconnaissance aircraft. The programme received extra impetus in 1980 when it was joined by Brazil, with EMBRAER chosen as the industrial partner. Procurement was signed initially for 79 AMXs for Brazil and 187 for Italy, plus six prototypes. The type's Rolls-Royce Spey Mk 807 turbofan powerplant was built under licence. The initial AMX flew in May 1984. Design features include HOTAS, INS, head-up and head-down displays, digital databus, active and passive ECM, and provision for air-to-air refuelling. By mid-1998, programme totals had increased to 332 aircraft, including 66 two-seat AMX-Ts (known in Brazil as A-1Bs). In these variants, a fuel bay behind the original cockpit is replaced by a second Martin-Baker Mk 10L ejection seat, causing some reduction in range. The first of three AMX-T prototypes initially flew in Italy on 14 March 1990, although funding problems delayed first flight of the Brazilian two-seat prototype until 14 August 1991. Radar-equipped versions of the AMX-T have also been considered in Brazil and Italy for enhanced all-weather, ECR and maritime strike roles, and Italian trials with the Exocet anti-ship missile proved successful. In the reconnaissance role, the AMX can either carry external photo or IR pods, or can be equipped with any one of three sensor pallets for internal carriage in the forward fuselage. The first operational AMI squadron received its first AMX on 7 November 1989. The first Brazilian A-1 unit began to receive its aircraft on 17 October 1989. In 1998 Venezuela announced its intention to purchase an advanced AMX-ATA variant and further prospects include a variant that is powered by a 13,500-lb st (60-kN) non-afterburning version of the Eurofighter's EJ200 turbofan.

Specification: AMX International AMX
Origin: Brazil/Italy
Type: single-seat close air support and reconnaissance aircraft
Armament: one internal 20-mm M61A1 cannon (or two internal 30-mm DEFA 554 cannon in Brazilian aircraft) plus a maximum ordnance load of 8,377 lb (3800 kg)
Powerplant: one Fiat/Piaggio/Alfa Romeo Avio/CELMA-built Rolls-Royce Spey RB.168 Mk 807 turbofan rated at 11,030 lb st (49.06 kN)
Performance: maximum level speed 'clean' at 36,000 ft (10975 m) 568 mph (914 km/h); maximum rate of climb at sea level 10,250 ft (3124 m) per minute; service ceiling 42,650 ft (13000 m); combat radius 345 miles (556 km) on a lo-lo-lo or 553 miles (889 km) on a hi-lo-hi attack mission with a 2,000-lb (907-kg) warload
Weights: operating empty 14,771 lb (6700 kg); maximum take-off 28,660 lb (13000 kg)
Dimensions: wing span 32 ft 9¾ in (10.00 m) over wingtip AAMs; length 44 ft 6½ in (13.58 m); height 15 ft¼ in (4.576 m); wing area 226.05 sq ft (21.00 m²)

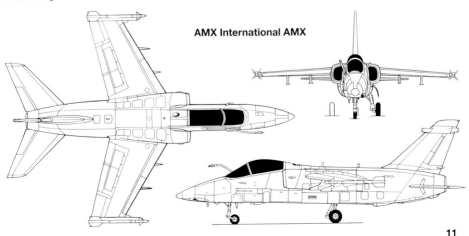

AMX International AMX

ANTONOV An-12 'CUB'

O.K. Antonov's design bureau at Kiev built its first large military transport in 1955 with the twin-turboprop An-8 becoming a standard type. From this was derived the civil An-10 with four engines and a pressurised fuselage, from which in turn came the mass-produced An-12 military transport with full-width rear loading doors. Oddly, most lack an integral ramp for vehicles, instead using a ramp carried separately and latched into position after the doors have been opened upwards on each side. Moreover, the main fuselage is unpressurised, though most versions have a pressurised passenger compartment to the rear of the pressurised flight deck. From its entry into service in 1959, the An-12 became the most important transport in Soviet military service. Indeed, although replacement by the Ilyushin Il-76 began in 1974, some 560 An-12s, out of 800 delivered, were still in front-line duty as transports in 1986. The majority of these aircraft were An-12B machines, this variant becoming the standard transport in Soviet service from 1963. Rebuilds for a multitude of special roles have been legion. These have included Elint (electronic intelligence) machines, known to NATO as 'Cub-B'. The An-12PP 'Cub-C' is an even more extensive EW rebuild with equipment housed in large nose/tail/canoe radomes conferring a significant active jamming capability. Construction of the An-12 in the USSR ceased in 1973, but unlicensed production of the aircraft in the People's Republic of China as the Shaanxi Y-8 is likely to have continued into the 21st century. Approximately 250 'Cub' transports serve with the Russian air forces; smaller numbers fulfil intelligence gathering roles with the AV-MF (Russian naval aviation). 'Cubs' also serve with CIS air arms in Belarus, Kazakhstan, Turkmenistan, Ukraine and Uzbekistan. Outside the CIS, An-12s are likely to remain in active service in Angola, Ethiopia, Iraq and Yemen.

Specification: Antonov An-12BP 'Cub-A'
Origin: USSR
Type: six-crew medium transport
Payload: maximum payload 44,092 lb (20000 kg); accommodation for 100 paratroops, these can be dispatched in about 45 seconds with the rear doors folded upward
Armament: two 23-mm NR-23 cannon in tail turret
Powerplant: four ZMDB Progress (Ivchyenko) AI-20K turboprops each rated at 4,000 ehp (2983 kW)
Performance: maximum speed 'clean' at optimum altitude 482 mph (777 km/h); maximum cruising speed at optimum altitude 416 mph (670 km/h); service ceiling 34,450 ft (10500 m); range 4,225 miles (6800 km) with maximum fuel and 2,236 miles (3600 km) with maximum payload
Weights: empty 61,728 lb (2800 kg); maximum take-off 134,480 lb (61000 kg)
Dimensions: wing span 124 ft 8 in (38.0 m); length 108 ft 7¼ in (33.1 m); height 34 ft 6½ in (10.53 m); wing area 1,310.01 sq ft (121.7 m²)

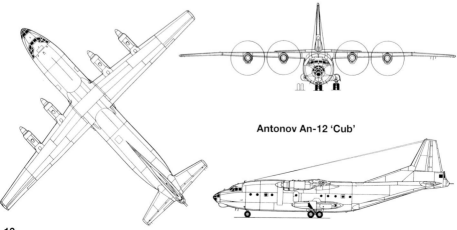

Antonov An-12 'Cub'

ANTONOV An-26 'CURL' SERIES

First seen in 1969, the Antonov An-26 'Curl-A' was the standard short-range Soviet tactical transport during the latter half of the Cold War. Developed from the previous An-24 design, it was first Soviet military transport aircraft to have a fully pressurised cargo hold. Production ended in 1985 after about 1,410 An-26s had been built, most of them for military operators. The type remains in widespread use. Small numbers of An-26s were converted as An-26RTR 'Curl-B' Elint/Sigint/EW platforms and have a profusion of swept blade antennas above and below the cabin. Painted as standard transports and often operating from the same bases, these aircraft remain in use with the Russian air force. Former East German 'special duties' An-26 aircraft were designated An-26ST. Similarly modified An-26 aircraft are also in Czech service. An unusually active combat role was undertaken by An-26s in Angola and Mozambique, where underfuselage bomb racks were fitted for the counter-insurgency role. Some An-26s, most notably those used in Afghanistan, also carried pylon-mounted chaff/flare dispensers. A fire-fighting version of the An-26 has also been developed as the An-26P, with tanks along the fuselage under the wing. Two other special-purpose types built as conversions are the An-26BRL for research into the nature of pack ice, and the An-26L navaid calibration type. Two major variants have been developed from the An-26. The An-30 'Clank' features a redesigned nose section with extensive glazing. Serving in the dedicated photographic and survey roles, it has only been built in small numbers. The An-32 'Cline' replaced the An-26 in production from 1977. It features Ivchyenko AI–20D Series 5 turboprops each rated at 5,043 ehp (3760 kW). These engines are mounted above the wing to give greater clearance for the increased-diameter propellers. The Indian air force operates An-32s under the local name 'Sutlej'.

Specification: Antonov An-26B 'Curl-A'
Origin: USSR
Type: five-crew light tactical transport aircraft
Payload: maximum payload 12,125 lb (5500 kg); (all An-26 versions) interior can be reconfigured for transport role with tip-up seats along the cabin sides to seat 38-40 passengers, or for casevac with 24 litters in the An-26M variant; parachute static line points fitted as standard
Powerplant: two ZMDB Progress (Ivchyenko) AI-24VT turboprops each rated at 2,820 ehp (2103 kW) and one Soyuz (Tumanskii) RU-19A-300 turbojet rated at 1,765 lb st (7.85 kN)
Performance: maximum level speed at 16,405 ft (5000 m) 336 mph (540 km/h); initial climb rate 1,575 ft (480 m) per minute; service ceiling 24,605 ft (7500 m); range 683 miles (1100 km) with maximum payload
Weights: empty 33,957 llb (15400 kg); maximum take-off 53,790 lb (24400 kg)
Dimensions: wing span 95 ft 9½ in (29.20 m); length 78 ft 1 in (23.80 m), height 28 ft 1½ in (8.58 m); wing area 807.1 sq ft (74.98 m²)

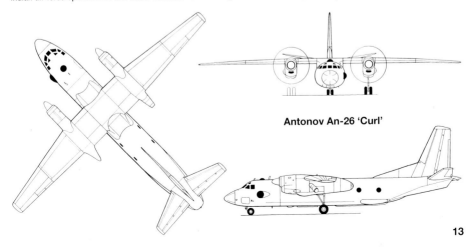

Antonov An-26 'Curl'

ANTONOV An-70

The An-70 is the result of a programme initiated in 1975 to create a successor to the An-12. The An-70 has typical airlifter layout, but has the distinction of being the first aircraft to fly with an all-propfan powerplant. Each D-27 engine drives a contra-rotating assembly of 14 scimitar-type blades (eight and six in the front and rear propellers respectively). Some 28 per cent of the airframe is made of composite materials, and other advanced features include a fly-by-wire control system. The An-70's pressurised hold has an inbuilt cargo-handling system that can be outfitted with seats for 300 troops or racks for 206 litters as alternatives to freight and/or vehicles or paratroops. The An-70 can air-drop individual items up to a limit of 44,092 lb (20000 kg). The hold's sill height can be varied to facilitate the loading and unloading of freight to and from vehicles of different truckbed heights. The An-70 is slightly larger than the proposed European Airbus A400M (for which requirement the An-70 has been recommended by Germany) but considerably smaller than the Boeing C-17 Globemaster III. The prototype An-70 made its first flight on 16 December 1994, but was lost on 10 February of the following year following an in-flight collision with its An-72 chaseplane. A second An-70 prototype that made its maiden flight on 24 April 1997 and was delivered for official trials in mid-1998. This too suffered serious damage in a crash-landing on 27 January 2001. While variants including commercial and export military airlifters have been proposed, the An-70 programme was struggling due to a general lack of funding and orders in 2000. It seems inevitable that this excellent aircraft will eventually gain limited orders, but is unlikely to achieve the success that it deserves.

Specification: Antonov An-70
Origin: Ukraine
Type: four-crew STOL medium transport
Payload: maximum payload 103,615 lb (47000 kg); standard payload from unpaved runway 66,138 lb (30000 kg); freight carried in standard rigid or flexible pallets; seating for 300 troops or 206 stretchers
Powerplant: four ZMKB Progress (Ivchyenko) D-27 propfan engines each rated at 13,800 shp (10290 kW)
Performance: (estimated) maximum speed 497 mph (897 km/h); cruising speed 466 mph (750 km/h) at between 29,520 and 39,380 ft (9000 and 12000 m); range 901 miles (1450 km) with a 77,161-lb (25000-kg) payload after a short take-off of 3,005 ft (915 m)
Weight: empty 160,500 lb (72800 kg); maximum take-off 286,596 lb (130000 kg)
Dimensions: wing span 144 ft 6 in (44.06 m); length 133 ft 7 in (40.73 m); height 53 ft 9 in (16.38 m)

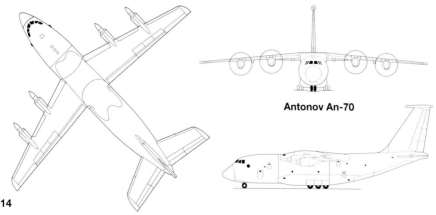

Antonov An-70

ANTONOV An-124 'CONDOR'

Only a small number of the 54 Antonov An-124 Ruslan aircraft delivered by late 1995 are assigned directly to the air transport arm of the Russian air forces, but there is provision for most if not all civil-registered aircraft to be called into military service. Named after Pushkin's legendary giant, the An-124 is in many respects comparable to the slightly smaller C-5 Galaxy. The An-124 remains the world's largest production aircraft, with only the one-off six-engined An-225 being bigger, and it has set a series of world records. Designed to meet a requirement issued by Aeroflot and the Soviet air forces for a long-range heavy transport to replace the turboprop-powered An-22 Antei, the An-124 first flew on 26 December 1982. The type entered service with the Soviet air forces in 1987. The aircraft has an upward-hinging 'visor-type' nose (with a folding nose ramp) and an enormous set of rear loading doors (with a three-part folding ramp). The vast cargo hold has a titanium floor with roller gangs and retractable cargo tie-down points. It is only lightly pressurised, although there is a fully pressurised upper passenger deck for up to 88 people. For ease of loading the aircraft can be made to 'kneel' in a nose-down position by retracting the nosewheels and supporting the nose on retractable feet. Equipped with fly-by-wire controls, the An-124 has a supercritical wing, and makes extensive use of composite materials for weight saving. It is capable of carrying virtually any load, including virtually all Russian armoured fighting vehicles, helicopters and other military cargo. An An-124-100M version of the An-124 with Western avionics, and an An-124-102, with EFIS flight deck and three-person crew, have also been offered to potential customers. Various other modifications, including the installation of Western engines, have also been proposed. Nevertheless, Russia remains the only military operator of the Ruslan.

Specification: Antonov An-124 Ruslan 'Condor'

Origin: Ukraine

Type: six-crew strategic airlifter

Payload: maximum payload 330,688 lb (150000 kg); cabin for 88 passengers aft of wing carry-through, plus up to 350 troops on lower deck; 16 air-droppable pallets each of up to 9,092 lb (4500 kg); 268 paratroops or 288 stretchers and 28 attendants

Powerplant: four ZMKB Progress (Ivchenko) D-18T turbofan engines each rated at 51,587 lb st (229.47 kN)

Performance: maximum cruising speed 537 mph (865 km/h) at optimum altitude; maximum certified altitude 39,380 ft (12000 m); range 2,795 miles (4500 km) with maximum payload and 7,456 miles (12000 km) with 88,184-lb (40000-kg) payload

Weights: empty 385,802 lb (175000 kg); maximum take-off 892,857 lb (405000 kg)

Dimensions: wing span 240 ft 5¼ in (73.30 m); length 226 ft 8½ in (69.10 m); height 69 ft 2 in (21.08 m); wing area 6,759.96 sq ft (628.00 m²)

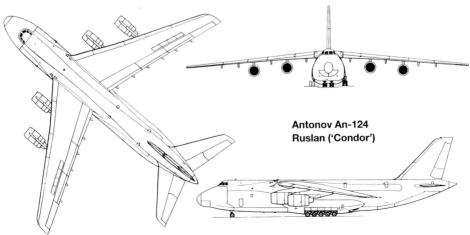

Antonov An-124 Ruslan ('Condor')

ATLAS CHEETAH

A November 1977 United Nations embargo on the delivery of weapons to South Africa forced the South African Air Force (SAAF) to place a high priority on a mid-life upgrade of the aircraft surviving from the 74 Dassault Mirage IIIs and related types received during 1963-70. The upgrade made extensive use of Israeli technology (a fact that was officially denied) and produced aircraft with similar capabilities and avionics to the Israeli Kfir. Some 16 Mirage IIIEZs were converted to Cheetah E standard, roughly equivalent to Kfir-C7, while 11 two-seater Mirage IIIDZs and D2Zs were modified as Cheetah Ds, being similar to the Kfir-TC7. Five more Cheetah Ds may have been produced from Kfir or Mirage airframes supplied by IAI. Cheetah D entered service with No 89 CFS from 1 July 1986, the single-seat Cheetah E following it into service with No 5 Sqn from March 1988. Cheetah D may also have briefly flown in the nuclear strike role in 1990, at a time when the SAAF's Buccaneers were phasing out of service and before South Africa dismantled its six nuclear weapons in 1992. With the retirement of the multi-role Cheetah E in October 1992, began the introduction of the previously secret Cheetah C. Equipped with a modern pulse-Doppler, track-while-scan EUM-2032 radar, this aircraft is formidable air defence aircraft, while the Cheetah E, with its simple ranging radar was optimised for ground attack. Cheetah C also introduces advanced avionics, a glass cockpit and HOTAS controls and employs an array of sophisticated weapons. Cheetah C entered service from late 1992 and deliveries were completed in June 1995. All 38 Cheetah Cs were built using Israeli-supplied airframe components (perhaps from surplus Kfirs or new-build) and used Atar 09K50 engines from South Africa's Mirage F1s, rather than the 09C engine of the earlier Kfirs. Surviving Cheetah Ds have been upgraded with the more powerful engine and other features of the Cheetah C. The Cheetah will continue in SAAF service until its final replacement by BAE Systems Hawk 100 and Saab/BAE Systems Gripen aircraft in 2012.

Specification: Atlas Cheetah C
Origin: South Africa
Type: single-seat multi-role fighter
Armament: two DEFA 552 30-mm internal cannon and up to 12,350 lb (5600 kg) of stores; Israeli-supplied Python 3 IR–guided AAMs and a Rafael active radar-guided AAM, and indigenous V3B Kukri and V3C Darter and U-Darter missiles; air-to-surface weapons include Mk 82/83 bombs, unspecified cluster bombs and indigenously-developed stand-off air-to-surface missile, submunitions dispensers and laser-guided bombs; other possible weapons include AM 39 Exocet anti-ship missiles
Powerplant: one SNECMA Atar 09K50 turbojet rated at 11,923 lb st (49.03 kN) dry and 15,873 lb st (70.82 kN) with afterburning
Performance: maximum speed 1,453 mph (2338 km/h) or Mach 2.20 at 39,370 ft (12000 m); maximum cruising speed 594 mph (956 km/h) at 36,090 ft (11000 m); service ceiling 55,775 ft (17000 m)
Weight: maximum take-off 35,700 lb (16200 kg)
Dimensions: wing span 26 ft 11¾ in (8.22 m); length (estimated) 51 ft 3¾ in (15.62 m) including probe; height 14 ft 11 in (4.50 m); wing area 374.60 sq ft (34.80 m²)

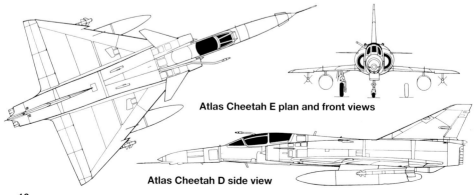

Atlas Cheetah E plan and front views

Atlas Cheetah D side view

ATLAS CSH-2 ROOIVALK

The Atlas (now Denel) Rooivalk (red kestrel) is the first operational result of a development programme launched in 1981 for an indigenous attack helicopter. The programme initially involved the XH-1 Alpha and XTP-2 Beta as concept-proving and systems test-beds. The definitive Rooivalk prototype, originally designated XH-2 (Experimental Helicopter No. 2), made its maiden flight on 11 February 1990. The type was later redesignated CSH-2 (Combat Support Helicopter No. 2) and, later still, XDM (Experimental Development Model). A second prototype, the ADM (Advanced Development Model) flew soon after this and was tasked with avionics and weapons development. Although it looks like an entirely new machine, the Rooivalk is based on a degree of reverse engineering of the Aerospatiale Puma, using the same engines (albeit in slightly uprated form) and main rotor. The stepped tandem cockpits for the pilot and co-pilot/gunner (rear and front respectively) have dual controls, as well as three CRT displays and a HUD in each. A gyro-stabilised turret at the nose contains an automatic target detection and tracking system which incorporates a laser rangefinder, FLIR and TV camera, and the two crewmen each have a helmet-mounted sight system. The SAAF has ordered an initial 16 examples as four operational evaluation and 12 operational helicopters. The full production standard Rooivalk will feature improved IR exhaust suppressors and enlarged sponson cheeks housing avionics and ammunition. A pair of external seats can be fitted to these cheeks, allowing a Rooivalk to pick up the crew of a downed helicopter, or to transport special forces soldiers. No16 Sqn, the SAAF's first Rooivalk unit, received its first AH-2A (as the aircraft is known in service) in May 1999, and will receive the last of its 12 examples in 2001.

Specification: Atlas CSH-2 Rooivalk
Origin: South Africa
Type: two-seat attack helicopter
Armament: one 20-mm Armscor GA-1 Rattler trainable cannon, or one trainable 30–mm DEFA 553 cannon turret-mounted under the nose, plus up to 3,446 lb (2032 kg) of stores including 18-round launchers for 2.68-in (68-mm) rockets, or four-round launchers for the Atlas Swift laser-guided anti-tank missile; air-to-air missiles can be carried at the wingtips
Powerplant: two Atlas Topaz (locally-upgraded Turboméca Makila 1A2) turboshaft engines each rated at 2,000 shp (1491 kW)
Performance: maximum cruising speed 172 mph (278 km/h) at optimum altitude; range 584 miles (940 km)
Weights: empty 13,029 lb (5910 kg); maximum take-off 19,290 lb (8750 kg)
Dimensions: main rotor diameter 51 ft 1½ in (15.58 m); length overall 61 ft 5½ in (18.73 m) with rotors turning; height 17 ft ¼ in (5.19 m); main rotor disc area 2,052.15 sq ft (190.64 m²)

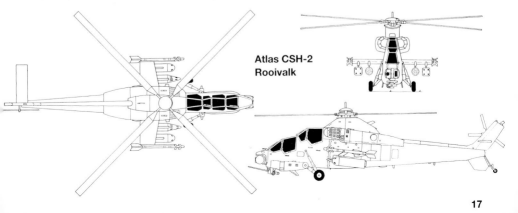

Atlas CSH-2
Rooivalk

BAE SYSTEMS HAWK

Originally designated Hawker P. 1182, the Hawk has been developed into a range of world-beating trainer and combat aircraft. No prototype was built, the first five aircraft off the line being allocated to flight trials, begun on 21 August 1974. Deliveries commenced in 1976, and in 2001 the Hawk T.Mk 1 and T.Mk 1A weapons trainer remained as the RAF's only basic/advanced jet trainer. There is no sign of a replacement despite rapidly dwindling airframe life among the badly overstretched fleet. In November 1981 the US Navy selected the Hawk as its new-generation trainer, and ultimately procured the Hawk Mk 60-based T-45A Goshawk (described separately). Export two-seat Hawk variants include the Mk 50 series, based closely on the Hawk T.Mk 1 and sold to customers including Finland, Indonesia and Kenya; the Mk 60 series with the uprated 5,700-lb st (225.40-kN) Adour Mk 861 engine for customers including Abu Dhabi, Dubai, Kuwait, Saudi Arabia, South Korea, Switzerland and Zimbabwe; and the heavily modified Mk 100 series. The later features a revised wing, with wingtip missile launch rails, advanced attack avionics and a 'chisel nose' housing optional FLIR or laser sensors. With its advanced/weapons training and formidable attack capabilities, the Mk 100 has been exported to Abu Dhabi, Malaysia and Oman. A radical and surprising development of the basic Hawk airframe is represented by the Mk 200 series. This single-seat air-superiority and ground-attack aircraft has an APG-66H radar in a revised nose radome and a pair of in-built 25-mm ADEN cannon beneath the cockpit floor. Exports of this variant have been made to Indonesia, Malaysia and Oman.

Specification: BAE Systems Hawk T.Mk 1
Origin: United Kingdom
Type: multi-role trainer and attack/defence aircraft
Armament: centreline 30-mm ADEN cannon pod (optional) plus up to 1,500 lb (680 kg) of practice stores or the capability for a 5,660-lb (2567-kg) weapon load; Hawk T.Mk 1A wired to carry AIM-9L AAMs for point defence role
Powerplant: one 5,200-lb (23.12-kN) thrust Rolls-Royce/Turboméca Adour Mk 151-01 turbofan
Performance: maximum speed 645 mph (1038 km/h); dive limit Mach 1.2; combat radius 345 miles (556 km) with 5,660-lb (2567-kg) weapon load, or 645 miles (1039 km) with 3,000-lb (1361-kg) load
Weights: empty 8,040 lb (3647 kg); maximum take-off 17,085 lb (7750 kg)
Dimensions: wing span 30 ft 9¾ in (9.39 m); length, excluding probe 36 ft 7¾ in (11. 17 m); height 13 ft 1¼ in (3.99 m); wing area 179.6 sq ft (16.69 m²)

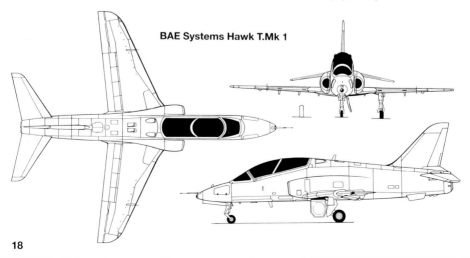

BAE Systems Hawk T.Mk 1

Australia is receiving 33 Hawk Mk 127 aircraft for use in the lead-in fighter trainer role. The aircraft have advanced digital cockpits, which resemble those of the Royal Australian Air Force's Hornet fighters.

BELL 205/UH-1 IROQUOIS

Developed from the previous Model 204, the ubiquitous Bell Model 205 utility helicopter was first flown in 1961. Bell built 3,573 UH-1Hs for US forces and a further 1,317 were exported. Model 205 variants still remain important within the US Army in 2001, despite most having been moved over to the Army National Guard. A significant development of the Model 205 has been the twin-engined Model 212, in service in its basic form as the UH-1N, and also licence built by Agusta-Bell. The Model 212 remains in widespread military service, most significantly with the USMC, to which the first machine was delivered in 1971. The Marine Corps intends to upgrade about 100 of its UH-1Ns to UH-1Y standard. This will share common systems, engines and components with the AH-1Z gunship. Improvements include uprated 1,690-shp (1260-kW) General Electric T700-GE-401 engines that will drive a new four-bladed main rotor system. The fully NVG-compatible cockpit will have four colour multi-function displays, mission and weapons computers, advanced communication and navigation equipment. The UH-1Y will also gain an AN/AAQ-22 Star SAFIRE thermal imaging system in the FLIR under the nose, plus greatly improved self-protection systems. The UH-1Y will have significantly increased speed, manoeuvrability, range, crashworthiness and lift capability, plus enhanced battlefield survivability. The useful load will be increased to 6,935 lb/3146 kg) and the 30-minute maximum cruise speed will be a fast 191 mph (308 km/h). First delivery to the Marines is scheduled for 2004. In addition, Bell and Agusta-Bell produce the Model 412 and AB 412 respectively, based on the Model 212, but with a four-bladed main rotor as standard. This aircraft has also found many military customers.

Specification: Bell UH-1N Iroquois
Origin: USA
Type: utility helicopter
Armament and payload: maximum useful payload over 3,000 lb (1360 kg); up to 13 passengers or six litters and a corpsman; armament includes 2.75-in (70-mm) rockets plus cabin-mounted guns comprise 7.62-mm M240, 12.7-mm GAU-16 and 7.62-mm GAU-17 Minigun
Powerplant: two General Electric GE T400-CP-400/401/402 turboshaft engines each rated at 900 shp (671 kW)
Performance: maximum speed 149 mph (240 km/h); maximum ceiling 10,000 ft (3048 m); range with internal fuel only 265 miles (426 km); maximum endurance 2 hours with 20 minutes of fuel remaining
Weights: basic empty 6,800 - 7,250 lb (3084 - 3289 kg); maximum gross 10,500 lb (4762 kg)
Dimensions: main rotor diameter of 48 ft 0 in (14.63 m); fuselage length 53 ft 3 in (16.23 m); height 13 ft 1 in (3.99 m); main rotor disc area 1810 sq ft (168.10 m²)

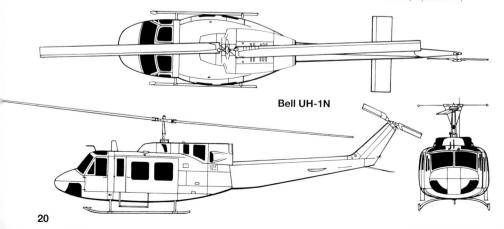

Bell UH-1N

Developed from the civil Model 206A JetRanger helicopter, the US Army's OH-58 Kiowa served extensively in Vietnam in the light observation and scout roles. The Model 206 was built in significant numbers for military service and remains in widespread use with the US Army in upgraded OH-58C form. Numerous foreign air arms also operate the military Model 206A/Bs primarily in the training role. The type also serves as a trainer with the US Navy as the TH-57 SeaRanger and with the US Army as the TH-67A Creek. The Model 406 was developed to meet a US Army requirement for a helicopter capable of observation duties, as well as support of attack helicopters and direction of artillery fire. The Model 406 introduced a mast-mounted sight, specialised avionics and a four-bladed main rotor with composite blades. Some 424 OH-58Ds were converted from previous OH-58 models in a process that was completed in 1998. The first OH-58D prototype made its maiden flight on 6 October 1983. Deliveries began in December 1985, and the first deliveries to a Europe-based unit took place in June 1987. Under Operation *Prime Chance*, 15 OH-58Ds were modified from September 1987 for operations against Iranian fast patrol boats in the Persian Gulf: provision was made for Stinger AAMs and Hellfire ATGMs in addition to 0.5-in (12.7-mm) machine-gun pods and rocket launchers. The armament options of the *Prime Chance* OH-58D were retained for an armed OH-58D version, designated as the OH-58D(I) Kiowa Warrior, to which standard all OH-58Ds have been upgraded. Taiwan is the only operator of new-build full-standard OH-58Ds, receiving 26 examples from July 1993. Saudi Arabia operates 15 of the simplified Model 406CS Combat Scout variant.

Specification: Bell OH-58D(I) Kiowa Warrior
Origin: USA
Type: two-seat scout and attack light helicopter
Armament: four FIM-92 Stinger or AGM-114 Hellfire missiles, or two seven-tube launchers for 2.75-in (70-mm) Hydra 70 air-to-surface unguided rockets, or one 0.5-in (12.7-mm) machine-gun pod, or a mix of these weapons
Powerplant: one Allison T703-AD-700 turboshaft rated at 650 shp (410 kW)
Performance: maximum speed 147 mph (247 km/h) at 4,000 ft (1220 m); initial climb rate 1,540 ft (469 m) per minute; hovering ceiling 10,000 ft (048 m) in ground effect; range 257 miles (413 km)
Weights: empty 3,289 lb (1492 kg); maximum take-off 5,500 lb (2495 kg)
Dimensions: main rotor diameter 35 ft (10.67 m); length overall 41 ft 2½ in (12.58 m) and fuselage 34 ft 3 in (10.44 m); height 12 ft 10½ in (3.93 m); main rotor disc area 962.11 sq ft (89.38 m²)

**Bell Model 406/
OH-58D(I)
Kiowa Warrior**

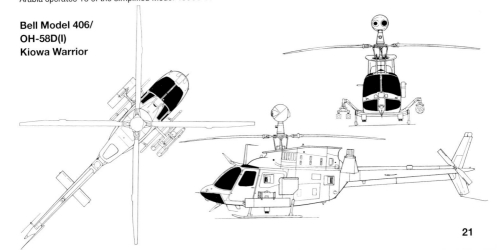

BELL 209/AH-1 HUEYCOBRA

In 7 September 1965 Bell flew the prototype of the world's first dedicated attack helicopter. Based on the Model 204 utility helicopter, the Model 209 introduced a new slim fuselage with a fighter-type cockpit. The pilot sits high in the rear with a co-pilot/gunner lower in the front directing the fire of a wide range of weapons mounted on lateral stub wings or under the nose. The AH-1G HueyCobra went into production in 1966 and over 1,000 were delivered in the first four years. The AH-1G saw extensive service in Vietnam. The AH-1J SeaCobra was the first twin-engine version, for the US Marine Corps, with a 1,800-shp (1343-ekW) T400 installation; in 1974-5 a batch of 202 with TOW missiles was supplied to Iran. The AH-1Q was an interim US Army version with TOW missiles, produced by conversion from AH-1G airframes, while the AH-1S, fitted with the 1,800-shp (1343-ekW) T53-703 engine was a production HueyCobra with TOW capability and other improvements. A number of AH-1Q aircraft were also modified to -1S standards, while AH-1S model aircraft were themselves modified into a number of variants. In addition, the AH-1P was produced by conversion of AH-1S helicopters with flat-plate canopies and other revisions. This confusing situation was resolved in 1987, when all surviving US Army HueyCobras were updated to a common AH-1F standard. Fuji-Bell has produced the AH-1S as an equivalent to the AH-1F for the JGSDF. Having evolved through the AH-1J and TOW-capable AH-1T, in 2001, the USMC's SeaCobra is represented by the AH-1W SuperCobra. This Hellfire-toting machine will be upgraded in a similar manner to the USMC UH-1N fleet to AH-1Z standard, featuring a four-bladed rotor and many other changes for continued service well into the 21st century. Both single- and twin-engined Model 209s have been widely exported.

Specification: Bell AH-1W SuperCobra
Origin: USA
Type: two-seat close support, attack and anti-armour helicopter
Armament: one chin-mounted M-197 three-barrelled 20-mm cannon; maximum ordnance 2,466 lb (1119 kg) including eight TOW or Hellfire ATGMs, seven- or 19-shot 2.75-in (70-mm) rocket pods, 5-in (127-mm) Zuni rockets, cluster munitions, napalm, AIM-9 and Stinger IR AAMs and drop tanks; qualified for AGM-65 Maverick AGMs
Powerplant: two 1,625-shp (1212-kW) General Electric T700-GE-401 turboshafts; transmission limited to 2,032 shp (1515 kW) for take-off and 1,725 shp (1286 kW) for continuous running
Performance: maximum level speed 'clean' at sea level 175 mph (282 km/h); range 395 miles (635 km) with standard fuel
Weights: empty 10,200 lb (4627 kg); maximum take-off 14,750 lb (6691 kg)
Dimensions: main rotor diameter 48 ft (14.63 m); fuselage length 45 ft 6 in (13.87 m), height overall 14 ft 2 in (4.32 m); main rotor disc area 1,809.56 sq ft (168.11 m²)

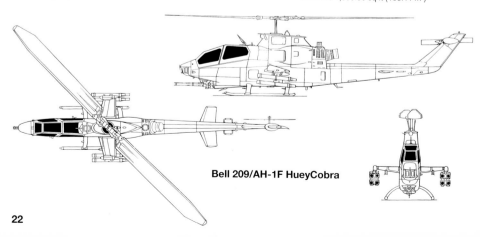

Bell 209/AH-1F HueyCobra

BELLBOEING V-22 OSPREY

In the early 1980s Bell Helicopter Textron and Boeing Vertol began collaboration to develop a larger derivative of the XV-15 tilt-rotor demonstrator for the Joint Services Advanced Vertical Lift Aircraft programme. Combining the vertical lift capabilities of a helicopter with the fast-cruise forward flight efficiencies of a fixed-wing turboprop aircraft, the resulting V-22 Osprey was awarded full-scale development in 1985. Mounted in wingtip nacelles, the engines can be swivelled through 97.5° and drive three-bladed prop-rotors through interconnected drive shafts. For shipboard stowage, the mainplanes pivot centrally to rotate along the fuselage top, the prop-rotor blades also folding in parallel. Initial requirements called for 913 Ospreys, comprising 522 MV-22A assault versions for the USMC and US Army; 80 USAF CV-22s for long-range special forces transport; and 50 USN HV-22s for combat SAR, special warfare and fleet logistic support. The USN also foresaw a need for up to 300 SV–22As for ASW. Flight-testing started on 19 March 1989, but the programme suffered a serious setback on 21 July 1992 with the crash of the fourth prototype. Already under financial and political review, a serious reappraisal of the Osprey programme followed, with the ultimate conclusion that 300 (later 425) aircraft would be acquired for the USMC only. The MV-22A can carry up to 24 troops, or 12 litters and medical attendants. In September 1994 production authorisation was granted for this batch, plus 48 Ospreys for the USN and 50 for the USAF. The loss of three V-22s during testing in 2000 cast a further shadow over the programme, but this most important of future combat aircraft should be reaching IOC with the USMC during 2001/2002. Deliveries to the USAF and US Navy are currently scheduled for 2003 and 2010 respectively.

Specification: BellBoeing MV-22A Osprey
Origin: USA
Type: land-based and shipborne multi-mission tilt-rotor transport
Payload: up to 20,000 lb (9072 kg) of freight carried internally, or 15,000 lb (6804 kg) of freight carried externally
Powerplant: two Allison T406-AD-400 turboshafts each rated at 6,150 shp (4586 kW) for take-off and 5,890 shp (4392 kW) for continuous running
Performance: maximum cruising speed at sea level 316 mph (509 km/h) in aeroplane mode; tactical range 1,382 miles (2224 km) after VTO at 44,619 lb (21146 kg) with 12,000–lb (5443-kg) payload
Weights: empty equipped 31,886 lb (14463 kg); maximum take-off 60,500 lb (27442 kg) for STO
Dimensions: rotor diameter, each 38 ft (11.58 m); wing span 50 ft 11 in (15.52 m) including nacelles; length, fuselage excluding probe 57 ft 4 in (17.47 m); height over fins 17 ft 7⅖ in (5.38 m); wing area 382.00 sq ft (35.59 m²); total rotor disc area 2,268.23 sq ft (210.72 m²)

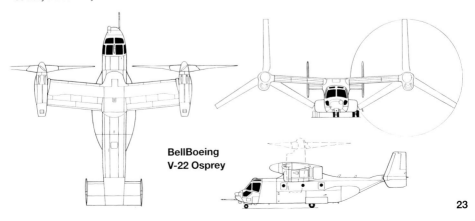

**BellBoeing
V-22 Osprey**

BOEING AH-64A APACHE

Designed in 1972-3 to meet the US Army's need for an AAH (Advanced Attack Helicopter), the AH-64A has taken over the mantle of the world's premier attack helicopter from the Bell AH-1 HueyCobra. The first Hughes YAH-64 prototype flew on 30 September 1975, the programme coming under the jurisdiction of McDonnell Douglas from August 1985 and Boeing from 1997. Features of the Apache include two T700 engines flat-rated to provide high emergency power, with large 'Black Hole' IR-suppressing exhaust systems, a large flat-plate canopy with boron armour, multi-spar stainless steel and glassfibre rotor blades designed to withstand 23-mm hits, comprehensive avionics and weapon fits, and numerous features to protect the crew, including crash-resistant seats and an airframe designed to withstand ballistic impact from guns up to 12.7-mm calibre. The Apache's primary sensor is the Martin Marietta TADS/PNVS (Target Acquisition and Designation Sight/Pilot's Night Vision System) that combines a low-light level TV, laser designator and FLIR. Both crew members use various sophisticated sensors and systems for the detection and attack of targets, including the IHADSS (Integrated Helmet And Display Sighting System) which provides a monocular helmet-mounted designator/sight. Some 827 AH-64As were eventually procured by the US Army and the helicopter entered service in July 1986. The helicopter was first blooded in combat during Operation *Just Cause* over Panama in December 1989, and went on to serve with devastating effect during the 1991 Gulf War – Apaches fired the first shots of that short-lived conflict. AH-64As have been exported to Egypt, Greece, Israel, Saudi Arabia and the United Arab Emirates.

Specification: Boeing AH-64A Apache (604th aircraft onwards)
Origin: USA
Type: two-seat attack helicopter
Armament: one M230 Chain Gun 30-mm cannon with 1,200 rounds; (principal armament) up to 16 AGM-114A Hellfire ATGMs; 19-shot 2.75-in (70-mm) Hydra 70 rocket pods; optional AIM-9L, AIM-92A Stinger and Mistral AAMs and Sidearm ARMs
Powerplant: two General Electric T700-GE-701C turboshafts each rated at 1,800 shp (1342 kW)
Performance: maximum level and cruising speed 'clean' 182 mph (293 km/h); initial vertical climb rate at sea level 2,500 ft (762 m) per minute; service ceiling 21,000 ft (6400 m); range 300 miles (428 km) with internal fuel
Weights: empty 11,387 lb (5165 kg); maximum take-off 21,000 lb (9525 kg)
Dimensions: main rotor diameter 48 ft (14.63 m); fuselage length 49 ft 1½ in (14.97 m); height overall 15 ft 3½ in (4.66 m); main rotor disc area 1,809.5 sq ft (168.11 m²)

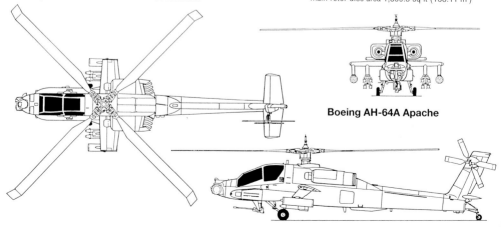

Boeing AH-64A Apache

The Apache suffered from a protracted and sometimes controversial early history. Criticism of its combat effectiveness was dispelled by highly successful operational use in Operation *Desert Storm* in 1991. The Apache has become the standard by which attack helicopters are judged, and has secured several major export orders.

BOEING AH-64D LONGBOW APACHE

Beginning in the late 1980s, the US Army planned a series of upgrades to its AH-64A fleet. The major upgrade is centred around the Northrop Grumman APG-78 Longbow millimetric-wavelength fire-control radar allied to new AGM-114L Hellfire 2 missiles. During 1992 McDonnell Douglas converted four AH-64As with this radar to act as proof-of-concept aircraft for a variant designated AH-64D. The designations AH-64B and AH-64C for interim variants were later dropped so that the AH-64D Apache became the second operational Apache variant. Longbow is readily identifiable by the mast-mounted antenna for its radar. It allows the AGM-114L to be fired in an autonomous fire-and-forget mode, whereas the laser-guided Hellfire requires external designation or use in conjunction with the TADS, and as such is a line-of-sight and non fire-and-forget weapon. The APG-78 radar can detect, classify and prioritise 12 targets simultaneously, and can see through the fog and smoke that currently foils IR or TV sensors. The AH-64D also features improvements in targeting, battle management, cockpit, communications, weapons and navigation systems. The forward avionics bay is expanded, and the landing gear fairings are extended forward to accommodate some of the new equipment. Entering service in 1995, early aircraft lack the radar system fitted to the definitive AH-64D Longbow Apache that followed from 1997. Early in 1999 the US Army finally decided that 530 AH-64As would be upgraded to D standard, for which 500 Longbow systems would be procured, and that the other 218 surviving AH-64As would be passed to the Air National Guard as a partial replacement for its Bell AH-1s. The AH-64D will also be flown by Israel, the Netherlands and the UK (where it is built under licence for the RAF by Westland as the WAH-64D).

Specification: Boeing AH-64D Longbow Apache
Generally similar to the Boeing AH-64A Apache except for the following respects:
Type: two-seat, radar-equipped attack helicopter
Armament: principal armament of up to 16 AGM-114L Hellfire 2 long-range, radar-guided, fire-and-forget ATGMs on four underwing hardpoints, additional two hardpoints give provision for four Stinger, four Mistral or two AIM-9 Sidewinder AAMs (Starstreak missile evaluated) or two AGM-122 Sidearm ARMs
Performance: maximum level and cruising speed 'clean' 165 mph (265 km/h), maximum vertical climb rate at sea level 2,415 ft (736 m) per minute; service ceiling 19,400 ft (5915 m); range 253 miles (407 km) with internal fuel
Weights: empty 11,800 lb (5352 kg)
Dimensions: height overall 16 ft 1 in (4.90 m) to top of mast-mounted radome

Boeing AH-64D Longbow Apache

BOEING B-52H STRATOFORTRESS

By normal standards long since rendered obsolete due to its great vulnerability to SAMs, the mighty Boeing B-52 Stratofortress has seen two would-be successors fall by the wayside. It remains a major element in one of the three US strategic deterrents and will continue to give valuable service well into the 21st century. The B-52 began life in 1948 as a turboprop successor to the B-50. In 1949, a change to Pratt & Whitney J57 turbojet powerplant was made and the XB-52 prototype made its maiden flight on 15 April 1952. The B-52 evolved through progressively improved B-52A to B-52G models, the latter remaining in service to late 1994. The ultimate B-52H is characterised by two major changes: introduction of TF33 turbofans that give greater thrust in concert with a considerably reduced specific fuel consumption, and structural changes which permit the B-52 to fly at low altitudes without excessive fatigue problems. The final B-52H was rolled out in June 1962 and with the B-1B and B-2A entering service in only limited numbers, the B-52H has been constantly upgraded to enable it to remain a credible front-line type. With the B-1B increasingly assuming the free-fall nuclear role of the B-52H, this latter type has been reallocated to the force projection role, with weapons that now include the AGM-86C conventionally-armed variant of the nuclear 'cruise' missile and Have Nap missiles. The importance of the B-52H to the USAF's continued need for warplanes with global reach while carrying very heavy warloads is demonstrated by the fact that comprehensive upgrades for the remaining aircraft, both in terms of avionics and weapons systems, are still planned. And although a re-engining programme has apparently been dropped, the type is still scheduled to remain in service until 2044.

Specification: Boeing B-52H Stratofortress
Origin: USA
Type: long-range strategic heavy bomber
Armament: one 20-mm Vulcan six-barrelled cannon in tail turret housing, plus up to 50,000 lb (22680 kg) of ordnance including AGM-86C conventional-warhead cruise missiles, B61 or B83 free-fall thermonuclear bombs, AGM-142 Have Nap (Rafael Popeye) stand-off precision-guided attack missiles and up to 51 750-lb (340-kg) Mk 117 or 1,000-lb (454-kg) Mk 83 conventional free-fall bombs
Powerplant: eight Pratt & Whitney TF33-P-3 turbofans, each rated at 17,000 lb st (75.62 kN)
Performance: maximum speed 595 mph (958 km/h) at optimum altitude; service ceiling 55,000 ft (16765 m); range over 10,000 miles (16093 km) without inflight-refuelling
Weights: maximum take-off 505,000 lb (229088 kg)
Dimensions: wing span 185 ft (56.39 m); length 160 ft 10⁄₁₀ in (49.05 m); height 40 ft 8 in (12.40 m); wing area 4,000 sq ft (371.60 m²)

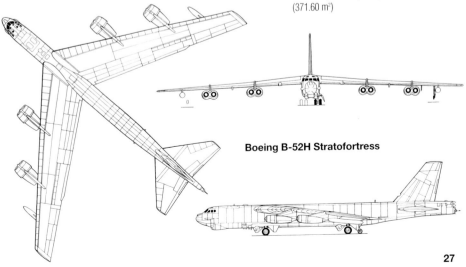

Boeing B-52H Stratofortress

BOEING C-17 GLOBEMASTER III

On 29 August 1981 McDonnell Douglas (since 1997 incorporated into Boeing) was selected to proceed with a design to fulfil the USAF's C-X requirement for a new heavy cargo transport. Although the aircraft reached initial operational capability only in January 1995, it is now revitalising the USA's strategic airlift capability. The winning design was designated C-17A, and later received the name Globemaster III. Retaining the now-classic military transport aircraft configuration, the C-17 also incorporates advanced-technology features such as winglets, a supercritical wing section and high-performance turbofans with thrust reversers. The C-17 can routinely operate from airfields previously denied to jet-powered transports. The cockpit is state-of-the-art, with four multi-function displays, and a HUD for each pilot. Flight control is effected by a fly-by-wire system, and the pilots each have a control column rather than the conventional yoke. After an earlier full-scale development schedule had been abandoned, the single prototype of the C-17A made its maiden flight on 15 September 1991. Deliveries to the 17th Airlift Squadron at Charleston AFB, South Carolina, began in June 1993. Continued opposition to the C-17 reduced procurement from 210 aircraft to 120 by 1991, and subsequently to an even lower minimum of 40 aircraft. The controlling and radical reduction of production costs and the manifest capabilities of the type then saw the previous total of 120 reinstated for delivery by 2005. A further 15 have been added later for the support of the US Special Forces, and the prospect of another 45 standard airlifters for the USAF is under possible consideration. In addition, the Royal Air Force's No.99 started operating four leased C-17As in 2001.

Specification: Boeing C-17A Globemaster III
Origin: USA
Type: three-crew heavy transport
Payload: maximum payload 169,000 lb (76658 kg), including up to 102 troops/paratroops on stowable seats in the cabin; 48 litters, three AH-64 Apache helicopters, or air-droppable platforms up to a weight of 110,000 lb (49896 kg)
Powerplant: four Pratt & Whitney F117-PW-100 turbofan engines, each rated at 40,700 lb st (181.04 kN)
Performance: normal cruising speed 507 mph (816 km/h) at 28,000 ft (8535 m); range 5,408 miles (8704 km) on a ferry flight without inflight refuelling, or 2,762 miles (4445 km) with a 160,000-lb (72576-kg) payload and no inflight refuelling
Weights: empty 277,000 lb (125647 kg); maximum take-off 585,000 lb (265356 kg)
Dimensions: wing span 169 ft 10 in (51.76 m) including winglets; length 174 ft 0 in (53.04 m); height 55 ft 1 in (16.79 m); wing area 3,800 sq ft (353.02 m²)

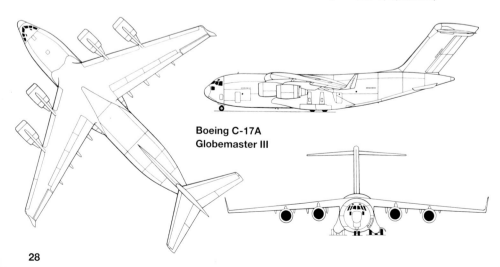

Boeing C-17A
Globemaster III

The C-17 has experienced one of the most remarkable turnarounds in aviation history. In the late 1980s the programme was poorly managed, behind schedule and over budget. Today, the C-17 has dramatically improved the USAF's airlift capability, and its production effort has won industry awards. During Operation *Allied Force* in 1999 the type was the only airlifter capable of hauling outsized loads into the poorly-equipped airport in Tirana, Albania.

BOEING C-135 SERIES

Boeing's decision to go ahead with its self-funded four-jet transport project in 1952 was heavily influenced by the fact that the USAF would almost certainly buy a version as an inflight-refuelling tanker for SAC. In the event the USAF bought 732, produced at 20 or more a month at a price below $6 million each. Smaller than the commercial Model 707, the KC-135 Stratotanker still constitutes the majority of the USAF's front-line tanker fleet in 2001, with 549 aircraft serving in KC-135E/R and T models. The KC-135E is basically the original KC-135A re-engined with TF33 turbofans, while the -135R represents a thorough upgrading and re-engining of former KC-135As with F108 turbofans. Formerly dedicated to refuelling the Lockheed SR-71, the KC-135Q has also been re-engined with F108 engines as the KC-135T, and now supports the F-117 Nighthawk and other covert programmes. France's *l'Armée de l'Air* operates the C-135FR, with modifications to the 'flying-boom' refuelling system allowing it to refuel probe-equipped receivers. Underwing refuelling pods have recently been added and these items have also been acquired for USAF KC-135Rs. Singapore and Turkey also fly small numbers of KC-135Rs. A profusion of C-135 variants served with the USAF on a range of test and special duties during the Cold War, although many have now been retired or converted back to tanker standard. The major operational variant is the RC-135, which remains among the USAF's most important strategic reconnaissance assets. Serving in the electronic and signals intelligence-gathering roles worldwide, these are under the control of the 55th Strategic Wing at Offutt AFB, Nebraska. Operational variants comprise the RC-135S, V and W, and are characterised by 'thimble' nose radomes, bulged cheek fairings that house mission equipment and a profusion of antennas and various fairings on the fuselage.

Specification: Boeing KC-135R Stratotanker

Origin: USA

Type: inflight refuelling tanker with secondary transport capability

Payload: maximum payload 83,000 lb (37650 kg)

Powerplant: four CFM International F108-CF-100 turbofans, each rated at 97.86 kN (22,000 lb st)

Performance: maximum level speed at high altitude 610 mph (982 km/h); cruising speed at 35,000 ft (10670 m) 532 mph (856 km/h); maximum rate of climb at sea level 1,290 ft (393 m) per minute; service ceiling 45,000 ft (13715 m); operational radius 2,879 miles (4633 k) to offload 24,000 lb (10886 kg) of fuel

Weights: operating empty 106,306 lb (48220 kg); maximum take-off 322,500 lb (146284 kg); internal fuel 203,288 lb (92210 kg)

Dimensions: wing span 130 ft 10 in (39.88 m); length 136 ft 3 in (41.53 m); height 41 ft 8 in (12.70 m); wing area 2,433.00 sq ft (226.03 m²)

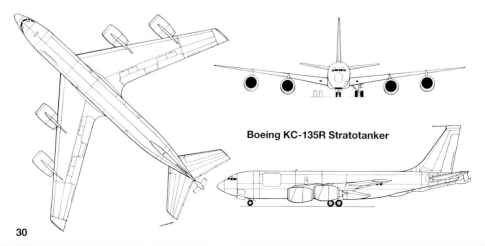

Boeing KC-135R Stratotanker

BOEING E-3 SENTRY

The Boeing E-3A Sentry is essentially a flexible, jamming-resistant, mobile and survivable airborne radar station. The Airborne Warning and Control System (AWACS) is tasked primarily with airborne surveillance, but can also act as a command and control centre. Boeing was awarded a contract on 23 July 1970 to provide two EC-137D prototypes. Based on the airframe of the Model 707-300B airliner, these added a large 30-ft (9.14-m) diameter rotodome above the rear fuselage to house the antenna for the search radar. Other essential avionics antennae are housed within the wing, fuselage and tail unit. The cabin is fitted with equipment bays and SDCs (Situation Display Consoles) for the AWACS specialist officers. The first test aircraft flew on 5 February 1972 and the first production E-3A was delivered to the USAF on 24 March 1977. The E-3A has been replaced in USAF service by the E-3B and E-3C, with upgraded APY-2 radar, higher-speed computers and secure communications facilities. The E-3C also has five additional operator consoles. In 2001 the USAF AWACS force numbers 18 E-3B/C aircraft, while NATO continues to fly the 17 survivors of 18 jointly funded E-3As. Based at Geilenkirchen, Germany, these have been extensively updated, most recently with the addition of the AN/AYR-1 ESM system. E-3s powered by CFM56 engines serve with France (four E-3Fs), Saudi Arabia (five E-3As) and the UK (seven E-3D Sentry AEW.Mk 1s). The E-3 remains invaluable to the USAF's front-line force, and the service is currently considering upgrading its E-3s with the 'glass' flightdeck of the Next Generation Model 737 and the Eagle system (to detect and track theatre ballistic missiles), with an IRST sensor and a laser rangefinder. Major upgrades are also planned for the radar, computer and navigation systems, as well as re-engining with CFM56 (F108) powerplants.

Specification: Boeing E-3C Sentry
Origin: USA
Type: airborne early warning and command post aircraft
Powerplant: four Pratt & Whitney TF33-P-100/100A turbofans, each rated at 21,000 lb st (93.41 kN)
Accommodation: basic operational crew of 17 comprising flight crew of four, plus 13 mission specialists
Armament: two hardpoints under inner wings give provision to carry four AIM-9L/M Sidewinder short-range AAMs for self defence
Performance: maximum level speed at high altitude 530 mph (853 km/h); service ceiling 29,000 ft (8840 m); operational radius 1,002 miles (1612 km) for a 6-hour patrol without flight refuelling; endurance more than 11 hours without inflight refuelling
Weights: operating empty 171,950 lb (77996 kg); maximum take-off 325,000 lb (147420 kg)
Dimensions: wing span 145 ft 9 in (44.42 m); length 152 ft 11 in (46.61 m); height 41 ft 9 in (12.73 m); wing area 3,050 sq ft (283.35 m²)

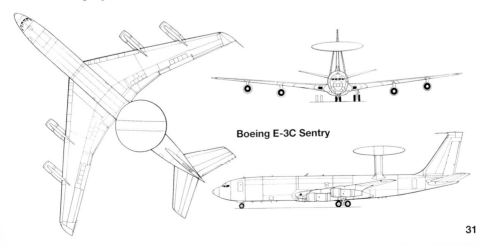

Boeing E-3C Sentry

BOEING F-15E EAGLE

Trials of the F-15 in the air-to-ground role began during 1982 when McDonnell Douglas modified the second TF-15A two-seater as the 'Strike Eagle' as a private venture. The 'Strike Eagle' was seen as a possible replacement for the F-111, and emerged as the winner of an evaluation over its rival, the General Dynamics F-16XL, for the USAF's Enhanced Tactical Fighter programme. The first production F-15E made its maiden flight on 11 December 1986, the 'Strike Eagle' name not being adopted. With the new avionics and equipment for the 'mud-moving' role, the F-15E is very much a second-generation Eagle. The weapons system operator (WSO) in the rear cockpit employs four multi-purpose CRT terminals for radar, weapon selection and monitoring of enemy tracking systems. The WSO also operates the F-15E's primary systems: the APG-70 synthetic aperture radar and the AAQ-13 navigation/AAQ-14 targeting pods of the Lockheed Martin LANTIRN nav/attack system. The navigation pod incorporates its own terrain-following radar, which can be linked to the aircraft's flight control system to allow automatic coupled terrain-following flight. The F-15E was initially powered by the F100-PW-220 turbofan, but the improved F100-PW-229 was installed in all aircraft delivered from August 1991, and also retrofitted in earlier aircraft. The first operational F-15Es were delivered to the 4th TFW, Seymour Johnson AFB, North Carolina in 1989. The type made its combat debut during Operation *Desert Storm*, and proved outstanding in this and subsequent combat actions. The USAF procured 209 F-15Es, all of which had been delivered by July 1994, with small attrition-replacement orders continuing into 2001. Exports have been made to Saudi Arabia, which took delivery of 72 F-15S aircraft between 1995 and 2000. These have downgraded avionics and downgraded LANTIRN pods, and also lack fuselage-mounted conformal fuel tanks. Israel took delivery of 25 examples of a similar variant, designated F-15I Ra'am (Thunder), between 1998 and 1999.

Specification: Boeing F-15E Eagle
Origin: USA
Type: two-seat strike and attack aircraft
Armament: one internal 20-mm M61A1 Vulcan six-barrel cannon and up to 24,250 lb (11000 kg) of ordnance, including Mk 82, Mk 83, Mk 84 bombs and GBU-10, -12 and -15 PGMs, CBU-52, -58, -71, -87, -89, -90, -92 or -93 cluster bombs, up to five B57 or B61 free-fall nuclear bombs, AGM-65 Maverick, AGM-88 HARM ARMs and AGM-130 ASMs, plus up to four AIM-7M Sparrows and four AIM-9 Sidewinders, or eight AIM-120 AMRAAMs
Powerplant: two Pratt & Whitney F100-PW-229 turbofan engines each rated at 29,100 lb st (129.4 kN) with afterburning
Performance: maximum speed more than 1,650 mph (2655 km/h) or Mach 2.5 at high altitude; initial climb rate over 50,000 ft (15240 m) per minute; radius 790 miles (1271 km) on a typical mission with maximum warload
Weights: empty 31,700 lb (14379 kg); maximum take-off 81,000 lb (36741 kg)
Dimensions: wing span 42 ft 9¾ in (13.05 m); length 63 ft 9 in (19.43 m); height 18 ft 5½ in (5.63 m); wing area 608.00 sq ft (56.48 m²)

Boeing F-15E Eagle

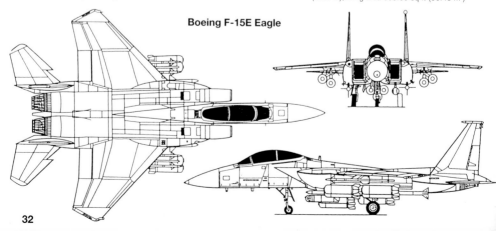

The USAF's 200+ F-15Es are the force's most capable strike/attack aircraft. There are seven front-line squadrons: four are CONUS-based units, with a further two in England and one in Alaska (illustrated).

BOEING F/A-18A/C HORNET

The world's premier naval fighter originated as a more sophisticated naval derivative of the Northrop YF-17 that was pitted successfully against the General Dynamics YF-16 in the USN's Air Combat Fighter programme of 1976. The first of 11 trials Hornets made its maiden flight on 18 November 1978. Production of the initial F/A-18A single-seat version eventually totalled 371 aircraft, the first US Navy squadron receiving its aircraft in 1983. The F/A-18 offers much greater weapons delivery accuracy than its predecessors, and is a genuinely multi-role aircraft, with remarkable dog-fighting ability. Its advanced APG-65 multi-mode radar has become the benchmark fighter radar. The F/A-18 made its combat debut during the *El Dorado Canyon* action against Libya in April 1986, and was heavily commit-ted to action during Operation *Desert Storm* in 1991. The F/A-18A was superseded by the F/A-18C, which remained the principal single-seat pro-duction model up to 1999, some 347 having been ordered for US service. The first F/A-18C made its maiden flight on 3 September 1986. This version introduced compatibility with the AIM-120 AMRAAM and the IIR version of the AGM-65 Maverick missile, as well as improved avionics and a new NACES ejection seat. After 137 baseline F/A-18Cs had been delivered, pro-duction switched to a night attack version with equipment including GEC Cat's Eye pilot's night vision goggles compatibility, an AAR-50 TINS pod, Kaiser AVQ-28 raster HUD, externally-carried AAS-38 FLIR targeting pod and colour multi-function displays. The first night-attack Hornet was deliv-ered on 1 November 1989. The Hornet's versatility has led to substantial export sales. Canada was the first foreign customer, taking delivery of 98 single-seat CF-188A aircraft, while Australia followed with an order for 57 AF-18A. Spain purchased 60 EF-18As (local designation C.15) and later acquired 24 former US Navy F/A-18As from late 1995. F/A-18Cs have been delivered to Kuwait (32 KAF-18Cs), Switzerland (26) and Finland (57).

Specification: Boeing F/A-18C Hornet
Origin: USA
Type: single-seat carrierborne and land-based fighter and strike/attack warplane
Armament: one internal 20-mm M61A1 Vulcan six-barrel cannon, plus up to 15,500 lb (7031 kg) of ordnance including AIM-120, AIM-7 and AIM-9 AAMs; AGM-65, AGM-84E SLAM, AGM-88 HARM and AGM-154 JSOW AGMs; AGM-62 Walleye, GBU-10, -12 and -16 PGMs; AGM-84 Harpoon AShMs; Mk 80 series bombs; CBU-59 cluster bombs, and B57 and B61 nuclear free-fall bombs
Powerplant: two General Electric F404-GE-402 turbofans each rated at 17,700 lb st (78.73 kN) with afterburning
Performance: maximum speed over 1,190 mph (1915 km/h); radius over 460 miles (740 km) on a fighter mission or 662 miles (1065 km) for an attack mission
Weights: empty 23,832 lb (10810 kg); maximum take-off 33,585 lb (15234 kg) for a fighter mission or 48,253 lb (21888 kg) for an attack mission
Dimensions: wing span 37 ft 6 in (11.43 m) without tip-mounted missiles; length 56 ft (17.07 m); height 15 ft 3½ in (4.66 m); wing area 400.00 sq ft (37.16 m²)

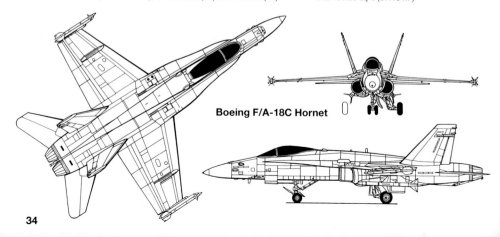

Boeing F/A-18C Hornet

The Hornet is one of the most successful of contemporary warplanes. Nearly 1,500 have been built, including 1,048 examples for the US Navy and Marine Corps. The initial F/A-18A model remains in limited US service and the majority of the 24 front-line Hornet units are equipped with the night attack capable F/A-18C model. The type supplants the F-14 Tomcat aboard US Navy carriers, with a standard carrier air wing now embarking three Hornet squadrons.

BOEING F/A-18B/D HORNET

Development of a two-seat version of the Hornet was undertaken concurrently with that of the single-seater. Two examples of the TF-18A, later redesignated the F/A-18B, featured in the original contract. Basically similar to the single-seater, the F/A-18B possesses identical equipment and virtually identical combat capability. Procurement of the F/A-18B for the USN and USMC ended with the 40th example, and this version has never been employed by front-line forces. The second two-seat version is the F/A-18D, which is broadly similar to the single-seat F/A-18C. F/A-18B/Ds serve with the US Navy's two principal Hornet training units, VFA-106 and VFA-125. F/A-18Bs also equip two reserve units, one of which (VFC-12) is an aggressor squadron. Some 31 baseline F/A-18Ds were built before production changed to the F/A-18D, which is the two-seat counterpart of the night-attack F/A-18C; 109 'D night' examples were built . The night-attack version of the F/A-18D replaced the Grumman A-6 Intruder used by the USMC's all-weather attack squadrons; it equips six frontline units and a training squadron. Originally dubbed F/A-18D+, the aircraft features 'uncoupled' cockpits, usually with no control column in the rear cockpit (although this item can be refitted) but two sidestick weapons controllers. Marine Corps F/A-18Ds have served with distinction during combat operations, including *Desert Storm* in 1991 and Kosovo in 1999. Production of two-seat Hornets has also been undertaken for the export market, and all customers to date have ordered examples. Equipment and designations vary according to local requirements, but these machines are basically similar to their US service equivalents. Deliveries were undertaken to Australia (18 ATF-18As, essentially an F/A-18B), Canada (40 CF-18Bs for service with the local designation CF-188B), Kuwait (eight KAF-18Ds) and Spain (12 EF-18Bs, operated under the local designation CE.15). The F/A-18D variant has been ordered by F/A-18C operators, these comprising Finland (seven) and Switzerland (eight). Malaysia has uniquely ordered only the two-seat variant in the form of eight F/A-18Ds. Thailand contracted for eight examples of the F/A-18C/D but later cancelled its order. Among options that can be specified by customers are APG-73 radar, -402 EPE powerplants and AIM-120 AMRAAM armament.

Specification: Boeing F/A-18B Hornet. Generally similar to the Boeing F/A-18C Hornet except for the following respects:
Type: two-seat attack aircraft
Performance: combat radius 634 miles (1020 km) on an attack mission
Weights: empty 31,700 lb (14379 kg); normal take-off 33,585 lb (15234 kg) for a fighter mission; maximum take-off 47,000 lb (21319 kg) for an attack mission

Boeing (McDonnell Douglas) F/A-18D Hornet

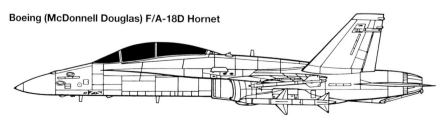

After one of the most drawn out and controversial procurement programmes of recent years, Switzerland eventually ordered the Hornet to replace ageing Mirage III and F-5 aircraft. The Swiss air force received 26 F/A-18Cs and eight F/A-18D two-seaters (illustrated), all with -402 engines, APG-73 radar and AIM-120 missiles. All but two of the aircraft were locally assembled by SF at Emmen, and all had been delivered by 1999.

BOEING F/A-18E/F SUPER HORNET

The first of McDonnell Douglas's (Boeing from 1997) Hornet upgrade concepts to reach fruition is the F/A-18E Super Hornet. The first F/A-18E made its maiden flight in November 1995 and the first aircraft was formally accepted into service with VFA-122 on 15 January 1999. The avionics upgrade is centred on the Raytheon APG-73 radar as already fitted to late versions of the F/A-18C. The IDECM (Integrated Defensive Electronic Counter Measures) system has three major elements: an ALR-67(V)3 RWR, ALQ-214 radio-frequency counter measures system and ALE-55 fibre-optic towed decoy system; the last two are still under development, so the F/A-18E is initially being operated with the ALE-50 towed decoy system. The cockpit of the F/A-18E is similar to that of the F/A-18C with the exception of a larger flat-panel display in place of the current three HDDs. The enlarged airframe incorporates measures to reduce radar cross section and includes a fuselage lengthened by 2 ft 10 in (0.86 m), an enlarged wing characterised by a thicker section and two more hardpoints, enlarged LERXes, and horizontal and vertical tail surfaces. The Super Hornet also has a structure extensively redesigned to reduce weight and cost without sacrificing its strength. The F/A-18E/F also features a new quadruplex digital 'fly-by-wire' control system without the Hornet's mechanical back-up system. The F/A-18F Super Hornet is the two-seat development of the F/A-18E, with the rear cockpit equipped with the same displays as the front cockpit and otherwise configured for alternative combat or training roles. The USN had originally planned to procure a total of 1,000 Super Hornets, but in 1997 the total was reduced to 548. Any delay in the service debut of the JSF to a time later than 2008-10, however, will see the number of Super Hornets rise to 748. An F/A-18F C³W electronic combat variant has been proposed as a replacement for the Grumman EA-6B Prowler. This will be capable of both active jamming as well as lethal SEAD.

Specification: Boeing F/A-18E Super Hornet
Origin: USA
Type: single-seat carrierborne and land-based multi-role fighter, attack and maritime air superiority warplane
Armament: one 20-mm M61A2 Vulcan rotary six-barrel cannon with 570 rounds, plus up to 17,750 lb (8051 kg) of disposable stores, similar weapons options to F/A-18C
Powerplant: two General Electric F414-GE-400 turbofan engines each rated at 22,000 lb st (97.86 kN) with afterburning
Performance: maximum speed over 1,190 mph (1915 km/h) at high altitude; radius 681 miles (1095 km) on a hi-hi-hi interdiction mission with four 1,000-lb (454-kg) bombs, two AIM-9 Sidewinder AAMs and two drop tanks, or 173 miles (278 km) on a 135-minute maritime air superiority mission with six AAMs and three drop tanks
Weights: empty 30,564 lb (13864 kg); maximum take-off 66,000 lb (29937 kg)
Dimensions: wing span 44 ft 8½ in (13.62 m) including tip-mounted AAMs; length 60 ft 1¼ in (18.31 m); height 16 ft (4.88 m); wing area 500.00 sq ft (46.45 m²)

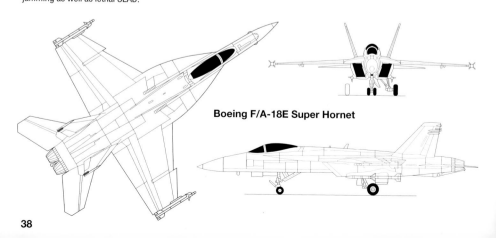

Boeing F/A-18E Super Hornet

The Super Hornet will form the cornerstone
of the US Navy's combat capability well into
the 21st century. Established at NAS
Lemoore on 15 January 1999, VFA-122
'Flying Eagles' was the first Super Hornet
squadron. The squadron's training role is
reflected in its motto: 'We Train the Experts'.

BOEING X-32

Both Boeing and Lockheed Martin were invited to proceed into the Concept Demonstration Program phase of the JSF (Joint Strike Fighter) competition in 1996. The JSF concept involves a single basic type being procured in different variants for service in disparate roles by the USAF, USN, USMC and Britain's Fleet Air Arm. Both CTOL and STOVL versions are to be offered for operations from both land bases and ships, with the type earmarked to replace the F-16, F/A-18, AV-8B and Sea Harrier FA.Mk 2. Other NATO operators may also select the JSF to replace their F-16 fleets in the first two decades of the 21st century. Current predictions suggest that as many as 2,800 aircraft may be produced for the US market alone, making the JSF by far the most valuable military aircraft project in the short to medium term. Boeing's design had previously featured a diamond-delta wing and forward swept underfuselage engine air intake, but in January 1999 the company announced its intention to adopt a more conventional swept wing, aftswept air intake and all-moving tailplane. Nevertheless, Boeing's X-32A flight demonstrator will still be of the earlier design configuration, since Boeing considers that at this early stage any differences in performance between the X-32 and any prototype JSF will be insignificant. Boeing unveiled both the X-32A and X-32B on 14 December 1999. Scoring something of a coup over Lockheed Martin, Boeing was able to fly its X-32A on 18 September 2000 before its rival could fly an X-35. Subsequent problems however, saw Lockheed able to regain the lost ground however, but Boeing plans to fly the first X-32B STOVL aircraft in the spring of 2001. A decision on the winning competitor is expected in September 2001.

Specification: Boeing X-32
Origin: USA
Type: single-seat CTOL (X-32A) or STOVL (X-32B) attack and strike aircraft
Armament: one 27-mm advanced derivative of Mauser BK 27 cannon, plus 14,000-18,000 lb (6350-8165 kg) of stores carried internally and under four wing hardpoints; internal bays in fuselage sides for AIM-120 AMRAAM and bombs, four wing stations for up to 10,000 lb (4536 kg) of weapons
Powerplant: (X-32A) one Pratt & Whitney JSF119-614C turbofan; (X-32B) one Pratt & Whitney JSF119-614S turbofan incorporating Rolls-Royce lift module and spool duct
Performance: not available
Weights: not available
Dimensions: (approximate) (X-32A) wing span 36 ft 0 in (11.00 m); (X-32B) wing span 30 ft 0 in (9.10 m); length 45 ft 0 in (13.70 m); height 13 ft 4 m); wing area 540 sq ft (50.00 m²)

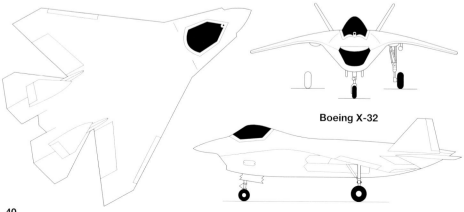

Boeing X-32

BOEING HELICOPTERS CH-47 CHINOOK

Though the US Army was initially interested in the Vertol 107 (which became the H-46 Sea Knight), in 1959 it finally picked a much bigger project, under development since 1956.The prototype Boeing Vertol Model 114 Chinook flew on 21 September 1961, and since then over 1,160 have been built, including 136 from Agusta (Meridionali) in Italy and 54 by Kawasaki in Japan (CH-47J). The original CH-47A reached the US Army in December 1962, and Vertol built 349 before delivering 108 CH-47Bs with more powerful engines, followed by 233 CH-47Cs with 3,750-shp (2798-ekW) engines, increased fuel and, as a retrofit, glass fibre blades and blade-inspection systems. Boeing and Meridionali have sold Chinooks all over the world, export models including the Canadian CH-147 and RAF Chinook HC.Mk 1. The HC.Mk 1 was delivered with two cargo hooks, one rated at 19,841 lb (9000 kg) and the other at 24,912 lb (11300 kg), and comprehensive nav/com avionics. Between 1982 and 1998 over 480 of the US Army's Chinooks were remanu-factured to CH-47D standard with greatly enhanced capability; the RAF has also upgraded 32 of its surviving Chinooks to this standard as Chinook HC.Mk 2s and is also receiving a further eight new-build HC.Mk 2s, as well as nine HC.Mk 3s, which are similar to the US Army's MH-47E special mis-sions helicopter. Other nations operating Chinooks upgraded to CH-47D standard include Australia, Greece, Italy, the Netherlands and Spain. As well as the special missions variants, Boeing also offers the Chinook in CH-47D International Chinook and CH-47SD 'Super D' forms for export. In addition, the CH-47F Improved Cargo Helicopter has been proposed as a new produc-tion version of the Chinook, which will serve the US Army through to 2033.

Specification: Boeing Helicopters CH-47D Chinook
Origin: USA
Type: medium transport helicopter
Armament: provision for two door-mounted 7.62-mm machine-guns or Miniguns
Payload: maximum payload 22,798 lb (10341 kg); crew 2/4; plus up to 44 troop seats, or 24 stretchers plus two attendants
Powerplant: two Textron Lycoming T55-L-712 turboshafts each rated at 3,750 shp (2796 kW) for take-off
Performance: maximum cruising speed at optimum altitude 159 mph (256 km/h); operational radius between 115 and 35 miles (185 and 56 km) with maximum internal and external payloads
Weights: empty 22,379 lb (10151 kg); maximum take-off 50,000 lb (22679 kg)
Dimensions: main rotor diameter, each 60 ft (18.29 m), fuselage length 51 ft (15.54 m); height to top of rear rotor head 18 ft 11 in (5.77 m); main rotor disc area (total) 5,654.86 sq ft (525.34 m²)

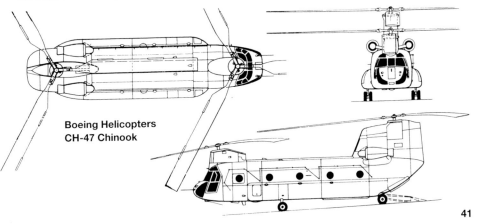

**Boeing Helicopters
CH-47 Chinook**

BOEING/BAE T-45 GOSHAWK

In 1981 the US Navy selected a modified version of the BAe Hawk trainer as the aircraft component of its T45 Training System. In May 1986 an engineering development contract was awarded to McDonnell Douglas (now Boeing), as the US prime contractor, with BAE Systems (formerly BAe) the principal subcontractor. Two versions were proposed: a 'wet' T-45A outfitted for carrierborne operation and a 'dry' T-45B restricted to land-based training and dummy carrier landing practice; the latter version was dropped. The T-45 is based on the airframe of the basic Hawk Mk 60, but features a new forward fuselage deepened to house a new twin-wheel nose gear, redesigned main gear units, a taller fin and tailplane of increased span, a single ventral fin, fuselage side-mounted airbrakes, an arrester hook and small fins ahead of and below the tailplanes. The T-45 also has full-span leading-edge slats plus USN standard cockpit instrumentation and radios. The three prototype T-45s were delivered to the US Navy in October 1990. The first production T-45A made its maiden flight on 16 December 1991 and initial carrier qualifications began in the same month. Plans to re-engine the T-45 with an American-built powerplant have been mooted; the Allied-Signal F124 turbofan was flight-tested in September 1997, without the modification proceeding further. Incorporated from the 84th production machine, the T-45C upgrade adds a much improved digital 'glass' 'Cockpit 21' with two MFDs; this is being retrofitted to earlier aircraft. The original total of 268 T-45s was later trimmed to 197 Goshawks. Since the introduction of the T-45, the training task is being accomplished with 25 per cent fewer flying hours using 42 per cent fewer aircraft and 46 per cent fewer personnel.

Specification: Boeing/BAE Systems T-45A Goshawk
Origin: USA/UK
Type: two-seat land-based but carrier-compatible intermediate and advanced trainer
Armament: provision made for single hardpoint under each wing for carriage of a rack for practice bombs, rocket pods or extra fuel; centreline hardpoint can also carry stores for use in the weapons training role
Powerplant: one Rolls-Royce/Turboméca F405-RR-401 turbofan engine rated at 5,845 lb st (26 kN)
Performance: maximum speed 620 mph (997 km/h) at 8,000 ft (2440 m); initial climb rate 6,982 ft (2128 m) per minute; service ceiling 42,250 ft (12875 m); range 1,152 miles (1854 km)
Weights: empty 9,399 lb (4263 kg); maximum take-off 12,758 lb (5787 kg)
Dimensions: wing span 30 ft 9¾ in (9.39 m); length 39 ft 3⅛ in (11.97 m) including probe; height 14 ft (4.27 m); wing area 176.90 sq ft (16.69 m²)

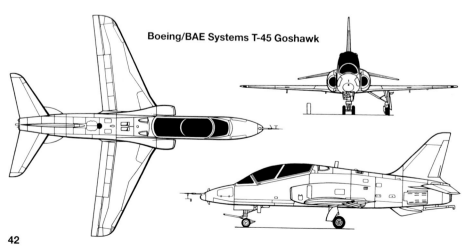

Boeing/BAE Systems T-45 Goshawk

The Goshawk deploys from land bases to the USS *John F. Kennedy* (CV-67), the US Navy's principal training aircraft carrier. The T-45 fleet is assigned to three squadrons, one based at NAS Meridian, Mississippi, and two based at NAS Kingsville, Texas. The baseline T-45A is being upgraded to T-45C standard; the sole external distinguishing feature is the addition of a small antenna GPS behind the cockpit.

BOEING/SIKORSKY RAH-66 COMANCHE

The US Army's ambitious LHX (Light Helicopter Experimental) programme called for a new armed reconnaissance/scout helicopter to replace the service's force of 3,000 AH-1s, OH-6s and OH-58s. A request for proposals was issued in June 1988, and 23-month demonstration and validation contracts were placed with two industrial teamings: the 'Super Team' (Bell and McDonnell Douglas) and the 'First Team' (Boeing and Sikorsky). In April 1991 the designation and name RAH-66 Comanche were selected and the First Team was announced as winner. The Comanche is designed for minimum observability and is based on a 'stealthy' airframe built largely of composite materials. Its advanced avionics are designed for maximum commonality with the F-22 Raptor, and include dual triplex fly-by-wire control systems with sidestick cyclic pitch controllers, a 'glass' cockpit with two large liquid-crystal displays in each cockpit, advanced crew helmet displays and sights, a comprehensive self-protection suite, and provision for Longbow radar (currently planned to be installed in only one out of three RAH-66s). Development has been slowed by technical considerations as well as political antipathy and budgetary delays. The definitive programme emerged in 1995, and called for two YRAH-66 flying prototypes (the first flying on 4 January 1996) plus six 'early operational capability' helicopters with reconnaissance equipment but no armament for trials from 2001. A production decision is expected in 2003, with low-rate production aircraft being delivered in 2004/5 and the establishment of the first operational unit in 2007. In 1998 the planned total was 1,292 helicopters with the possibility of 389 to be added later.

Specification: Boeing/Sikorsky RAH-66 Comanche
Origin: USA
Type: two-crew reconnaissance, attack and air combat helicopter
Armament: (planned) one 20-mm three-barrel cannon with 500 rounds in undernose turret, plus up to three Hellfire ATGMs or six Stinger AAMs on a launcher extended from each of the two weapons bays; optional stub wings (above weapons bays) capable of carrying up to eight Hellfires or 16 Stingers
Powerplant: two LHTEC T800-LHT-801 turboshaft engines each rated at 1,432 shp (1068 kW)
Performance: (estimated) maximum speed 198 mph (319 km/h) at 4,000 ft (1220 m); range 1,450 miles (2334 km) with drop tanks
Weights: (estimated) empty 8,951 lb (4060 kg); maximum take-off 17,408 lb (7896 kg)
Dimensions: main rotor diameter 39 ft 0½ in (11.90 m); length overall, rotors turning 46 ft 10¼ in (14.28 m); height 11 ft 0¾ in (3.37 m); main rotor disc area 1,197.1 sq ft (111.22 m²)

**Boeing/Sikorsky
RAH-66 Comanche**

BRITISH AEROSPACE NIMROD

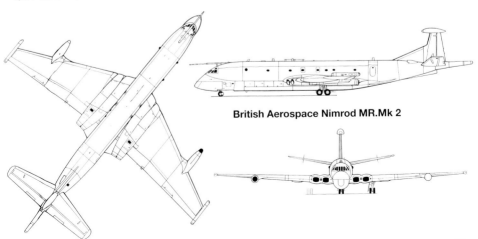

In 1964 Hawker Siddeley began development of a maritime reconnaissance aircraft to replace the ageing, piston-engined Shackleton in service with RAF Coastal Command. Its HS.801 design used the airframe of the de Havilland Comet as a basis, but incorporated a ventral weapons pannier to give a new 'double bubble' cross section and powerplant of four Spey turbofans. The prototype made its maiden flight on 23 May 1967 and the first of 46 production Nimrod MR.Mk 1s flew on 28 June 1968. The type entered service in October 1969. Eleven MR.Mk 1s were later converted in the early 1980s to Nimrod AEW.Mk 3 standard in an abortive programme to provide the RAF with a new airborne early warning aircraft. From 1975 MR.Mk 1s were upgraded to MR.Mk 2 standard, the first such conversion being redelivered to the RAF in August 1979. This variant introduced a completely new avionics and equipment suite, including a GEC central tactical system, a Thorn EMI Searchwater radar and an acoustics system compatible with modern sonobuoys. The addition of an inflight-refuelling probe for the 1982 Falklands war created the Nimrod MR.Mk 2P – the 'P' was subsequently dropped in the late 1990s. Wingtip-mounted Loral ESM pods were added later. Several Nimrods detached to Oman for Operation *Desert Storm* were modified with an underwing FLIR, BOZ ECM pod and a towed radar decoy. During the mid-1990s, BAe was selected to update 21 Nimrods to MRA.Mk 4 standard. This involves a virtual total rebuild of the airframe, installation of 15,000-lb st (66.73-kN) BMW Rolls-Royce BR.710 turbofans, strengthened undercarriage and new avionics and sensor suites that will maintain the Nimrod's capabilities at a very high standard. The programme is scheduled to deliver these revitalised machines between 2002 to 2007. Three further aircraft designated Nimrod R.Mk 1 serve in the electronic intelligence-gathering role. A crashed R.Mk 1 was replaced by converting a 'spare' MR.Mk 2 airframe in 1997.

Specification: British Aerospace Nimrod MR.Mk 2
Origin: United Kingdom
Type: maritime reconnaissance, anti-submarine warfare, anti-ship and search and rescue aircraft
Armament: maximum ordnance 13,500 lb (6124 kg) including AIM-9 Sidewinder AAMs for self-defence, AGM-84 Harpoon AShMs, Stingray torpedoes, bombs or depth charges
Powerplant: four Rolls-Royce RB.168-20 Spey Mk 250 turbofans each rated at 12,140 lb st (54.00 kN)
Performance: maximum speed 575 mph (926 km/h) at optimum altitude; maximum cruising speed at optimum altitude 547 mph (880 km/h); patrol speed on two engines 230 mph (370 km/h); service ceiling 42,000 ft (12800 m); range 5,758 miles (9266 km); typical unrefuelled endurance 12 hours; endurance 19 hours with one inflight refuelling
Weights: empty 86,000 lb (39010 kg); maximum overload take-off 192,000 lb (87090 kg)
Dimensions: wing span 114 ft 10 in (35 m); length 126 ft 9 in (38.63 m); height 29 ft 8½ in (9.08 m); wing area 2,121 sq ft (197 m²)

British Aerospace Nimrod MR.Mk 2

BRITISH AEROSPACE SEA HARRIER

The versatility and effectiveness of a maritime version of the Harrier were clear as early as 1966, but it was not until May 1975 that the go-ahead was given for development of a dedicated naval variant. Compared to the RAF's Harrier GR.Mk 3, this introduced a new forward fuselage seating the pilot higher to provide space for extra avionics which included a Blue Fox multi-mode radar. The type was intended to be multi-role, and gained the the designation FRS for fighter/reconnaissance/strike (for which latter role it carried a lightweight version of the free-fall WE177 weapon). The first of an initial batch of 24 Sea Harrier FRS.Mk 1s for the Royal Navy flew on 20 August 1978. Subsequently, a further 10 were ordered, followed by 14 in July 1982 (seven of the latter replacing attrition in FAA service, including the Falklands war) and a further nine in 1984. The Indian navy was the sole export customer, ordering 23 Sea Harrier FRS.Mk 51s. The Sea Harrier proved of vital importance in the conflict to regain the Falklands Islands in 1982, scoring 22 confirmed victories for no losses during air combat. The shortcomings of the Sea Harrier highlighted by the conflict led to an ambitious mid-life upgrade. On 19 September 1988, BAe flew the first prototype conversion of the Sea Harrier FRS.Mk 2 (later F/A.Mk 2 and now designated FA.Mk 2). This features a multi-function CRT cockpit with HOTAS controls, increased weapons and stores capability, Pegasus Mk 106 powerplant (based on the Mk 105 of the AV-8B), and most importantly, a Blue Vixen radar in a re-contoured radome. The radar allows compatibility with the AMRAAM missile for beyond visual range engagements. On 24 December 1998, the last of 18 new-build FA.Mk 2s was delivered, this adding to the total of 31 machines produced by conversion from FRS.Mk 1 standard. Both Sea Harrier variants saw extensive combat over Bosnia in 1996.

Specification: British Aerospace Sea Harrier FA.Mk 2

Origin: United Kingdom

Type: ship-based STOVL attack, fighter and reconnaissance aircraft

Armament: two 30-mm ADEN cannon in under-fuselage pods (optional), maximum ordnance 8,000 lb (3630 kg) for STO, primary armament of four AIM-120B AMRAAMs or two AIM-120s and four AIM–9L/Ms; other stores include bombs, rockets, ALARM missiles and 190-Imp gal (864-litre) drop tanks

Powerplant: one Rolls-Royce Pegasus Mk 106 turbofan rated at 21,500 lb st (95.64 kN)

Performance: maximum level speed 'clean' at sea level more than 736 mph (1185 km/h); combat radius 460 miles (750 km) on a hi-hi-hi interception mission with four AAMs

Weights: operating empty 14,052 lb (6374 kg); maximum take-off 26,200 lb (11884 kg)

Dimensions: wing span 25 ft 3 in (7.7 m); length 46 ft 6 in (14.2 m); height 12 ft 2 in (3.70 m); wing area 201 sq ft (18.6 m²)

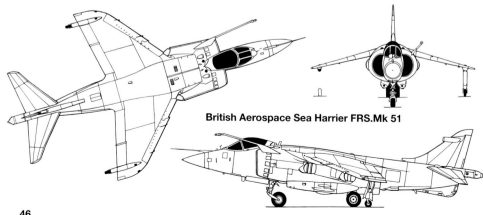

British Aerospace Sea Harrier FRS.Mk 51

The Sea Harrier FA.Mk 2 is viewed by some as
the world's finest operational naval fighter.
The FA.Mk2 is an extremely advanced
derivative of the first generation FRS.Mk 1
that was retired from Fleet Air Arm service in
1995. The upgrade is centred around the Blue
Vixen radar, which is acknowledged as
among the most capable multi-mode units
fitted to any fighter.

BRITISH AEROSPACE VC10

Included in the production run of 54 Vickers VC10s and Super VC10s were 14 transports for the RAF which combined features of both variants. Apart from having the short VC10 fuselage, almost all engineering features of the VC10 C.Mk 1 were those of the Super VC10, including uprated engines, stronger structure, wet (integral tank) fin, extended leading edge and increased gross weight. To meet RAF requirements the C.Mk 1 also had an Artouste APU fitted in the tail, a large cargo door and a floor strengthened for heavy freight. Thirteen aircraft (the 14th being an RB.211 engine test-bed) were fitted with inflight-refuelling probes and, between 1991 and 1992, these gained a Mk 32 HDU (hose-drum unit) beneath each outer wing. Known as VC10 C.Mk 1Ks these dual-role tanker/transports continue to give exemplary service with No10. To meet the RAF's need for tankers, No101 received nine former civil aircraft completely rebuilt by BAe Bristol. Five British Airways VC10s became VC10 K.Mk 2 tankers and four East African Model 1154 Supers became VC10 K.Mk 3 tankers. The RAF bought the last 14 British Airways Supers, three of which were cannibalised and the rest stored for possible conversion into tankers at a later date. On 30 July 1993, the first of five VC10 K.Mk 4s, converted from the stored air-frames, was flown for the first time. These triple-point tankers do not have extra fuel tanks and are used for short-range operations. The K.Mk 2 and K.Mk 3 were generally brought to C.Mk 1 standard, but have no passenger windows and sealed-cargo doors. Five large double-skinned tanks were added above the floor, and three HDUs installed, a Mk 17B in the rear fuse-lage and a Mk 32 under each outer wing. The VC10 served during the 1991 Gulf War and during NATO operation *Allied Force* against Serbia in 1999.

Specification: British Aerospace VC10 C.Mk 1K

Origin: United Kingdom

Type: long-range transport aircraft and inflight-refuelling tanker

Payload: maximum payload of provision for all-passenger interior with 150 aft-facing seats; mixed passenger/cargo or all-cargo interior; VIP interior for royal families or heads of state; or up to 78 stretchers for casevac role

Powerplant: four Rolls-Royce Conway RCo.43 Mk 301 turbofans each rated at 21,800 lb st (96.97 kN)

Performance: typical cruising speed 550 mph (886 km/h), initial rate of climb 3,050 ft (930 m) per minute, service ceiling 42,000 ft (12800 m); range with maximum payload 4,720 miles (7600 km)

Weights: empty 146,000 lb (66226 kg); maximum take-off 323,000 lb (146513 kg)

Dimensions: wing span 146 ft 2 in (44.55 m); length (excluding probe) 158 ft 8 in (48.36 m); 39 ft 6 in (12.04 m); wing area 2,932 sq ft (272.38 m²)

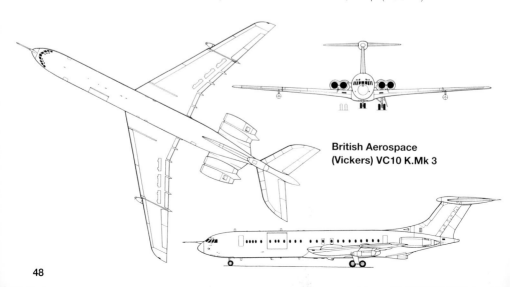

**British Aerospace
(Vickers) VC10 K.Mk 3**

BRITISH AEROSPACE/McDONNELL DOUGLAS HARRIER GR.MK 7

The Harrier GR.Mk 7 is basically the RAF equivalent of the USMC's night attack variant of the AV-8B Harrier II. Fitted with the same standard of equipment and avionics, it lacks the rear fuselage chaff/flare dispensers, however. The variant is easily distinguished from the AV-8B and the RAF's previous Harrier GR.Mk 5 by twin undernose forward hemisphere antennas for the Marconi Zeus ECM system. The GR.Mk 7 also has an NVG-compatible cockpit fitted with a digital colour map. The first GR.Mk 7s ordered as such were 34 aircraft requested during 1988. The first GR.Mk 5 converted to Mk 7 standard flew for the first time on 20 November 1989. It was soon decided that all RAF Harrier IIs would be retrofitted to this configuration, and Harrier IIs Nos 42-60 were completed as GR.Mk 5As with provision for GR.Mk 7 avionics. Conversions of these aircraft (plus a damaged GR.Mk 5) began during December 1990. From aircraft No77 all RAF Harriers were fitted with the so-called 100 per cent LERX (Leading-Edge Root Extension), for improved turn performance. The first production GR.Mk 7 was delivered in May 1990. By late 1992 some No1 Sqn aircraft already had their FIN1075 INAS upgraded to FIN1075G standards, with the incorporation of a GPS receiver. No1 received GR.Mk 7s during late 1992, and became the first front-line unit to start night-attack training in earnest. The Harrier is one the RAF's three principal warplanes, and is scheduled to receive new equipment and armament in line with upgrades to the Jaguar and Tornado forces. Harrier GR.Mk 7s dropped Paveway II LGBs on Serb positions in Bosnia in late August 1995, and saw extensive service in *Allied Force* in 1999. The RAF's requirement for a trainer fully representative of the second-generation Harrier's performance led to the purchase of 13 Harrier T.Mk 10s. These are based on the TAV-8B, the last example being delivered on 26 October 1995.

Specification: British Aerospace/McDonnell Douglas Harrier GR.Mk 7
Origin: United Kingdom/USA
Type: single-seat STOVL attack and close-support aircraft
Armament: maximum ordnance 10,800 lb (4899 kg) for STO, including 1,000-lb (454-kg) bombs, CPU-123 Paveway II laser-guided bombs, CRV-7 rockets, AIM-9 Sidewinders and 250-Imp gal (1135-litre) drop tanks
Powerplant: one Rolls-Royce Pegasus Mk 105 turbofan rated at 21,500 lb st (95.64 kN)
Performance: maximum speed at sea level 662 mph (1065 km/h); range 460 miles (750 km) 684 miles (1001 km) on a hi-lo-hi attack mission after STO with seven 500-lb (227-kg) bombs
Weights: empty 13,968 lb (6336 kg); maximum take-off 31,000 lb (14061 kg) for STO
Dimensions: wing span 30 ft 4 in (9.25 m); length 46 ft 4 in (14.12 m); height 11 ft 7¾ in; wing area 238.70 sq ft (22.18 m²)

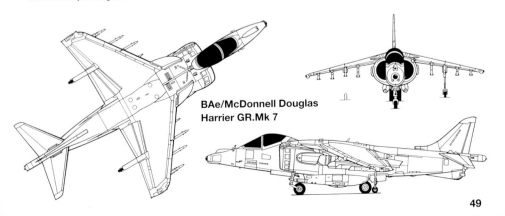

BAe/McDonnell Douglas Harrier GR.Mk 7

CASA C.101 AVIOJET

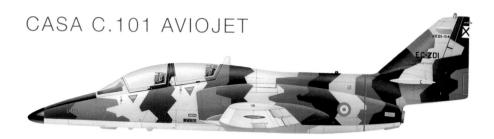

On 16 September 1975 the Spanish *Ministerio del Aire* signed a contract with CASA for the development of a new jet trainer capable of carrying a wide range of weapons. Design was assisted by Northrop (USA) and MBB (West Germany), but after the completion of the flight development programme, which began on 27 June 1977, the entire production was handled by CASA, except for items such as the US powerplant and Dowty Rotol nose landing gear. Features include a low-powered turbofan of good fuel economy, tandem stepped seating with Martin-Baker zero/zero seats, manual controls apart from powered ailerons, and a large bay in the belly into which can be fitted a range of stores packages. CASA initially delivered 60 C.101EB-01s for the Spanish air force, which gained the designation E.25 Mirlo. A second contract covered a further 28 aircraft and all surviving machines received a nav/attack system upgrade between 1990–1992. Fitted with a 3,700-lb (16.46-kN) thrust TFE731-3 engine and provision for full armament, the C.101BB was the original export model. Chile became the first export customer; it received 14 C.101BB-02s, four Spanish-built and ten assembled by ENAER. Locally designated T-36 Halcon (hawk), these were intended for advanced training but were later modified with ranging radar to serve as A-36BB tactical weapons trainers. First flown on 16 November 1983, the C.101CC dedicated attack variant introduced an uprated 4,700-lb (20.91 kN) thrust TFE731-5-1J engine. Exports have been made to Chile (23 C.101CC-02), Honduras (four C.101BB-03) and Jordan (16 C.101CC-04). The C.101DD is the most advanced Aviojet variant. First flown on 25 May 1985, it has HOTAS controls, a HUD and compatibility with the AGM-65 Maverick ASM. Intended as an improved trainer with a secondary light attack capability, it has failed to gain orders.

Specification: CASA C.101EB Aviojet
Origin: Spain
Type: trainer and light tactical aircraft
Armament: (C.101BB) one 30-mm DEFA cannon beneath the fuselage, or twin 12.7-mm (0.5-in) M3 machine-guns, or a reconnaissance camera pod, ECM pod or laser designator in a fuselage bay; plus up to 2,205 lb (1000 kg) of stores under six wing hardpoints
Powerplant: one Garrett TFE731-221 turbofan rated at 3,500 lb (15.57 kN) thrust
Performance: maximum speed, 'clean' at 25,000 ft (7620 m) 493 mph (793 km/h); combat radius on a lo-lo-hi mission with four 551-lb (250-kg) bombs and 30-mm gun, 3 minutes over target and 30-minute reserves 236 miles (380 km); ferry range with 30-minute reserves 2,245 miles (3613 km)
Weights: empty 7,385 lb (3350 kg); maximum take-off 12,345 lb (5600 kg)
Dimensions: wing span 34 ft 9½ in (10.6 m); length 40 ft 2¼ in (12.25 m), height 13 ft 11¼ in (4.25 m); wing area 215.3 sq ft (20.00 m²)

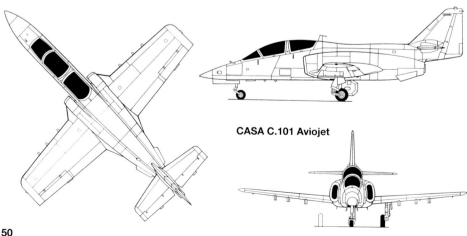

CASA C.101 Aviojet

CESSNA T-37/A-37 DRAGONFLY

When Cessna Aircraft flew the prototype XT-37 on 12 October 1954, it was the world's second purpose-designed military jet primary trainer after the Fouga Magister. Unlike the French trainer, the USAF adopted side-by-side seats. The T-37A entered service in 1957, and has been the USAF's standard undergraduate pilot trainer ever since. Over four decades of service, the 'Tweet' has proved to be a reliable, simple and versatile trainer. From 1989 the USAF's surviving T-37s were cycled through a structural upgrade. Only in June 1999 was the first production T-6A Texan II (the turboprop aircraft selected as its replacement) delivered to the USAF. Following 534 T-37As came 447 T-37Bs with more powerful J69 engines, improved navaids and provision for wingtip tanks. Cessna also built 269 T-37Cs with a limited light attack capability. In 1963 Cessna developed a dedicated light attack derivative of the T-37, converting two T-37Bs as YAT-37D prototypes. These were fitted with greatly increased power from two General Electric J85 engines, armour protection, an internal 0.3-in (7.62-mm) Minigun, ground-attack avionics, eight wing hardpoints and wingtip tanks. Following 39 T-37Bs converted to A-37A standard, Cessna built 577 examples of the definitive A-37B model. This featured an airframe stressed to 6g and an IFR probe. A-37s saw combat in Vietnam and were exported to Chile, Colombia, Ecuador, Guatemala, Thailand and South Vietnam. At least 130 A-37Bs were converted to OA-37B standard with modified avionics for FAC duties with the USAF, the last one being retired in 1992. A-37s and OA-37Bs drawn from USAF stocks continue to serve extensively with Latin American air arms in operational training and light attack roles. Operators in 2001 comprise Chile, Ecuador, Guatemala, Honduras, Peru and El Salvador, as well as Thailand and South Korea. The T-37C remains in limited service.

Specification: Cessna OA-37B Dragonfly
Origin: USA
Type: two-seat light attack and forward air controller aircraft
Armament: one 7.62-mm (0.3-in) GAU-213/A7 Minigun in nose, eight wing hardpoints (four inner pylons rated at 870 lb /394 kg each, next 600 lb/272 kg, outers 500 lb/ 227 kg); stores include 500-lb (227-kg) Mk 82 free-fall bombs, rocket launchers
Powerplant: two General Electric J85-17A turbojets each rated at 2,850 lb st (12.68 kN) thrust
Performance: maximum speed, clean 524 mph (843 km/h), initial climb rate 6,990 ft (2130 m) per minute; service ceiling 41,765 ft (12730 m); range at high altitude with maximum payload (including 4,100 lb/ 1860 kg of ordnance) 460 miles (740 km)
Weights: empty 6,211 lb (2817 kg); maximum take-off 14,000 lb (6350 kg)
Dimensions: wing span (over wingtip tanks) 35 ft 10½ in (10.93 m): length (excluding probe) 28 ft 3¼ in (8.62 m), height 9 ft 2 in (2.80 m); wing area 183.90 sq ft (17.09 m²)

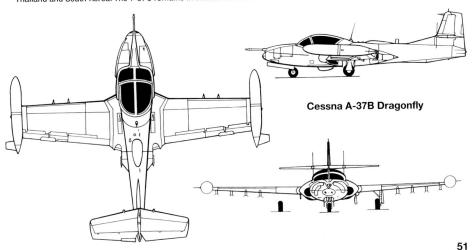

Cessna A-37B Dragonfly

CHENGDU F-7 SERIES

Licensed production of the MiG-21 and its variants by China – both for the home country and for export – has been significant. Copies of the basic MiG-21F-13 (J-7 I in Chinese service, F-7A for export) were sold to Albania and Tanzania. From 1979 Chengdu began to build the improved J-7 II in large numbers for the PLAAF. The export variant of the J-7 II is known as F-7B and is compatible with the MATRA R550 Magic missile. Two large orders – each of approximately 90 aircraft – were secured from Egypt and Iraq (the latter customer losing several in air combat during *Desert Storm*). A further 22 were sold to Sudan. The F-7M Airguard was developed specifically for export and featured two extra underwing hardpoints (total four) able to carry PL-7 short-range AAMs or drop tanks, an uprated engine, a strengthened airframe, a Marconi HUD and weapon aiming computer and GEC-Marconi Type 226 Skyranger ranging radar. Pakistan has been the lead export customer for the F-7M and its derivatives. It considered licence manufacture of the F-7M but finally opted for 20 F-7P derivatives with Western avionics, the ability to carry both PL-5 and AIM-9 AAMs and Martin-Baker Mk 10L zero/zero ejection seats. Pakistan also received 100 F-7MPs with revised cockpit layouts, improved navigation avionics and FIAR Grifo 7 fire-control radars in place of the original Skyranger units. All Pakistani F-7s are designated as F-7P. The F-7M and its sub-variants have also been sold to Bangladesh (16), Iran (at least 18), and Myanmar (24). Sri Lanka's F-7BS and Zimbabwe's F-7 IIN aircraft are based on the F-7B but have the F-7M's four-pylon wing. Two variants that entered PLAAF service in the early 1990s retain the armament capability of the F-7M. The J-7E is an upgraded J-7 II with a cranked (double delta) wing and provision to carry PL-8 missiles, while the J-7 III is basically equivalent to the Soviet MiG-21MF and also serves with the Chinese navy.

Specification: Chengdu F-7M Airguard
Origin: People's Republic of China
Type: single-seat interceptor and ground-attack fighter
Armament: two 30-mm Type 30-1 fixed forward-firing cannon, plus up to 5,511 lb (2500 kg) of stores; including PL-2, -2A, -5, -7, -8 or R550 air-to-air missiles, pods for 57-mm (18-shot) or 90-mm (seven-shot) rockets, plus bombs from 50 kg to 500 kg (110 lb–1,102 lb)
Powerplant: one Liyang (LMC) WP-7B(BM) turbojet engine rated at 13,448 lb st (59.82 kN) with afterburning
Performance: maximum speed 1,350 mph (2175 km/h) at high altitude; initial climb rate 35,433 ft (10800 m) per minute; service ceiling 59,700 ft (18200 m); combat radius 373 miles (600 km) on a hi-lo-hi interdiction mission with two 331-lb (150-kg) bombs and three drop tanks
Weights: empty 11,629 lb (5275 kg); normal take-off 16,603 lb (7531 kg)
Dimensions: wing span 23 ft 5⅚ in (7.15 m); length 48 ft 10 in (14.89 m) including probe; height 13 ft 5½ in (4.103 m); wing area 247.58 sq ft (23.00 m²)

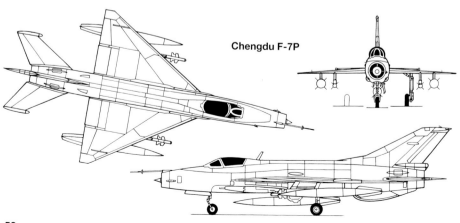

Chengdu F-7P

DASSAULT MIRAGE III/5/50

The delta-winged Mirage III is one of the most successful fighters in history. In a programme stretching until 1995, Dassault built over 1,400 Mirage IIIs and derivatives for service with 21 countries. The Mirage III-001 prototype made its maiden flight in 1956, and was followed by the first production Mirage IIIC interceptors for the *Armée de l'Air* in 1960. Other major variants were the IIIB/D trainer, IIIE multi-role, radar-equipped fighter and IIIR for reconnaissance. The Mirage 5 was optimised for clear-weather day attack; it lacked radar but featured extra fuel and weapons-carrying capability. The Mirage 50 was powered by an uprated Atar 09K50 engine. In 2001 Mirage III/5/50s remain important front-line types with the air forces of Argentina, Brazil, Chile, Colombia, Egypt, Pakistan, Peru and Venezuela. Mirages remain in limited service, in reserve or are in storage in Abu Dhabi, France, Gabon, Libya and Zaïre. Most current operators have upgraded their aircraft to various degrees. Most upgrades are centred around improvements in radar, avionics, nav/attack and self-defence system. Canards have also been added to improve the Mirage's poor field performance and turn rate. Pakistan is the last major Mirage III/5 operator. Its existing force has been augmented with second-hand aircraft acquired from Australia, France and the Lebanon. Existing Mirage IIIs and 5s can also be upgraded to Mirage 50 standard as is the case with Venezuela's Mirage 50EV/DVs. Chile operates arguably the most capable aircraft. Its Mirage 50CNs have been upgraded with Israeli assistance to Pantera standard (above) and share features of the IAI Kfir. Chile also operates ex-Belgian Mirage 5s that were progressively upgraded to MirRSIP, and later Elkan, standard.

Specification: Dassault Mirage 50
Origin: France
Type: single-seat multi-role fighter
Armament: two internal DEFA 552A 30-mm cannon with 125 rounds per gun, plus up to 8,818 lb (4000 kg) of ordnance; air-to-air weapons include R.530 and Magic AAMs
Powerplant: one SNECMA Atar 9K-50 turbojet rated at 11,023 lb st (49.03 kN) dry and 15,873 lb st (70.82 kN) with afterburning
Performance: maximum level speed 'clean' at 39,370 ft (12000 m); 1,453 mph (2338 km/h); initial climb rate 36,614 ft (11000 m) per minute; service ceiling 59,055 ft (18000 m); combat radius 817 miles (1315 km) on a hi-hi-hi interception mission with two AAMs and three drop tanks
Weights: normal take-off 22,046 lb (10000 kg); maximum take-off 32,407 lb (14700 kg)
Dimensions: wing span 26 ft 11½ in (8,22 m); length 51 ft 0⅔ in (15.56 m), height 14 ft 9 in (4.5 m); wing area 374.6 sq ft (34.85 m²)

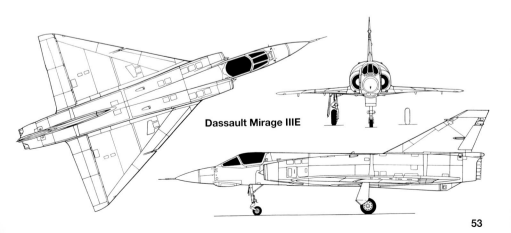

Dassault Mirage IIIE

DASSAULT MIRAGE F1

14-15

Dassault's successor to the Mirage III dispensed with the traditional delta layout and adopted a more conventional configuration. The resulting Mirage F1 has 40 per cent more internal fuel in a smaller airframe, a much shorter field length, three times the supersonic endurance, twice the tactical radius at low levels and all-round better manoeuvrability. The prototype F1 first flew in 1966. The F1C all-weather interceptor reached *l'Armée de l'Air* units in 1973, and when production ended in 1992, some 762 aircraft of all versions had been built. F1 variants follow a similar designation system applied to earlier Mirage IIIs and include the F1A simplified for day attack, F1B and F1D dual-control trainers, multi-role Mirage F1E, F1CR multi-sensor reconnaissance platform and F1C-200 with fixed IFR probe. The arrival of the Mirage 2000 saw the conversion of surplus F1C airframes to F1CT standard as tactical fighter-bombers. The F1 was exported widely and has seen extensive combat with the majority of its operators; conflicts have included the Persian Gulf 'tanker war' (during which Iraq's Exocet-armed F1EQs attacked oil tankers in international waters), South Africa's 'externals' into neighbouring countries and *Desert Storm*. The F1 remains in widespread service in 2001. France operates two squadrons each of F1CRs and F1CTs, a conversion unit equipped with trainers and a small detachment of F1C interceptors for the defence of Djibouti. Other operators comprise Greece, Iraq, Jordan, Kuwait, Libya, Morocco, and Spain. Jordan's elderly F1CJ/EJs are being replaced by F-16s. Iraq was the largest export customer, acquiring 108 F1EQs to various standards. Combat losses during *Desert Storm*, and the loss of 24 F1s to Iran, have left some 30-35 currently in service. The remaining significant operator is Spain, whose force of F1CE/F1EEs has recently been augmented by 12 ex-Qatari F1EDA/DDAs.

Specification: Dassault Mirage F1C
Origin: France
Type: single-seat interceptor
Armament: two internal DEFA 553 30-mm cannon with 135 rpg; standard intercept load of two Super 530 and two R550 Magic AAMs; practical maximum load of 8,818 lb (4000 kg); typical French weapons for ground attack include ARMAT ARM, AS.30L ASM, AM.39 Exocet AShM, 250-kg bombs , BGL-400 400-kg (881-lb) LGB
Powerplant: one SNECMA Atar 9K-50 turbojet rated at 11,023 lb st (49.03 kN) dry and 15,785 (70.21 kN lb st) with afterburning
Performance: maximum speed 'clean' at 36,090 ft (11000 m) 1,453 mph (2338 km/h); initial climb rate 41,930 ft (12780 m) per minute; service ceiling 65,615 ft (20000 m); combat radius 264 miles (425 km) on a hi-lo-hi attack mission with 14 551-lb (250-kg) bombs
Weights: empty 16,315 lb (7400 kg), maximum take-off 33,510 lb (15200 kg)
Dimensions: wing span 30 ft 6¾ in (9.32 m); length 50 ft 2½ in (15.30 m); height 14 ft 9 in (4.50 m); wing area 269.11 sq ft (25.00 m²)

Dassault Mirage F1AZ

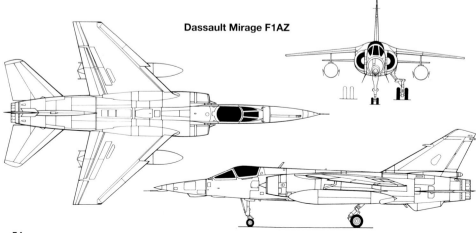

Ecuador received 16 single-seat F1JAs and a pair of twin-seat trainers between 1978 and 1980. They are armed with French Magic 2 air-to-air missiles for intercept missions, but carry up to eight Israeli P-1 bombs for ground attack.

DASSAULT MIRAGE 2000B/C

For the third generation of its Mirage warplane series, Dassault returned to the delta configuration – using negative longitudinal stability and an FBW FCS – to eliminate many of the shortcomings of a conventionally controlled delta. This combination confers the resulting Mirage 2000 with exceptional manoeuvrability. A high-priority development programme was launched to ensure a service debut in 1982. The first of five prototypes made its maiden flight in March 1978. Delivery of 124 production 2000C single-seat interceptors began to the *Armée de l'Air* in 1983. Three units were equipped, with early aircraft fitted with M53-5 engines and RDM radar. The 38th 2000C introduced the definitive initial standard with the M53-P2 engine and RDI radar optimised for look-down/shoot-down intercepts with Super 530D semi-active radar-homing AAMs. The 2000B is the two-seat conversion trainer equivalent of the 2000C; it dispenses with both cannon and features a small fuselage stretch to accommodate a second seat. All trainers retain full combat capability and have RDI radar (except first 15 aircraft) and M53-5 engines. Orders were terminated in 1991 as an economy measure after the completion of 30 production 2000Bs. Export series aircraft are designated 2000E (single-seat) and 20000ED (trainer). Aircraft similar to early production French 2000B/Cs were built for Egypt (20), India (49) and Peru (12), while Mirages with upgraded EW suites were built for Abu Dhabi (36) and Greece (30). Abu Dhabi's order also included eight 2000RAD reconnaissance variants able to carry SLAR, LOROP and other podded sensors. The much-improved 2000-5 introduced RDY multi-mode radar (compatible with MICA AAMs), improved cockpit systems and an upgraded EW suite. Some 37 French 2000Cs were upgraded to 2000-5F standard in 1994-97. Exports have been made to Taiwan in 1997-98 and subsequently to Qatar.

Specification: Dassault Mirage 2000-5
Origin: France
Type: single-seat multi-role fighter
Armament: two 30-mm DEFA 554 fixed forward-firing cannon in the lower part of the forward fuselage, plus maximum load of 13,889 lb (6300 kg); standard intercept load of four MICA and two Magic 2 missiles (to be replaced later by IR-homing MICA); for attack options see specification for Mirage 2000D
Powerplant: one SNECMA M53-P2 turbofan engine rated at 14,462 lb st (64.33 kN) dry and 22,046 lb st (98.06 kN) with afterburning
Performance: maximum speed 1,451 mph (2335 km/h) or Mach 2.2 at high altitude and Mach 1.2 at low level; initial rate of climb 56,000 ft (17060 m) per minute; service ceiling 60,000 ft (18290 m); operational range 898 miles (1445 km) with six missiles
Weights: empty 16,534 lb (7500 kg); combat weight 20,944 lb (9500 kg); maximum take-off 33,069 lb (15000 kg)
Dimensions: wing span 29 ft 11½ in (9.13 m); length 48 ft 0¾ in (14.65 m); height 17 ft 0¾ in (5.20 m); wing area 441.33 sq ft (41.00 m²)

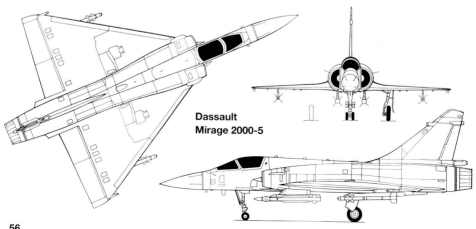

**Dassault
Mirage 2000-5**

Taiwan received 48 single-seat Mirage 2000-
5Eis optimised for air defence missions.
Equipping three squadrons, these are
essentially similar to the 37 French 2000-5Fs
and are armed with MATRA BAe Magic 2 and
MICA missiles. The standard intercept loadout
comprises four MICA and two Magics. The
Taiwanese order also included 12 2000-5Di
trainers.

DASSAULT MIRAGE 2000D/N

In 1979 Dassault was contracted to produce two prototypes of the Mirage 2000P (*Pénétration*) that were intended to replace the ageing Mirage IVP in the nuclear strike role. Later designated 2000N (*Nucléaire*), this version of the 2000B trainer features a strengthened airframe to cope with high-subsonic, low-level flight and an Antilope 5 terrain-following radar that provides automatic terrain following down to 300 ft (91 m) at speeds up to 691 mph (1112 km/h). The primary armament is the 1,874-lb (850-kg) Aerospatiale ASMP stand-off tactical strike missile. This has a dual yield of 150- or 300-KT and a range of over 50 miles (80 km) from low-altitude launch. The 2000N achieved IOC in July 1988 and was built in two versions: N-K1 dedicated nuclear strike (31 built) and N-K2 with additional conventional attack capability (46 built). Delays with the Rafale programme generated a requirement for more aircraft solely for conventional attack. The resulting 2000N' (*N Prime*) flew in prototype form in 1990. The designation was later changed to 2000D (*Diversified*) and 75 examples were built for delivery from 1993. These differ from the 2000N by having an upgraded countermeasures suite and cockpit systems with more integrated HOTAS controls. The key to much of the 2000D's precision attack capability is the PDCLT laser designator/ TV/thermal imaging pod. Carried beneath the starboard air intake, it allows the 2000D to direct weapons such as the AS 30L laser-guided missile or BGL 1000 LGB. In 2001 the *Armée de l'Air* fielded three squadrons each of 2000Ds (all based at Nancy) and 2000Ns (two units at Luxeuil and one at Istres). In 1997 Abu Dhabi ordered 30 new-build Mirage 2000-9 long-range attack aircraft. Later designated 2000-5 Mk II, these will be joined by all 33 remaining examples of Abu Dhabi's earlier batch (including 2000D-DA trainers) upgraded to 2000-9 standard.

Specification: Dassault Mirage 2000D-D generally similar to the Mirage 2000-5 except in the following parameters
Type: two-seat attack aircraft
Armament and other stores: (cannon not fitted); precision attack weapons include AS 30L laser guided ASMs, AM39 Exocet AShMs, GBU-10, GBU-12 and BGL 1000 2,183-lb (990-kg) LGBs, APACHE and SCALP stand-off submunitions dispensers and ARMAT ARMs combined with PDCLT and Atlis II targeting pods; free-fall weapons include MATRA 250 free-fall retarded bombs, BM 400 modular bombs, BAP 100 anti-runway bombs, Belouga cluster bombs and Durandal airfield denial weapons, LR F4 18-shot 68-mm rocket launchers and CC630 gun twin 30-mm cannon pods; two Magic 2 AAMs carried for self-defence
Performance: range 575 miles (925 km) on a lo-lo-lo attack mission
Weights: empty 16,755 lb (7600 kg); clean take-off 24,165 kg (10960 kg); maximum take-off 37,480 lb (17000 kg)
Dimensions: height 16 ft 10¾ in (5.15 m)

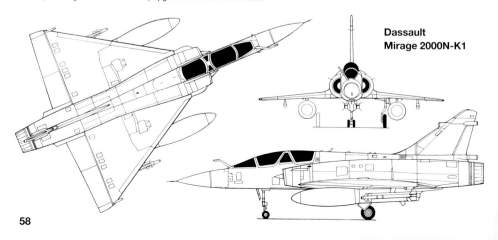

**Dassault
Mirage 2000N-K1**

Previously designated M2000-9, the 2000-5 Mk II programme was developed specifically for Abu Dhabi. The requirement called for a long-range attack aircraft that was also capable of carrying six MICAs. Indigenous weapons include the Black Shaheen, a development of the SCALP EG/Storm Shadow weapon being produced for the RAF and *Armée de l'Air*.

DASSAULT RAFALE

The Dassault Rafale will form the cornerstone of French air power until well into the 21st century. The programme began with the Rafale A technology demonstrator that was first flown on 4 July 1986. This established the basic aerodynamic design and evaluated the delta canard configuration, performance, FBW control system and composite-based structure. The generic Rafale D (*Discret*, or stealthy) – prototype for the *Armée de l'Air* versions – is slightly smaller and lighter. The Rafale features some of the very latest avionics systems including RBE2 multi-mode radar (the first in Europe with two-plane electronic scanning), advanced pilot's helmet with sight and display, Spectra countermeasures system and OSF – a jam-resistant passive optronic surveillance and imaging system with laser rangefinder. The *Aéronavale* will acquire the single-seat Rafale M interceptors and strike/attack aircraft for operation from the carrier *Charles de Gaulle*. This is similar to land-based counterparts but features major reinforcement of the landing gear, plus a 'jump-strut' that allows automatic unstick rotation. The *Aéronavale's* has a requirement for 86 examples, but procurement is likely to be limited to 60 aircraft initially. The *Armée de l'Air* plans to acquire 82 single-seat Rafale Cs and 130 two-seat Rafale Cs. These will be designated as Rafale F and will be delivered in several standards: F1 optimised for the air-to-air role but lacking ASMP capability, OSF and Spectra; F2 with improved air-to-surface capability (including the SCALP SOM dispenser) and the definitive Rafale F3 with improved radar. The 20,907-lb st (93.00-kN) M88-3 turbofan will become standard later in the programme. Milestones were marked with the first flights of the prototype Rafale C in May 1991 and Rafale M in December 1991, and the Rafale B in April 1993. The Rafale M will be the first operational Rafale variant and is scheduled to enter service in 2001. The *Armée de l'Air* will receive F1-specification Rafales in 2002.

Specification: Dassault Rafale D
Origin: France
Type: single-seat multi-role warplane
Armament: one 30-mm GIAT/DEFA M791B cannon, plus maximum load of 20,944 lb (9500 kg); principal weapons include up to eight MICA AAMs for interception, single ASMP stand-off nuclear missile for strike or two APACHEs or SCALPs for attack
Powerplant: two SNECMA M88-2 turbofan engines each rated at 10,950 lb st (48.7 kN) dry and 16,400 lb st (72.9 kN) with afterburning
Performance: maximum speed 1,189 mph (1913 km/h) or Mach 1.8 at 36,090 ft (11000 m); radius of action on a low-level penetration mission with 12 551-lb (250-kg) bombs, four MICA AAMs and three external fuel tanks 655 miles (1055 km)
Weights: empty equipped 19,973 lb (9060 kg); maximum take-off 42,989 lb (19500 kg) increasing to 54,012 lb (24500 kg) in later-production aircraft
Dimensions: wing span 35 ft 5¼ in (10.80 m) with tip-mounted AAMs; length 50 ft 1¼ in (15.27 m); height 17 ft 6¼ in (5.34 m); wing area 491.93 sq ft (45.70 m²)

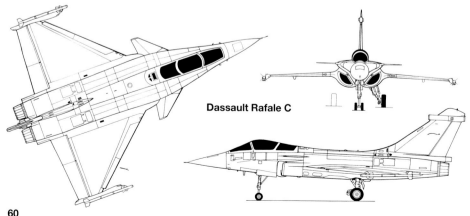

Dassault Rafale C

This pre-production Rafale B carries two APACHE weapons. Combat experience from the Gulf War led to an increase in procurement of the two-seat Rafale B. Initially planned to serve mainly as a trainer conversion, this will become instead the *Armée de l'Air's* principal operational variant. The first of 130 production two-seaters made its maiden flight in November 1998. In *Armée de l'Air* service, early Rafales will initially replace the Jaguar and the oldest Mirage 2000C interceptors.

DASSAULT/DORNIER ALPHA JET

The Alpha Jet was designed in the late 1960s to meet a joint Franco-German requirement for a jet trainer and light attack aircraft. It was seriously delayed by the formation of multi-national production programmes for both the aircraft and its two powerplants, so that although the prototype flew on 26 October 1973, the type did not enter service for a further six years. The two original partners bought 350 aircraft. France received 176 E (*Ecole*, or trainer) versions while West Germany received 175 A (*Appui*, or attack) models equipped with an advanced nav/attack system, as well as a ventrally-mounted 27-mm Mauser cannon pod. Exports of new-build trainers were made to Belgium (33), Egypt (26 Alpha Jet MS1 models), Ivory Coast (7), Morocco (24) Qatar (6), Nigeria (24) and Togo (5). Egypt later procured 15 MS2 attack variants with improved avionics that included a TMV630 laser rangefinder; seven MS2s were also supplied to Cameroon. With the thawing of the Cold War and the transfer of German fast-jet crew training to the USA, the Luftwaffe retired its Alpha Jet fleet from 1992. Of these, 50 were supplied to Portugal in 1994, while Thailand received 25 in 2000 to replace OV-10 Broncos in the COIN and border patrol roles. Finding itself barely capable of supporting the RAF's training needs due to its chronic shortage of Hawk trainers, Britain has also acquired ex-German Alpha Jets. Twelve have been procured, some to fly test and target facilities missions, the rest to act as a spares source. In 2001 approximately 90 Alpha Jet Es remain in service with five *Armée de l'Air* squadrons (three at Tours and two at Cazaux). A further 13 aircraft equip the '*Patrouille de France*', the national aerobatic team. The *Armée de l'Air* is considering the upgrade of perhaps 50 Alpha Jets with new systems to serve as lead-in trainers for the Mirage 2000-5F and Rafale, both of which have advanced 'glass' cockpits.

Specification: Dassault/Dornier Alpha Jet E
Origin: France/Germany
Type: basic and advanced trainer
Armament: provision for a belly pod containing one 30-mm DEFA cannon with 150 rounds for armament training or close support; maximum load of 5,511 lb (2500 kg); weapons include 275-, 551- and 881-lb (125-, 250- and 400-kg) free-fall bombs, Belouga cluster dispensers, 18-shot 68-mm rocket launchers, practice carriers for bombs and rocket launchers, 30-mm gun pods (carried underwing), plus provision for Magic or AIM-9 AAMs
Powerplant: two SNECMA/Turboméca Larzac 04-C6 turbofans each rated at 2,976 lb st (13.24 kN)
Performance: maximum speed clean at sea level 621 mph (1000 km/h); operational radius 361 nm (670 km; 416 miles) on a lo-lo-lo training mission with two drop tanks
Weights: empty 7,374 lb (3345 kg); maximum take-off 16,535 lb (7500 kg)
Dimensions: wing span 29 ft 10¾ in (9.11 m); length 40 ft 3¾ in (12.29 m), height 13 ft 9 in (4.19 m), wing area 188.4 sq ft (17.5 m²)

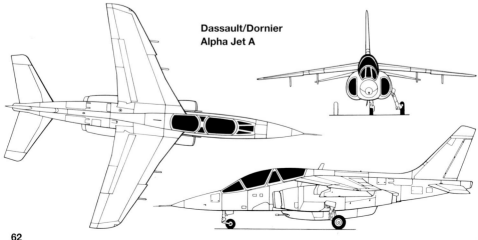

Dassault/Dornier Alpha Jet A

EH INDUSTRIES EH 101

The EH 101 has its roots in a UK project to replace the Sea King. The design was later revised to meet Italian navy as well as Royal Navy requirements. Westland and Agusta established European Helicopter Industries Ltd, which received a formal go-ahead in February 1984 for nine prototypes and subsequent development of what now became the EH 101. The first prototype made its maiden flight in October 1987. Aside from its principal ASW role, the EH 101 is also envisaged for utility and transport missions. Some roles can be performed using the same basic fuselage as the naval helicopter but, alternatively, the EH 101 can be fitted with a modified rear fuselage incorporating a ventral ramp/door. Systems and equipment vary with role and customer. The initial Royal Navy variant is the Merlin HM.Mk 1 which is equipped with a Blue Kestrel 360° search radar. The first of 44 on order was delivered in 1998. The Italian navy EH 101s (16 on order plus eight on option) are powered by GE T700-GE-T6A engines, each rated at 1,714 shp (1278 kW). In 2000 the RAF began to receive the first of 22 Merlin HC.Mk 3 medium-lift transports. These can accommodate a maximum of 45 troops or up to 12,000 lb of freight carried internally or as a slung load. The first customer for the utility variant was to have been Canada, which ordered 15 EH 101s for SAR duties, along with 35 naval variants. The entire Canadian programme was subsequently cancelled on budget and political grounds, but, in January 1998, the Canadian government placed a new order for 15 examples of the revised AW320 Cormorant SAR version for delivery between 2000 and 2003. Further development of the EH 101 could result in an AEW version of the type required by both the Italian navy and Royal Navy.

Specification: EH Industries Merlin HM.Mk 1
Origin: Italy/UK
Type: one/two-crew shipborne and land-based anti-submarine and utility helicopter
Armament: maximum load of 2,116 lb (960 kg); weapons comprise four Marconi Sting Ray homing torpedoes (Mk 46 for Italian ASW version); other options include two Sea Eagle, Marte 2, AM 39 Exocet and AGM-84 Harpoon AShMs for ASV mission
Powerplant: three Rolls-Royce/ Turboméca RTM 322-01 turboshaft engines each rated at 2,312 shp (1724 kW)
Performance: cruising speed 173 mph (278 km) at optimum altitude; service ceiling 15,000 ft (4575 m); range 656 miles (1056 km); endurance 5 hours
Weights: empty 23,149 lb (10500 kg); maximum take-off 32,188 lb (14600 kg)
Dimensions: main rotor diameter 61 ft (18.59 m); length 74 ft 10 in (22.81 m) with the rotors turning; height 21 ft 10 in (6.65 m) with the rotors turning; main rotor disc area 2,922.60 sq ft (271.51 m²)

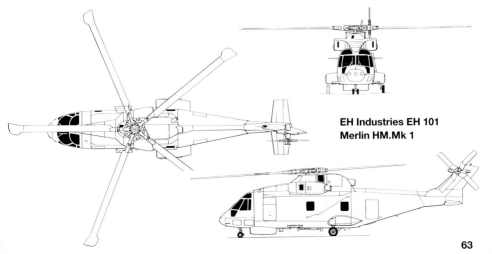

**EH Industries EH 101
Merlin HM.Mk 1**

EMBRAER EMB-312 TUCANO

The Brazilian EMBRAER Tucano is one of the world's most successful turbo-prop trainers, and its light attack derivatives are gaining significant orders. Design of the EMB-312 Tucano (toucan) high-performance trainer started in 1978 in response to a *Força Aerea Brasileira* (FAB – Brazilian air force) specification. First flown on 16 August 1980, the prototype Tucano was followed by 133 production aircraft designated T-27 for the FAB. Designed to provide a jet-like flying experience, the Tucano has a long cockpit with vertically staggered ejection seats and a single power lever governing both propeller pitch and the engine rpm. Tucanos have also been delivered to Argentina (30), Colombia (14), Egypt (54), France (50), Iran (25), Iraq (80), Honduras (12), Paraguay (6), Peru (30) and Venezuela (31); a further 27 aircraft have been built for undisclosed customers. The Tucano's most notable export success came in March 1985, when it won a British order for an aircraft to replace the RAF's Jet Provosts in the basic training role. The resulting Tucano T.Mk 1 was produced under licence by Shorts. This model featured a range of modifications including British equipment and a more powerful Garrett engine. Shorts built 130 examples for the RAF and further aircraft for Kenya (12) and Kuwait (16). In June 1991 EMBRAER announced the EMB-312H (later EMB-314) Super Tucano with a stretched fuselage, an uprated PT6A engine, an NVG-compatible, Kevlar-armoured cockpit and FLIR. This type has higher performance and greater agility, as well as the ability to carry a heavier load. In August 1995 the FAB ordered full development of the ALX variant of the EMB-314. Intended for light attack, Amazon border patrol and weapons training, some 99 aircraft have been ordered, comprising 49 single-seat A-29 attack machines, 20 two-seat AT-29s with night attack capability and 30 AT-29 advanced trainers.

Specification: EMBRAER EMB-312 Tucano
Origin: Brazil
Type: two-seat basic flying and armament trainer
Armament: up to 2,205 lb (1000 kg) of stores carried on four underwing hardpoints; weapons include C2 0.30-in (7.62-mm) machine-gun pods, 250-lb (113-kg) Mk 81 bombs, 25-lb 913-kg) practice bombs, and seven-shot Avibras rocket launchers
Powerplant: one Pratt & Whitney Canada PT6A-25C turboprop engine rated at 750 shp (559 kW)
Performance: maximum speed 278 mph (448 km/h) at 10,000 ft (3050 m); cruising speed 255 mph (411 km/h) at 10,000 ft (3050 m); initial climb rate 2,231 ft (680 m) per minute; service ceiling 30,000 ft (9145 m); typical range 1,145 miles (1844 km) with internal fuel
Weights: empty 3,991 lb (1810 kg); maximum take-off 7,000 lb (3175 kg)
Dimensions: wing span 36 ft 6½ in (11.14 m); length 32 ft 4¼ in (9.86 m); height 11 ft 1¾ in (3.40 m);); wing area 208.82 sq ft (19.40 m²)

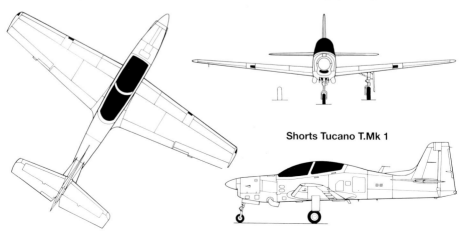

Shorts Tucano T.Mk 1

EUROCOPTER DOLPHIN/PANTHER

Military derivatives of the twin-engined civil SA 365 and SA 366 Dauphin serve in various forms with 21 air arms. Sales were limited to small numbers principally for utility and VIP transport duties. The biggest customer was the US Coast Guard (USCG) which bought 99 HH-65A Dolphins for the short-range recovery SAR role. Dedicated military versions are derived from the civil AS 365N Dauphin 2. The AS 365F is intended primarily for the anti-ship role, and features search radar, a towed MAD 'bird', AShM armament and avionics for mid-course targeting update of ship-launched AShMs. A SAR variant has an advanced EFIS flightdeck, a rescue winch and an automatic navigation system. Eurocopter also offers a more advanced ASW derivative equipped with dunking sonar, upgraded MAD, and torpedo armament. Military variants have since been redesignated in the Eurocopter France AS 565 Panther series. Saudi Arabia received four SAR/surveillance AS 565MBs and 20 AS 565SBs for ASW duties. Abu Dhabi bought seven AS 565SAs for ASW while Israel bought AS 565SAs (local name Atalef/Bat). France has 18 unarmed AS 565MA variants for SAR, sea surveillance and aircraft-carrier plane guard ('Pedro') duties. The Panther is also marketed in three basic land-warfare forms; armed AS 565AB; anti-tank AS 565CA and unarmed utility AS 565UB. Brazil acquired 36 AS 565AAs (local designation HM-1) primarily for general transport. In the PRC, the AS 365N has been built under licence as the Harbin Z-9 Haitun for the PLA Army Aviation Corps and PLA Naval Aviation. Harbin also markets an anti-tank variant.

Specification: Eurocopter AS 565SA Panther
Origin: France
Type: two-seat light naval utility helicopter
Armament: maximum load 1,323 lb (600 kg); weapons include four AS15TT light AShMs or two Mk 46 lightweight torpedoes
Powerplant: two Turboméca Arriel 1M1 turboshaft engines each rated at 749 shp (558 kW)
Performance: maximum cruising speed 170 mph (274 km/h) at sea level; initial climb rate 1,378 ft (420 m) per minute; service ceiling 15,010 ft (4575 m); hovering ceiling 8,530 ft (2600 m) in ground effect; combat radius 155 miles (250 km) on an anti-ship mission with four missiles
Weights: empty 4,938 lb (2240 kg); maximum take-off 9,370 lb (4250 kg)
Dimensions: main rotor diameter 39 ft 2 in (11.94 m); length 44 ft 10⅝ in (13.68 m) with rotor turning; height 13 ft ¾ in (3.98 m); main rotor disc area 1,205.26 sq ft (111.97 m²)

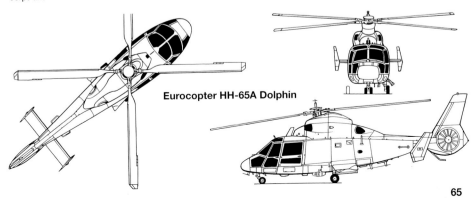

Eurocopter HH-65A Dolphin

EUROCOPTER GAZELLE

The Gazelle is a successful light utility helicopter that remains in widespread service in 2001 with some 25 operators. The type originated in a mid-1960s Sud Aviation project. The X.300 design, soon redesignated SA 341, achieved high speed and manoeuvrability through the adoption of a powerful turboshaft, an aerodynamically-shaped cabin and covered tail-boom, and advanced rotor technology. It also featured a revolutionary fenestron tail rotor. The Gazelle was part of an Anglo-French helicopter agreement of 1967 that also included the Puma and British-designed Lynx. The SA 340 prototype flew on 7 April 1967, and manufacture of the revised SA 341 began on 6 August 1971. Current operational military versions of the basic SA 341 comprise the British army Gazelle AH.Mk 1 (SA 341B), French army (ALAT) SA 341F and export SA 341H. The AH.Mk1 remains a key type in Army Air Corps service and, of 212 built, some 70 were fitted with magnifying sights to act as target-finders for missile-armed Lynx attack helicopters. ALAT received 170 SA 341Fs and converted 40 to carry HOT missiles as SA 341Ms, and 62 with an M621 20-mm cannon and SFOM 80 sight as SA 341F/Canon helicopters. The SA 342 is an improved SA 341 variant that introduced the uprated 858-shp (640-kW) Astazou XIVH engine. Military exports began with the SA 342K, the latter soon replaced by the SA 342L with an improved fenestron. The ALAT equivalent is designated SA 342M and over 200 have been delivered, armed with four HOT ATGMs. For the 1991 Gulf War, 30 were converted to SA 342M/Celtic standard, with a pair of Mistral AAMs. The definitive anti-helicopter Gazelles are the 30 conversions to SA 342M/ATAM standard. Gazelles built in the former Yugoslavia by SOKO are armed with AT-2 'Sagger' ATGMs.

Specification: Eurocopter France SA 341F Gazelle
Origin: France/UK
Type: light utility helicopter
Armament: maximum payload 1,540 lb (700 kg); SA 341F/Canon carries a GIAT M621 20-mm cannon to starboard and a roof-mounted SFOM optical 80 sight
Powerplant: one Turboméca Astazou IIIA turboshaft rated at 590 shp (440 kW)
Performance: maximum cruising speed at sea level 164 mph (264 km/h); maximum rate of climb at sea level 1,770 ft (540 m) per minute; service ceiling 16,405 ft (5000 m); hovering ceiling 9,350 ft (2850 m) in ground effect and 6,560 ft (2000 m) out of ground effect; range 416 miles (670 km) with standard fuel
Weights: empty 2,028 lb (920 kg); maximum take-off 3,968 lb (1800 kg)
Dimensions: main rotor diameter 34 ft 5½ in (10.50 m); length overall, rotor turning 39 ft 3⅝ in (11.97 m); height overall 10 ft 5¼ in (3.18 m); main rotor disc area 932.08 sq ft (86.59 m²)

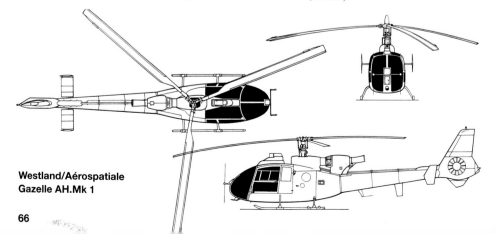

Westland/Aérospatiale Gazelle AH.Mk 1

EUROCOPTER PUMA/COUGAR

The SA 330 Puma was developed by Sud-Aviation to meet a French army specification for an all-weather medium transport helicopter. In 1967 it was also selected for the RAF and produced as a joint programme with Westland. Nearly 700 Pumas were built for at least 25 air forces and the type remains in widespread use. The RAF Puma HC.Mk 1 entered service in 1971 and is in the twilight of its career; it will shortly be replaced by the EH.101 Merlin. The basic SA 330Ba still serves in significant numbers with French army aviation. The ALAT's 130 surviving SA 330Bs have been progressively updated. The *Armée de l'Air* operates 29 Pumas, six of which in the combat SAR (CSAR) role. The Aérospatiale AS 332 Super Puma was devised as a successor to the Puma. It first flew on 13 September 1978 and entered service as the military AS 332B and 'stretched' AS 332M. Pumas and Super Pumas have been built under licence by IPTN in Indonesia. South Africa's Pumas were replaced from 1995 by the TP-1 Oryx, a Puma developed by Atlas that incorporates elements of the Super Puma upgrade, including Makila engines. In January 1990 the military developments of the AS 332 were renamed Cougar (later Cougar Mk I), renumbered AS 532 and accorded new variant suffixes, according to role and airframe (short- or long-fuselage). First flown in 1987 the Cougar Mk II introduced uprated 2,104-shp (1569-kW) Makila 1A2 powerplants. The Cougar serves with the ALAT as a battlefield surveillance and control aircraft with the HORIZON battlefield surveillance radar; it also supplements the basic SA 330B in the assault transport role. Dedicated CSAR variants serve with the air forces of France and Saudi Arabia. AS 332 Super Pumas and AS 532 Cougars are operated by 30 air arms.

Specification: Eurocopter France AS 532UC Cougar Mk I
Origin: France
Type: two/three-crew general-purpose tactical medium helicopter
Payload: accommodation for up to 21 troops; maximum external slung load of 9,921 lb (4500 kg)
Powerplant: two Turboméca Makila 1A1 turboshafts each rated at 1,877 shp (1400 kW)
Performance: maximum cruising speed 163 mph (262 km/h) at sea level; maximum climb rate at sea level 1,378 ft (420 m) per minute; service ceiling 13,450 ft (4100 m); range 384 miles (618 km) with standard fuel and 607 miles (977 km) at with two external tanks and one auxiliary internal tank
Weights: empty 9,546 lb (4330 kg); maximum take-off 19,841 lb (9000 kg) with internal load; maximum take-off 20,615 lb (9350 kg) with external slung load
Dimensions: main rotor diameter 51 ft 2¼ in (15.60 m); length 61 ft 4¼ in (18.70 m) with rotors turning; height 16 ft 1¾ in (4.92 m); main rotor disc area 2,057.42 sq ft (191.13 m²)

**Aérospatiale/Westland
Puma HC.Mk 1**

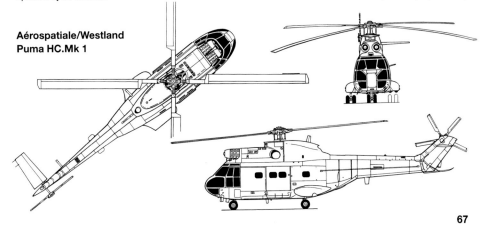

EUROCOPTER TIGER

The EC 665, known in France as the Tigre and in Germany as the Tiger, was planned in 1984 to meet French and German requirements for an advanced multi-role type for battlefield operations in the typical European scenario. After much deliberation Eurocopter received a contract to build five prototype/development helicopters in November 1989. Three were to be unarmed aerodynamic testbeds and the other two armed prototypes for the basically similar Tiger/Tigre anti-tank variants required by Germany and France (one prototype), and for a French escort helicopter variant. The basic type is of typical attack helicopter configuration with an airframe built largely of composite materials and optimised for high-survivability over the modern battlefield. The first prototype made its maiden flight in April 1991. Three versions are being developed in two basic layouts. The ALAT requires 100 HAC (*Hélicoptère Anti-Char*) anti-tank helicopters while the German army needs 212 UHT (*Unterstützungshubschrauber Tiger*) anti-tank/multi-role support helicopters. Both HAC and UHT share a common mast-mounted TV/FLIR/ laser rangefinder sighting system for the gunner, nose-mounted FLIR for the pilot and Trigat missile armament. The UHT may later be fitted with a turret-mounted 30-mm Mauser cannon. The Tigre HAP (*Hélicoptère d'Appui et de Protection*) is being developed for the French army, which requires 115 such examples for the escort and fire support roles. The HAP carries a chin turret-mounted 30-mm GIAT M30/781B cannon, STRIX roof-mounted sight plus armament of up to 68 SNEB 68-mm rockets and Mistral AAMs. In June 1999 both French and German governments signed a production contract for an initial batch of 160 helicopters. The first Tiger and Tigre are scheduled to enter German and French service in 2002 and 2003 respectively.

Specification: Eurocopter Tiger HAC/UHT
Origin: France/Germany
Type: two-seat anti-tank and close support helicopter
Armament: (primary) up to eight HOT 2/ HOT 3 ATMs (Trigat 2 projected available from 2006); plus four Stinger 2 (UHT) or Mistral (HAC) short-range AAMs; additional options include unguided 68-mm rockets, podded 12.7-mm guns and fuel tanks
Powerplant: two MTU/Turboméca/Rolls-Royce MTR 390 turboshaft engines each rated at 1,285 shp (958 kW) for take-off
Performance: maximum speed 167 mph (269 km/h) at optimum altitude; initial climb rate 2,106 ft (642 m) per minute; hovering ceiling 10,500 ft (3200 m) out of ground effect; range 497 miles (800 km) with standard fuel; endurance 3 hours 25 minutes
Weights: empty 7,275 lb (3300 kg); maximum take-off 13,448 lb (6100 kg)
Dimensions: main rotor diameter 42 ft 7¾ in (13.00 m); length 51 ft 10 in (15.80 m) with the rotors turning; height 17 ft ¾ in (5.20 m) to top of mast-mounted sight; main rotor disc area 1,428.76 sq ft (132.73 m²)

Eurocopter Tiger

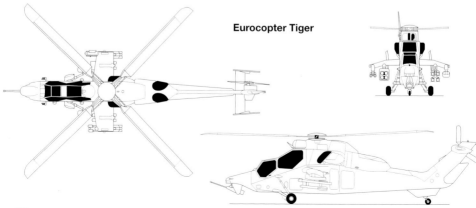

Eurocopter emphasises that the Tiger offers the latest technology, with 80 per cent of the airframe being of composite materials. Despite being badly affected by French/German defence cuts, which have resulted in lower production totals, the Tiger will shortly enter service with both French and German armies in two basic anti-tank and anti-helicopter/escort variants.

EUROFIGHTER 2000/TYPHOON

The Eurofighter Typhoon will form the cornerstone of European air power until well into the 21st century. Much experience of the type's main concepts were proven by the BAe EAP technology demonstrator programme of the late 1980s. These concepts include an unstable delta canard configuration, active digital FBW control system, a HOTAS cockpit and highly capable though complex avionics that even include direct voice command input. In June 1986 the Eurofighter consortium was formed by Germany, Italy, the UK and, later, Spain, to develop a new multi-role combat aircraft, optimised as a BVR interceptor with a secondary ground-attack capability. Other consortia have been formed to develop the EJ200 engine, ECR90 multi-mode radar, IRST and advanced DASS (defensive aids sub-system). DASS comprises an integrated package of missile approach, laser and radar-warning elements together with wingtip mounted ESM and ECM pods and fuselage-mounted chaff/flare dispensers and a towed radar decoy. An initial 1988 contract covered construction of eight prototypes (to be built in all of the partner countries). Funding was divided in proportion to the various national industrial participations, with respective national requirements being finally settled on in 2000 as a maximum of 297 for the UK, 180 for Germany, 130 for Italy and 103 for Spain. In addition, an export order for 60 Typhoons plus 30 options for Greece was signed in 1999 and other exports are likely. The first two Eurofighter 2000 prototypes, completed in Germany and the UK as DA.1 and DA.2 respectively, undertook their maiden flights on 27 March and 6 April 1994. These have been followed by six further prototypes (including a pair of two-seaters) that are used as testbeds for the EJ200 engine, ECR90 radar and for avionics and weapons integration. In 1998 Eurofighter 2000 received the name Typhoon, and the first production aircraft is expected to be rolled out in the second half of 2001.

Specification: Eurofighter Typhoon
Origin: UK/Spain/Italy/Germany
Type: single-seat air combat fighter with attack capability
Armament: one 27-mm Mauser BK27 cannon; maximum ordnance load of 17,637 lb (8000 kg); mix of AIM-120B AMRAAM (later Meteor FMRAAM) and ASRAAM or IRIS-T AAMS, for interception; air-to-ground weapons include Paveway III LGBs, Storm Shadow SOM dispensers, ALARM ARMs, Penguin AShMs, Brimstone anti-armour munitions
Powerplant: two Eurojet EJ200 turbofans each rated at 13,490 lb st (60.00 kN) dry and 20,250 lb st (90.00 kN) with afterburning
Performance: maximum speed 1,321 mph (2125 km/h) at 36,090 ft (11000 m); climb to 35,000 ft (10670 m) and Mach 1.5 in 2 minutes 30 seconds; radius 864 miles (1390 km) on an air-defence mission with three drop tanks for a 10-minute loiter
Weights: empty 24,239 lb (10995 kg); maximum take-off 50,705 lb (23000 kg)
Dimensions: wing span 35 ft 11 in (10.95 m) over tip-mounted ECM pods; length 52 ft 4¼ in (15.96 m); height 17 ft 4 in (5.28 m); wing area 538.21 sq ft (50.00 m²)

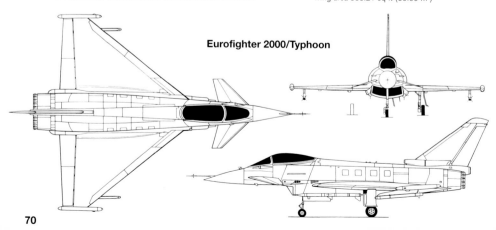

Eurofighter 2000/Typhoon

Both built by BAe (now BAE Systems), DA.2 (background) was the first British single-seater while DA.4 was the first two-seater, and is also the development prototype for the Eurofighter's ECR.90 radar. The two-seater retains full combat capability. The Eurofighter has been dogged by political delays and disagreement, but is unarguably one of the most important pan-European combat aircraft programmes. The aircraft has been making steady gains recently, and first examples are scheduled to be delivered to test units of the German, Italian and British air forces in 2002/2003. It is also likely to attain operational service before its main rivals – the F-22 and Rafale.

FAIRCHILD A-10 THUNDERBOLT II

Originally conceived as a COIN aircraft to help the US war effort in Southeast Asia, the A-10 emerged as a dedicated close air support aircraft with the primary role of destroying enemy armour. The A-10 was built around the 30-mm GAU-8 Avenger cannon, the most powerful gun ever flown. The A-10 was also required to carry large numbers of ground-attack stores and be survivable in the face of intense battlefield AA fire. Unpressurised and without radar, the A-10A remains austerely equipped in terms of avionics, but is a very hard-hitting and well-protected machine. The cockpit is protected from 23-mm cannon hits by a 'bath' of titanium armour. The nickname of 'Warthog' has largely stuck on account of the type's ungainly looks. However, the unconventional design is central to its ability to survive the lethal battlefield environment; the fuel-efficient turbo-fans of low IR signature are mounted above the rear fuselage and the A-10 can remain airworthy with an engine, tail or other parts inoperative or shot away. The A-10A first flew in production form on 21 October 1975 and entered USAF service in 1977. Much derided and destined for premature retirement prior to the 1991 Gulf War, the star performance of the A-10A and its identical, but Forward Air Control (FAC)-roled, OA-10A variant led to the type's continued leading presence in the USAF's front-line. Most current aircraft have received the LASTE modification which adds an autopilot and also considerably improves gun accuracy. Primarily armed with AGM-65 Maverick missiles in addition to the 30-mm gun, the A-10 has been a key player in subsequent USAF actions, including combat over the former Yugoslavia. Although a plan to supply second-hand A-10As to Turkey was aborted, the type will remain in US service well into the 21st century. The type currently equips nine active-duty, three AFRES and six ANG units.

Specification: Fairchild A-10A/OA-10A Thunderbolt II
Origin: USA
Type: single-seat FAC, close support and anti-tank aircraft
Armament: one GAU-8A 30-mm cannon; maximum theoretical ordnance load of 16,000 lb (7258 kg); weapons generally comprise AGM-65B/C Maverick air-to-surface missiles with IR- or TV-guidance, six LAU-68 seven-shot multiple launchers for 70-mm rockets, plus four AIM-9L/M Sidewinder missiles for self defence
Powerplant: two General Electric TF34-GE-100 turbofans each rated at 9,065 lb st (40.32 kN)
Performance: maximum level speed 'clean' at sea level 439 mph (706 km/h); initial climb rate 6,000 ft (1829 m) per minute; combat radius 288 miles (463 km) on a CAS mission
Weights: operating empty 24,959 lb (11321 kg); maximum take-off 22680 kg (50,000 lb)
Dimensions: wing span 57 ft 6 in (17.53 m); length 53 ft 4 in (16.26 m); height 14 ft 8 in (4.47 m); wing area 506.00 sq ft (47.01 m²)

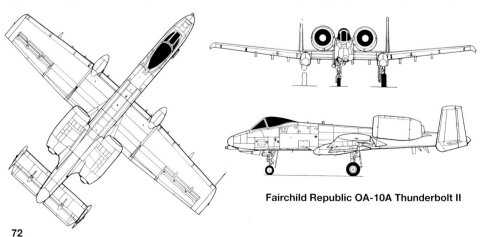

Fairchild Republic OA-10A Thunderbolt II

GENERAL DYNAMICS F-111

First flown on 21 December 1964, the F-111 scored several 'firsts'. It was the world's first attack aircraft with both supersonic speed and avionics for blind first-pass attack on a point target; the F-111 was also the world's first production aircraft to feature variable-sweep 'swing wings' and terrain-following radar. The F-111A/D/E and the 'definitive' F-111F served with the USAF's TAC, while SAC operated the FB-111A in the strike role. Grumman rebuilt 42 F-111As as EF-111A Raven electronic jamming platforms. F–111E/Fs and EF-111As served with distinction during *Desert Storm* but were retired a few years later. The Royal Australian Air Force (RAAF) was the sole export customer, receiving 24 F-111Cs in 1973; these combined the longer span wings of the FB-111A with the lower powered engines and avionics of the F-111A. Four were later modified as RF-111Cs with a multi-sensor reconnaissance pallet in the former internal weapons bay. In 1993-94 the RAAF acquired 15 ex-USAF F-111Gs, along with a number of Pave Tack laser-designation pods as previously used by the F–111F. The RAAF F-111s are tasked with anti-ship missions as well as precision and conventional attack, and give the RAAF the most formidable long-range attack and maritime attack capabilities in the region. As the type will form the core of the RAAF's offensive capability well into the 21st century, the entire fleet is being upgraded with new systems and weapons. The 21 surviving F–111C/RF-11Cs have been cycled through an avionics upgrade programme and also re-engined with the more powerful TF30-P-109 engine. A similar avionics upgrade is proposed for the F-111G fleet and this is also projected to confer autonomous laser designation capability. The four 'Recce Jets' (RF-11C) are also slated to have their reconnaissance suite upgraded. New weapons include the AGM-142E Have Nap stand-off missile with both blast and penetrating warheads. The current lack of an anti-radiation and area denial/hardened target weapons is being addressed.

Specification: General Dynamics F-111C (pre-engine upgrade)
Origin: USA
Type: two-seat long-range precision attack and interdiction aircraft
Armament: maximum load of 31,500 lb (14228 kg); weapons include AGM-84D Harpoon AShMs, AGM-84E SLAM missiles, AGM-142E stand-off missiles (in blast and penetrating (semi-hardened target) warhead versions), GBU-10/12/24 LGBs, GBU-15 EO-guided bombs, Mk 82/84 free-fall bombs, Mk 36 Destructor mines, Karinga cluster bombs, plus AIM-9L/M/P AAMs for self defence (projected to be replaced by MATRA/BAe AIM-132 ASRAAM)
Powerplant: two Pratt & Whitney TF30-P-3 turbofans each rated at 18,500 lb st (82.32 kN) with afterburning
Performance: range more than 2,925 miles (4707 km) with internal fuel
Weights: operating empty 47,481 lb (21537 kg); maximum take-off 100,000 lb (45360 kg)
Dimensions: wing span 63 ft (19.20 m) spread and 31 ft 11½ in (9.74 m) swept; length 73 ft 6 in (22.40 m); height 17 ft 1½ in (5.22 m); wing area 525.00 sq ft (48.77 m²) spread

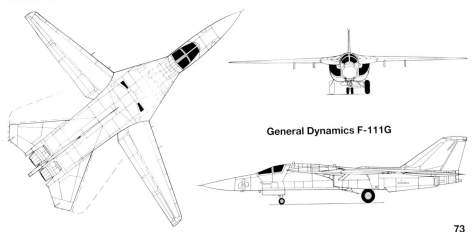

General Dynamics F-111G

GRUMMAN EA-6B PROWLER

The EA-6B remains an essential element of US naval air power and has taken part in all US major actions since it entered service in 1971. Since the retirement of the USAF's EF-111A Raven in 1997, the Prowler has assumed the full responsibility for the EW mission in US service, with joint USAF/USN squadrons operating the type. The Prowler was developed from the earlier EA-6A EW variant that saw service in Vietnam. Externally similar to the A-6 Intruder two-seat attack aircraft, the EA-6B featured a nose section extended by 4 ft 6 in (1.37 m) for a four-seat cockpit, and a distinctive fin pod to house the passive receivers for the ALQ-99 Tactical Jamming System (TJS). The Prowler's advanced ECM system is based upon the ALQ-99 TJS and up to ten 'noise' jamming transmitters can be carried in five self-powered external jammer pods. Delivery of production Prowlers began to the US Navy in January 1971; a total of 170 EA-6Bs was built until 1991. The jamming ability and capacity of the EA-6B has been progressively upgraded from 1973 through the introduction of the EXCAP (Expanded Capability), ICAP-1 (Increased Capability-1), ICAP-II and ADVCAP (Advanced Capability) initiatives. From 1995, the EA-6B acquired the ability to use more direct methods to counter the threat posed by enemy SAM sites. The EA-6B can now act as a 'shooter' with the AGM-88 HARM anti-radar missile. To keep the Prowler serving well into the next century, the remaining airframes are beginning to undergo ICAP-III development. This is replacing the ALQ-99 with improved TJS receivers and introduces a fully integrated communications jamming system to give the EA-6B the ability to react to the latest SAMs. The Prowler currently equips 16 US Navy and four USMC squadrons; five Navy squadrons provide electronic warfare support to USAF expeditionary units. It is expected to remain in service to at least 2015.

Specification: Grumman EA-6B Prowler
Origin: USA
Type: four-seat carrier-based electronic warfare and SEAD aircraft
Armament: (ADVCAP/Block 91) up to four AGM-88A HARM anti-radar missiles
Powerplant: two Pratt & Whitney J52-P-408 turbojets each rated at 11,200 lb st (49.8 kN)
Performance: (with payload of five external jammer pods) maximum level speed at sea level 610 mph (982 km/h); maximum rate of climb at sea level 10,030 ft (3057 m) per minute; service ceiling 38,000 ft (11580 m); range 1,099 miles (1769 km); take-off distance to 50 ft (15 m) 3,495 ft (1065 m); landing run 2,150 ft (655 m)
Weights: empty 31,572 lb (14321 kg); normal take-off with five external jammer pods 54,461 lb (24703 kg); normal take-off with five external jammer pods and maximum fuel 60,160 lb (27493 kg); maximum take-off 65,000 lb (29484 kg)
Dimensions: wing span 53 ft 0 in (16.15 m) extended and 25 ft 10 in (7.87 m) folded; length 59 ft 10 in (18.24 m); height 16 ft 3 in (4.95 m); wing area 528.90 sq ft (49.13 m²)

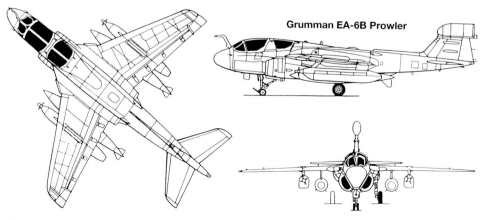

Grumman EA-6B Prowler

GRUMMAN E-2 HAWKEYE

Since entering service in 1964 the E-2 has protected US Navy carrier battle groups and acted as an airborne controller for their aircraft. One of very few types designed specifically for the AEW role, it was first flown in prototype form as long ago as October 1960. As a consequence of its ability to operate from aircraft carriers, the basic Hawkeye is extremely compact. A total of 59 production E-2As was delivered from January 1964; 51 were updated to E-2B standard, before production switched to the improved E-2C. The first E-2C flew on 23 September 1972 and Grumman built 139 for the US Navy when the line closed in 1994. However, low-rate production began again in 2000. External changes to the E-2 have been minor but its systems have been progressively updated. The E-2C was initially equipped with APS-125 search radar, but this was replaced by the AN/APS-139 in Group I aircraft from 1988 and the AN/APS-145 in the latest Group II E-2Cs. The latter radar allows a low-flying, fighter-sized aircraft to be detected at up to 253 miles (407 km) away with the E-2C flying at its operational altitude. A passive detection system gives warning of hostile emitters at ranges up to twice the radar detection range. After almost 30 years in service, the E-2C is still an evolving design, and Northrop Grumman is developing the even more capable E-2C Group II Plus or Hawkeye 2000; new-build aircraft are scheduled to enter US Navy service in late 2001. The E-2 currently equips 14 US Navy squadrons and is destined to remain in service until as least 2020. E-2Cs have been exported to Egypt (6), France (2), Israel (four, currently in storage), Japan (13), Singapore (4) and Taiwan (4). Many customers are upgrading their E-2s to a mix of Group II or Hawkeye 2000 standards.

Specification: Grumman E-2C Hawkeye (Group I configuration onwards)
Origin: USA
Type: carrierborne AEW aircraft
Powerplant: two Allison T56-A-427 turboprops each rated at 5,100 ehp (3803 kW)
Performance: maximum level speed 389 mph (626 km/h); maximum cruising speed at optimum altitude 374 mph (602 km/h); maximum rate of climb at sea level over 2,515 ft (767 m) per minute; service ceiling 37,000 ft (11275 m); unrefuelled time on station at 200 miles (320 km) from base 4 hours 24 minutes; endurance with maximum fuel 6 hours 15 minutes;
Weights: empty 40,484 lb (18363 kg); maximum take-off 54,426 lb (24687 kg)
Dimensions: wing span 80 ft 7 in (24.56 m); folded width 29 ft 4 in (8.94 m); rotodome diameter 24 ft 0 in (7.32 m); length 57 ft 6¾ in (17.54 m); height 18 ft 3¾ in (5.58 m); wing area 700.00 sq ft (65.03 m²)

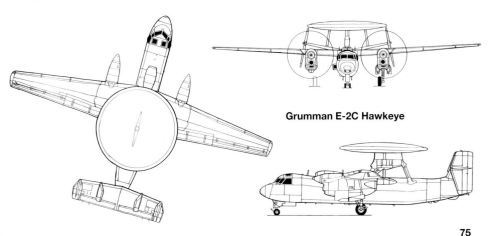

Grumman E-2C Hawkeye

GRUMMAN F-14 TOMCAT

During the late 1970s the Grumman F-14 Tomcat was widely regarded as the most important aircraft in the US Navy. Only the Tomcat was felt to be capable of defending the Carrier Battle Group from long-range cruise missile carriers, with its unmatched potential to fire off a salvo of up to six ultra long-range Phoenix AAMs against high- or low-flying targets, and then to deal with any 'leakers' with AIM-9s or the internal 20-mm cannon. However, the credibility of the Phoenix has been dented by a poor showing in combat and trials, while the F-14 still cannot carry today's leading AAM, the AIM-120 AMRAAM. AIM-54s fired at long range by F-14Ds in two recent, separate engagements at Iraqi MiG-25s and MiG-23s missed their targets. The original F-14A (which still outnumbers the re-engined F-14B and F-14D) remains severely constrained by the unreliability and limitations of its TF30 engines. The Tomcat's tactical reconnaissance capability has been enhanced in recent years by the addition of a digital TARPS reconnaissance pod and by the ongoing development of real-time data-links. The US F-14 force began assuming a limited clear-weather attack capability in 1992. Since 1995 the LANTIRN laser designation pod has been integrated across the F-14 fleet, in combination with a basic NVG-compatible cockpit. Work is progressing on integrating GPS-guided munitions, including JDAM. The F-14 has seen combat during recent operations over Bosnia and southern Iraq, usually mounting CAPs and also flying air-to-ground and reconnaissance sorties. All F-14As are scheduled for replacement by F/A-18E/Fs by 2003, the F-14Bs following by 2007, and the last F-14Ds retiring by 2008. The sole export customer was Iran, and of 79 F-14As received in the late 1970s, the IRIAF has a reported 28-30 in active service. These are based at Bushehr to protect Iran's vital oil installations. The Hawk SAM has been integrated onto at least two aircraft, possibly as a Phoenix replacement, and there remain rumours that Iran is developing a major F-14 upgrade.

Specification: Grumman F-14D Tomcat
Origin: USA
Type: two-seat carrier-based multi-role fighter
Armament: one M61A1 Vulcan 20-mm cannon with 675 rounds; air-to-air weapons comprise AIM-54C Phoenix, AIM-7M Sparrow and AIM-9M Sidewinder AAMs; air-to-ground weapons include GBU-10/-12/ -16/-24 LGBs, Mk 80 series bombs, Rockeye and CBU-59 cluster bombs, Gator mines; TARPS pod for reconnaissance
Powerplant: two General Electric F110-GE-400 turbofans each rated at 16,088 lb st (71.56 kN) dry and 27,000 lb st (120.1 kN) with afterburning
Performance: maximum level speed 'clean' 1,241 mph (1997 km/h) or Mach 1.88; maximum climb rate at sea level over 30,000 ft (9145 m); service ceiling over 53,000 ft (16150 m); range with maximum internal fuel and two external tanks over 1,842 miles (2965 km)
Weights: empty 41,780 lb (18951 kg); maximum take-off 74,349 lb (33724 kg)
Dimensions: wing span 64 ft 1½ in (19.54 m) spread, 38 ft 2½ in (11.65 m) swept; length 62 ft 8 in (19.10 m); height 16 ft (4.88 m); wing area 565.00 sq ft (52.49 m²)

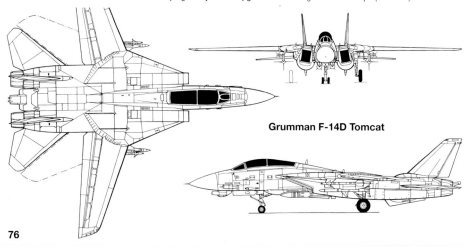

Grumman F-14D Tomcat

In 2001 the Tomcat equipped 11 front-line US Navy squadrons and a training unit. The front-line units comprise three As, five with Bs and three with Ds. In general each aircraft carrier embarks one squadron of Tomcats and three of Hornets. Tomcats also serve as adversary aircraft with the Naval Strike and Air Warfare Center at NAS Fallon, CA. They are painted in a variety of schemes to simulate fighters serving with potentially hostile countries such as Iran.

IAI KFIR

France's embargo of Mirage 5J fighters in 1967 forced Israel to establish an indigenous aircraft industry. This led directly to an unlicenced copy of the Mirage III as the Nesher; in 2001 upgraded examples remain in service with the Argentinian air force. The Nesher was developed by Israel Aircraft Industries into the canard-equipped Kfir (Lion Cub). Integration of the new US-supplied J79 engine required total redesign of the rear fuselage and a cooling inlet in the dorsal fin. The new forward fuselage was extended to house avionics, including the Elta 2001B ranging radar and a comprehensive weapons delivery and navigation suite. The prototype was flown in 1973 and production Kfir C2s entered service in the fighter-bomber role with the IDF/AF in 1975. The tandem two-seat Kfir-TC2 was developed as a weapon-system trainer and EW (electronic warfare) platform. Some 185 C2s and TC2s were built, including 12 C2s exported to Ecuador in 1982, and another 11 to Colombia in 1988-89. Both customers also received two Kfir-TC2s. Ecuador's Kfirs clashed with Peruvian fighters during border disputes in 1995 and, along with Mirage F1s, have made three confirmed aerial kills. Virtually all surviving Israeli Kfirs were upgraded to Kfir-C7 and TC7 standards from 1983. These have two additional hardpoints, further avionics improvements and have what are, effectively, HOTAS cockpits. Kfirs remain in service only as reserves in Israeli and possibly equip up to five squadrons. The latest export customer is Sri Lanka which acquired six C2s and two TC2s from Israel in 1996. Sri Lankan Kfirs have been used in offensive actions against the Tamil Tiger rebel group. IAI has developed the Kfir 2000 upgrade for application to surplus Israeli Kfir airframes made available for export. The main addition is a new radome housing an Elta EL-2032 multi-mode radar that allows delivery of PGMs. Some Ecuadorian Kfirs have been upgraded to Kfir CE configuration with Elta EL-2034-5 radar.

Specification: IAI Kfir-C7
Origin: Israel
Type: multi-role fighter/attack aircraft
Armament: two Rafael-built DEFA 553 30-mm cannon with 140 rpg, maximum ordnance of 13,415 lb (6085 kg), including Shafrir 2 and Python 3 IR AAMs; AGM-45 Shrike, AGM-65 Maverick and GBU-13 guided weapons, CBU-52/58 and Israeli-built TAL-1 and -2 CBUs, LAU-3A/-20A/-32A rocket launchers and Mk 82/83/84 series Israeli-derived/designed free-fall bombs;
Powerplant: one IAI Bedek Division-built General Electric J79-J1E turbojet rated at 11,890 lb st (52.89 kN) dry and 18,750 lb st (83.40 kN) with afterburning and 'combat boost' option
Performance: maximum level speed 'clean' at 36,000 ft (10975 m) more than 1,516 mph (2440 km/h); combat radius 548 miles (882 km) on a one-hour CAP
Weights: empty about 16,060 lb (7285 kg); maximum take-off 36,376 lb (16500 kg)
Dimensions: wing span 26 ft 11⅔ in (8.22 m); length 51 ft 4¼ in (15.65 m) including probe; height 14 ft 11¼ in (4.55 m); wing area 374.60 sq ft (34.80 m²)

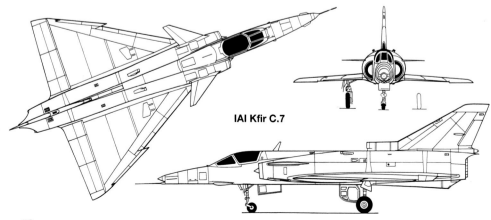

IAI Kfir C.7

ILYUSHIN IL-18 SERIES

Ilyushin's Il-18 was a major milestone in the development of Soviet commercial aviation. Its performance, capacity and reliability made it an obvious choice for adaptation of redundant airframes for military roles. The first such conversion was the Il-20M (NATO 'Coot-A') dedicated strategic Elint/radar reconnaissance aircraft. Fitted with a SLAR, cameras and other optical sensors, the 'Coot-A' can be regarded as the Soviet answer to the Boeing RC-135 series. The Il-22 'Coot-B' airborne command post variant was developed by the Myasischev design bureau and is available in two versions: the Il-18D-26 'Bizon' and Il-22M-11 'Zebra'. Both have a cylindrical pod on the fin, but have differing antennae arrays. Production comprised converted Il-18Ds and new-build aircraft. Four Il-20RTs built as dedicated tracking aircraft for space flight support remain in Russian air force and naval aviation (AV-MF) as trainers and transports. Il-18Ds and reconverted Il-22s also serve as staff/VIP transports. The Il-38 (NATO 'May') long-range maritime patrol and ASW aircraft entered service in 1968. Production comprised up to 65 aircraft. Search sensors include a Berkut STS (NATO 'Wet Eye') search radar and associated sonobuoys and a tail-mounted APM-73 MAD. The 'May' also carried out maritime SAR and reconnaissance roles for which some aircraft were retrofitted with the Vishnya Comint system. Most of the former Soviet Il-38s remain in use with the AV-MF. The sole export operator is the Indian Navy which received five Il-38s to equip INAS 315 Sqn at Dabolim. In 1999 the Indian 'Mays' received an upgraded mission avionics/ESM suite – possibly the Morskoy Zmey search and targeting system developed by the Leninets Holding Company. With continuing production of the Tu-142 'Bear-F', Russian Il-38s may adopt a shorter-range role, and due to their excellent reliability and safety record, are scheduled to remain in viable service up to at least 2012.

Specification: Ilyushin Il-38 'May'
Origin: Russia
Type: seven-crew ASW/maritime reconnaissance aircraft
Armament: two internal weapons bays for maximum load of 18,518 lb (8400 kg); weapons include AT-2 homing torpedoes, 250-kg (551-lb) PLAB-250-120 Lastochka depth charges, KAB-500PL Zagon guided and nuclear depth charges
Powerplant: four ZMDB Progress (Ivchyenko) AI-20M turboprops each rated at 4,190 shp (3126 kW)
Performance: maximum level speed at 19,685 ft (6000 m) 404 mph (650 km/h); minimum patrol speed 271 mph (350 km/h); service ceiling 32,808 ft (10000 m); range 5,903 miles (9500 km); combat radius with 3-hour patrol 1,367 miles (2200 km); patrol endurance with maximum fuel 12 hours
Weights: empty equipped 79,365 lb (36000 kg); maximum take-off 114,638 lb (66000 kg)
Dimensions: wing span 122 ft 8½ in (37.40 m); length 131 ft 6¾in (40.10 m); height 33 ft 1⅔ in (10.12 m); wing area 1,507.00 sq ft (140.00 m²)

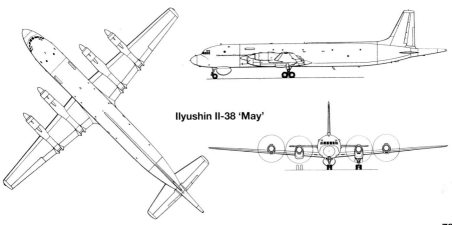

Ilyushin Il-38 'May'

ILYUSHIN IL-76 'CANDID' SERIES

The Ilyushin Il-76 'Candid' is a landmark Soviet-era design. Russia's first four-jet heavy transport, it was conceived and used to fly strategic military cargoes into front-line air bases in the most extreme operational conditions. The Il-76 prototype made its first flight in March 1971. The basic Il-76 'Candid-A' transport was built purely for military service, while the Il-76M 'Candid-B' is the military version of the civilian Il-76T 'Candid-A', with additional fuel, higher operating weights, a powered lifting ramp, full pressurisation, and freight-handling equipment inside the hold. The Il-76MD 'Candid-B' is a military version of the civil Il-76TD 'Candid-A' with uprated D-30KP-2 turbofans to maintain performance at higher ambient temperatures, increased fuel capacity and a strengthened wing. Apart from Russia, other military operators are Algeria, Belarus, China, Cuba, India, Iran, Iraq, Libya, North Korea, Syria and Ukraine. The tough, dependable airframe spawned many variants – some designed to do the basic transport job even better, and others which serve as indispensable combat support roles. A bewildering array of other specialised variants have been developed for roles including mobile hospital, cosmonaut training and airborne command post, airborne laser platform and firefighter. The Il-78 'Midas' is the Russian air force's standard IFR tanker, and is fitted with three UPAZ-1 external refuelling units (one under each wing and one at the rear fuselage). When fitted with fuselage fuel tanks the Il-78 can transfer up to 65 tonnes (143,300 lb)/ 84639 litres (18,618 Imp gal) of fuel at a combat radius of 620 miles (1000 km). The A-50 'Mainstay' is a variant developed by Beriev for the AWACS role with a Shmel search radar mounted in a large rotodome above the rear fuselage. Iraq has converted at least one and three Il-76s respectively to tanker and AWACS configurations.

Specification: Ilyushin Il-76M 'Candid-B'
Origin: Russia
Type: seven-crew long-range transport aircraft
Armament: two 23-mm Gryazev-Shipunov GSh-23L trainable rearward-firing two-barrel cannon in the tail turret
Payload: maximum payload 110,230 lb (50000 kg), accommodation for up to 140 troops, 125 paratroops or 108 passengers in three modules
Powerplant: four PNPP 'Aviadvigatel' (Soloviev) D-30KP turbofans each rated at 26,455 lb st (117.68 kN)
Performance: maximum level speed 528 mph (850 km/h); absolute ceiling 50,850 ft (15500 m); range with maximum payload 2,265 miles (3650 km), range with 44,090-lb (20000-kg) payload 4,535 miles (7300 km)
Weights: maximum take-off 418,875 lb (190000 kg)
Dimensions: wing span 165 ft 8 in (50.50 m); length 152 ft 10¼ in (46.59 m); height 48 ft 5 in (14.76 m); wing area 3,229.28 sq ft (300.00 m²)

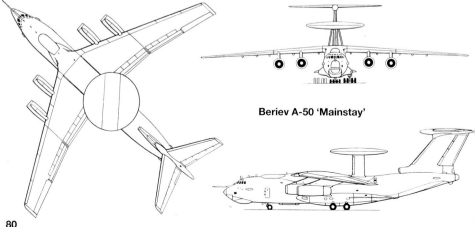

Beriev A-50 'Mainstay'

KAMAN SH-2 SEASPRITE

The H-2 Seasprite was conceived in response to a 1956 USN requirement for a high-speed, all-weather, long-range SAR, liaison and utility helicopter. The first single-engined prototype made its maiden flight on 2 July 1959. The sole variant remaining in US Navy service is the SH-2G, six of which were built as new plus a further 17 converted from the previous SH-2F model. The US Navy's SH-2Gs (16 in operational service) are the last remaining helicopters which fly the LAMPS I ASW mission. As the active-duty SH-60 fleet now carries the improved LAMPS III system, the Navy has re-roled the two Naval Reserve SH-2G squadrons to carry out new missions. These include long-range surveillance, anti-surface warfare, ASW, SAR, utility and airborne mine countermeasures missions. For the latter role, the SH-2G carries the Kaman-developed Magic Lantern device, a laser detector that finds mines from the water's surface to below the keel depth of most warships. The US Navy is slowly divesting itself of its smaller *Oliver Hazard Perry*-class (FFG-7) frigates, and foreign navies are scrambling to acquire these still-capable ships, plus helicopters to support them. Kaman is marketing rebuilds of up to 72 USN-surplus SH-2Fs. Egypt received 10 such SH-2G(E)s from October 1997. In June 1997 the Royal Australian Navy (RAN) and Royal New Zealand Navy (RNZN) contracted with Kaman for the delivery of 11 and four SH-2Gs: as well as the standard upgrade, these helicopters have a 'glass' cockpit, a digital mission suite and provision for Penguin Mk 2 anti-ship missile (RAN) and AGM-65 Maverick (RNZN) air-to-surface missile respectively. Both SH-2G(NZ)s and SH-2G(A)s entered service in 2001.

Specification: Kaman SH-2G Super Seasprite
Origin: USA
Type: ship-based ASW/utility helicopter
Payload: useful payload 5,070 lb (2299 kg)
Armament: provision for two 0.3-in (7.62-mm) M60 machine-guns in the cabin doors, plus up to 1,600 lb (726 kg) of stores, including two Mk 46 or Mk 50 torpedoes
Powerplant: two General Electric T700-GE-401/401C turboshafts each rated at 1,723 shp (1285 kW)
Performance: maximum speed 159 mph (256 km/h) at sea level; service ceiling 21,000 ft (6401 m); rate of climb 2,360 ft (719 m) per minute; radius 40 miles (65 km) for a patrol of 2 hours 10 minutes with one torpedo; maximum endurance 5.7 hours
Weights: empty 7,680 lb (3483 kg); maximum take-off 13,500 lb (6123 kg)
Dimensions: main rotor diameter 44 ft 4 in (13.51 m); length overall 52 ft 9 in (16.08 m) with rotors turning; height 15 ft ½ in (4.58 m) with rotors turning; main rotor disc area 1,543.66 sq ft (143.41 m²)

**Kaman SH-2G
Seasprite**

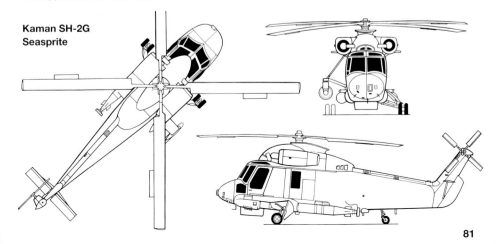

KAMOV Ka-50 'HOKUM'

The Ka-50 Chernaya Akula (black shark – NATO codename 'Hokum') was planned as a rival to the Mi-28 'Havoc' in a competition to provide the Soviet armed forces with a new battlefield attack helicopter. Kamov opted for a single-crew layout to save weight for more armour, more powerful armament, and a greater number of advanced sensors. The first of three V-80 prototypes made its maiden flight on 17 June 1982. In October 1986 the Ka-50 was selected for production. The core of the Ka-50's weapon system is the tube-launched Vikhr anti-tank missile, of which 16 are carried. The Ka-50's cannon has variable rates of fire and selective feed from two ammunition boxes. Survivability is enhanced by features including IR suppression of the hot exhaust gases, layered cockpit armour and chaff/flare dispensers in wing tip pods. The pilot can escape the aircraft via a K-37 ejection seat, after the rotor blades have been explosively separated. Later revision of the requirement to emphasise night combat capability led to a reassessment of the Ka-50, whose production was postponed, in the light of the two-seat Mi-28's apparently greater developability for the task. Kamov has thus developed the Ka-50N (Nochnoy, or nocturnal). The type first flew in 1997 and has a FLIR turret and mast-mounted radar. The Ka-52 Alligator ('Hokum-B') is a side-by-side two-seat conversion trainer and day/night combat derivative. It also features uprated TV3-117 engines and millimetric-wavelength radar. First flown in production form on 25 June 1997, the type has been ordered for Russian service. The Ka-50-2 export derivative, with Israeli avionics, has been offered to China, India and Turkey.

Specification: Kamov Ka-50 Chernaya Akula 'Hokum-A'
Origin: Russia
Type: single-seat battlefield air-combat and close-air support helicopter
Armament: one 30-mm 2A42 cannon, plus up to 6,614 lb (3000 kg) of disposable stores, including unguided rockets, and 9M120 Vikhr (AT-9 'Spiral') and Vikhr M (AT-16) laser-guided anti-tank missiles
Powerplant: two Klimov TV3-117VK turboshafts each rated at 2,193 shp (1635 kW)
Performance: maximum speed 186 mph (300 km/h) at optimum altitude; service ceiling 18,040 ft (5500 m); range 279 miles (540 km); endurance 1 hour 40 minutes with standard fuel
Weights: empty 17,196 lb (7800 kg); maximum take-off 23,810 lb (10800 kg)
Dimensions: rotor diameter, each 45 ft 7 in (14.50 m); length 52 ft 6 in (16.00 m) with rotors turning; height 16 ft 2 in (4.93 m); rotor disc area, total 3,555.00 sq ft (330.26 m²)

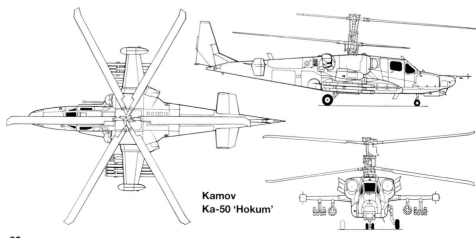

**Kamov
Ka-50 'Hokum'**

KAWASAKI OH-1

From the mid-1980s the Japan Defence Agency (JDA), began to consider a successor to the OH-6D light helicopters currently in service with the Japanese Ground Self-Defence Force. It was decided to procure an indigenous type for the scout/reconnaissance roles. In 1992 Kawasaki was selected as prime contractor with 60 per cent of the programme, the balance being allocated equally between Fuji and Mitsubishi. The three companies established the Observation Helicopter Engineering Team to develop the programme, on which detailed work began in 1992. The resulting OH-1 is a conventional machine that is relatively small and of typical gunship helicopter configuration. Its structure comprises, by weight, 40 per cent carbonfibre-reinforced plastics, and it features a 'fenestron' type tail rotor. Each crew member has two LCD colour multi-function displays, and the gunner has a HUD. The mission avionics include a trainable roof-mounted Kawasaki package (forward of the main rotor) with a Fujitsu thermal imager, NEC colour TV camera and NEC laser rangefinder. Protection is enhanced by the installation of an IR jammer on the helicopter's spine to the rear of the main gearbox. The first of six prototypes made its initial flight on 6 August 1996, and the first of a possible 150 to 200 OH-1s was delivered to the JGSDF on 24 January 2000. A total of 14 OH-1s has been ordered for delivery into 2001.The JDA may revise the OH-1 to meet its AH-X light attack helicopter requirement. This would probably feature MTR-390 or T800 engines, allowing the introduction of a heavier weapons load and revised mission avionics. The projected designation of the AH-X production model is AH-2.

Specification: Kawasaki XOH-1 (prototype)
Origin: Japan
Type: two-seat light scout and observation helicopter
Armament: maximum weapon load 291 lb (132 kg); weapons comprise four Toshiba Type 91 lightweight short-range IR-guided AAMs carried under stub wings for self defence
Powerplant: two Mitsubishi TS1-10 turboshafts each rated at 888 shp (663 kW)
Performance: maximum level speed approx. 172 mph (277 km/h); combat radius 124 miles (200 km); range 342 miles (550 km)
Weights: empty 5,401 lb (2450 kg); design gross weight 7,825 lb (3550 kg); maximum take-off 8,818 lb (4000 kg)
Dimensions: main rotor diameter 38 ft 0¾ in (11.60 m); fuselage length 39 ft 4½ in (12.00 m); height to top of rotor head 11 ft 1¾ in (3.40 m); main rotor disc area 1,136 sq ft (105.68 m²)

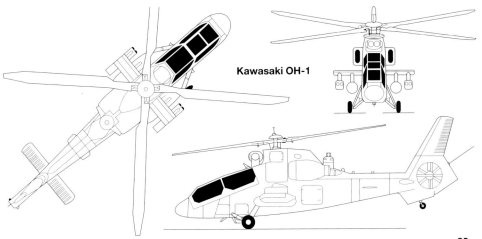

Kawasaki OH-1

KAWASAKI T-4

In September 1981 the Japanese Defence Agency selected Kawasaki's KA-851 design as the winning contender for development of a new intermediate flying trainer. The new type would replace Fuji T1F (T-1) and Lockheed T-33 aircraft in service with the Japanese Air Self-Defence Force (JASDF) in the late 1980s. Emphasis was placed on high subsonic manoeuvrability. Detail design was finalised by the end of 1983, and the construction effort of six XT-4 prototypes began in the spring of 1984. The construction effort was collaborative, with Fuji building the wing, rear fuselage and tail unit, Mitsubishi the centre fuselage and air inlets, and Kawasaki the forward fuselage. Power is provided by two F3 engines developed by IHI. As prime contractor, Kawasaki is also responsible for final assembly and test. All four flyable prototypes had flown by July 1986; the first prototype taking to the air on 29 July 1985. Successful trials led to full-scale production with the first production T-4 flying in June 1988. Deliveries began three months later to the 31st and 32nd Flying Training Squadrons of the 1st Air Wing at Hamamatsu. Small numbers of T-4s are attached to the instrument/communications flights of most operational squadrons, as well as the flights of regional headquarters and operational group flights for liaison duties. Nine T-4s form the mount of the 'Blue Impulse' national aerobatic display team. The T-4 features a licence-built Kaiser HUD and three external hardpoints (one underfuselage and two wingpoints) that allow it to have a secondary light attack tasking as well as a weapons training role. Kawasaki has proposed an enhanced version as possible replacement for the Mitsubishi T-2 in the dedicated armament training role. The JASDF has a requirement for 200 T-4s, and had received around 180 examples by 2001.

Specification: Kawasaki T-4
Origin: Japan
Type: two-seat intermediate trainer with secondary combat training & liaison roles
Armament: up to 4,409 lb (2000 kg) of weapons including free-fall or retarded bombs, 2.75-in (70-mm) unguided rockets, gun pods, and (as a possible retrofit) ASM-2 long-range, IIR-guided anti-ship missiles and AA-4 short-range AAMs
Powerplant: two Ishikawajima-Harima F3-IHI-30 turbofans each rated at 3,671 lb st (16.32 kN)
Performance: maximum level speed 'clean' at 36,000 ft (10975 m) 594 mph (956 km/h); maximum rate of climb at sea level 10,000 ft (3048 m) per minute; service ceiling 50,000 ft (15240 m); standard range 806 miles (1297 km)
Weights: empty 8,157 lb (3700 kg); normal take-off 12,125 lb (5500 kg); maximum take-off 16,534 lb (7500 kg)
Dimensions: wing span 32 ft 7½ in (9.94 m); length 42 ft 8 in (13.00 m); height 15 ft 1¼ in (4.60 m); wing area 226.05 sq ft (21.00 m²)

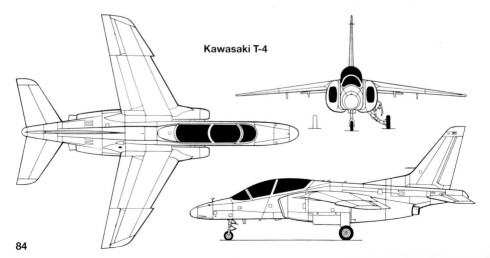

Kawasaki T-4

LOCKHEED C-5 GALAXY

The Lockheed C-5 Galaxy heavy logistics transport, now supported by the Lockheed Martin Corporation, is the workhorse of US strategic airlift capability. Key to the C-5's mission capability is its cavernous interior and 'roll-on/roll-off' capability with access to cargo at both ends of the aircraft. The C-5A first flew on 30 June 1968, and the first operational C-5A was delivered on 17 December 1969 with the last following in May 1973. The C-5A suffered initially from wing crack problems and cost overruns, but has since served well. Between 1981 to 1987 77 of the 81 production C-5As received wings of virtually new design and with greater corrosion resistance. From 1986 to 1989, the production line was re-opened to manufacture 50 improved C-5Bs that incorporated modifications and improvements resulting from experience with the C-5A. The type provides the most ton-miles at the fastest speed of any American airlifter, and is the largest aircraft routinely operated by US forces. Although not usually assigned airdrop duties, it can also drop paratroops. The C-5C designation is applied to two aircraft modified with sealed front visor and strengthened interior for the carriage of satellites and space equipment. In recent years the C-5A/B has suffered from serious reliability problems that result in low 'mission capable rates'. The USAF is addressing the shortfall in airlift capacity as a result of the C–141's retirement by considering a range of major modifications to keep its Galaxy fleet operational until 2030. Around 125 aircraft will receive new digital automatic flight controls, new cockpit displays and new communications and navigation equipment. In 2000 the USAF selected the General Electric CF6-80C2L1F turbofan to initially re-engine the 50 youngest C-5Bs. C-5A/Bs equip AMC, AFRC and ANG units. At least two C-5As assigned to AFSOC have a special forces role.

Specification: Lockheed C-5B Galaxy
Origin: USA
Type: strategic airlifter
Payload: maximum payload 261,000 lb (118387 kg); typical loads include two M1A1 Abrams main battle tanks, 16 3⁄4-ton trucks or 10 LAV-25 light armoured vehicles
Powerplant: four General Electric TF39-GE-1C turbofans each rated at 43,000 lb st (191.27 kN)
Performance: maximum speed 571 mph (919 km/h) at 25,000 ft 7620 m); maximum cruising speed 564 mph (908 km/h) at 25,000 ft (7620 m); initial climb rate 1,725 ft (525 m) per minute; service ceiling 35,750 ft (10895 m) at 615,000 lb (278960 kg); range 6,469 miles (10411 km) with maximum fuel or 3,434 miles (5526 km) with maximum payload
Weights: operating empty 374,000 lb (169643 kg); maximum take-off 837,000 lb (379657 kg)
Dimensions: wing span 222 ft 8½ in (67.88 m); length 247 ft 10 in (75.54 m); height 65 ft 1½ in (19.85 m); wing area 6,200.00 sq ft (575.98 m²)

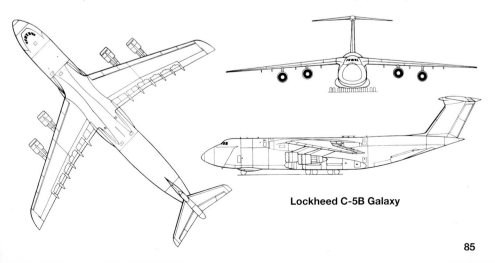

Lockheed C-5B Galaxy

LOCKHEED C-141 STARLIFTER

First flown on 17 December 1963, the C-141 StarLifter provided the USAF with a fast and capacious long-range jet transport. The C-141 features a fuselage of similar cross-section to that of the C-130 Hercules. Its wing is fitted with powerful high lift-devices for good low-speed handling and field performance. The first of two C-141A prototypes flew in December 1963. The type entered service in October 1964 and reached initial operational capability in April 1965, soon providing impressive confirmation of its capabilities on the 'air bridge' service to South-East Asia. During the 1970s, 270 of the surviving 274 C-141s were cycled through an upgrade programme that added a fuselage stretch of 7.11 m (23 ft 4 in) and IFR capability for true global airlift capacity. The overall cargo capacity of the resulting C-141B was increased by over 30 per cent, and the programme thus added the equivalent of 90 new aircraft in terms of capacity at low relative cost. The YC-141B prototype conversion made its first flight on 24 March 1977, and Lockheed completed the final C-141B on 29 June 1982. Throughout its career the StarLifter has been a workhorse of the USAF, flying regular supply missions around the world in addition to undertaking special requirements. Of inestimable value to the USAF is the StarLifter's sheer versatility; it can be rapidly reconfigured for many missions. Thirteen C-141B transports of the 437th Air Wing are equipped for the Special Operations Low Level (SOLL) support role, with increased survivability measures, including a FLIR turret beneath the nose, improved ECM systems and self-defence systems. Between 1997 and late 1999, the USAF upgraded 64 C-141s to C-141C standard exclusively for AFRC. These received 'glass cockpits', GPS, an all-weather flight control system and a defensive system incorporating missile warning receivers. The intensive utilisation of the C-141 fleet has extracted a heavy toll; the type is being rapidly replaced by the Boeing C-17A and is scheduled to be withdrawn from front-line service by 2004.

Specification: Lockheed C-141B StarLifter
Origin: USA
Type: strategic airlifter
Payload: maximum payload 90,880 lb (41222 kg) in up to 13 standard cargo pallets; C-141B can carry most US armed forces vehicles, aircraft engines, food supplies, fuel drums or nuclear weapons; palletised passenger seats for 166 people, canvas seats for 205 passengers or 168 paratroops
Powerplant: four Pratt & Whitney TF33-P-7 turbofans each rated at 21,000 lb st (93.41 kN)
Performance: maximum cruising speed 566 mph (910 km/h) at high altitude; economical cruising speed 495 mph (797 km/h) at high altitude; initial climb rate 2,920 ft (890 m) per minute; service ceiling 41,600 ft (12680 m); range 10280 km (6,390 miles) without payload 2,936 miles (4725 km) with maximum payload
Weights: empty 67186 kg (148,120 lb); maximum take-off 155580 kg (343,000 lb)
Dimensions: wing span 159 ft 11 in (48.74 m); length 168 ft 3½ in (51.29 m); height 39 ft 3 in (11.96 m); wing area 3,228.00 sq ft (299.88 m²)

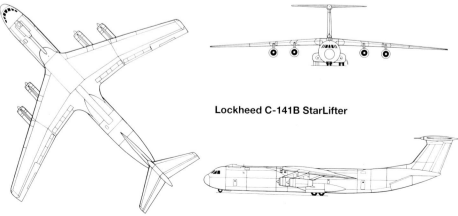

Lockheed C-141B StarLifter

LOCKHEED F-104 STARFIGHTER

In 2001 Lockheed's classic F-104 Starfighter serves with just one operator, the Italian air force (AMI), but continues to form the core of its air defence force. The AMI received 205 F-104S aircraft developed and built under licence by Aeritalia in the 1970s. A total of 153 aircraft were upgraded to ASA (*Aggiornamento Sistema d'Arma*, or armament system modernisation) standard between 1986 to 1991. Introduction of a FIAR R21G/M1 Setter non-coherent Doppler radar allowed a look-down/shoot-down capability over a maximum range of around 22 miles (35 km). The upgrade also introduced Aspide Mk 1A and 20-mm M61 cannon armament, AN/ALQ-70/ AN/ALQ-73 ECM systems and provision for the all-aspect AIM-9L AAM. In the light of the considerable delays to the Eurofighter programme, the AMI decided to upgrade further some of the best ASA airframes to the new ASA-M standard. These have received new avionics (including fitment of an inertial platform, GPS, radio and systems for the main aircraft functions). Only 49 single-seaters and 15 two-seaters were modified, the first example of which was delivered in late 1998 to the first unit, the 23° *Gruppo* of 5° *Stormo*. The single-seat F-104S ASA-M serve with four interceptor groups, while TF-104G ASA-M trainers equip another group for operational training. The Starfighter is a fondly regarded aircraft, but today is not a fighter compatible with modern missions and tactics, although its speed, climb rate and acceleration performance are still more than adequate. The Starfighter was only nominally involved in the air operations over Kosovo in 1999, mostly sitting alert, due to the fact that it lacks a good interception radar system, does not have RWR or IFF systems, and has a limited operational range. The AMI is to lease F-16s as interim interceptors, and intends to replace its F-104s with the first Eurofighter EF2000s in 2004.

Specification: Alenia (Aeritalia) F-104ASA
Origin: Italy
Type: single-seat air defence fighter
Armament: maximum ordnance 3400 kg (7,495 lb); standard intercept load comprises two Selenia Aspide 1A semi-active monopulse radar-guided AAMs and two AIM-9L Sidewinder IR-guided AAMs
Powerplant: one General Electric J79-GE-19 turbojet rated at 11,870 lb st (52.80 kN) dry and 17,900 lb st (79.62 kN) with afterburning
Performance: maximum level speed 'clean' at 36,000 ft (10975 m) 1,450 mph (2333 km/h), and at sea level 910 mph (1464 km/h); maximum initial rate of climb 55,000 ft (16764 m) per minute; service ceiling 58,000 ft (17680 m); combat radius 775 (1247 km) with maximum fuel
Weights: empty 6760 kg (14,903 lb); normal take-off 9840 kg (21,693 lb); maximum take-off 14060 kg (30,996 lb)
Dimensions: wing span 21 ft 11 in (6.68 m) without tip tanks; length 54 ft 9 in (16.69 m); height 13 ft 6 in (4.11 m); wing area 196.10 sq ft (18.22 m²)

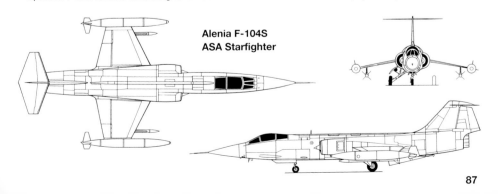

**Alenia F-104S
ASA Starfighter**

LOCKHEED F-117 NIGHTHAWK

From experience with two XST technology demonstrators, Lockheed's 'Skunk Works' developed the world's first operational tactical warplane to use low observable, or stealth, technology to reduce vulnerability to radar detection. Developed in great secrecy, the first of five FSD prototypes flew in 1981, and in 1983 the first USAF unit was declared operational. The F-117A was officially acknowledged by the Pentagon in 1988, and in 1989 the type finally went into action during the US invasion of Panama. The F-117 made a significant contribution to Operation *Desert Storm*; 42 aircraft flew from Saudi Arabia on nightly missions against high priority targets in Iraq and occupied Kuwait. The F-117A struck Serbian targets during Operation *Allied Force* in 1999 and suffered its first operational loss. In USAF planning the F-117 is used for attacks against 'highly leveraged' targets such as C³I centres, air defence sector centres, key bridges and airfields. The F-117A uses a highly accurate INS to put it in the right position to begin the attack. A FLIR and DLIR are used to acquire the target. PGMs are guided to a direct hit on the target by a laser boresighted with the DLIR. After the Gulf War, the F-117 came out of the USAF's 'black' or beyond top secret programmes and was integrated into the war-fighting capabilities of ACC. In 1990 Lockheed began an Offensive Capability Improvement Program for the 57 F-117As remaining out of 59 production and five pre-series aircraft delivered. The object was to increase combat effectiveness by reducing cockpit workload. The upgrade added a new FMS, new cockpit instrumentation with full colour MFDs, digital moving map and a new turret-mounted IRADS. The INS was replaced by a new ring laser gyro system that later integrated GPS. All aircraft had been upgraded by 1995. F-117s currently equip the 49th Fighter Wing at Holloman AFB, NM. Future upgrades with a new digital databus are being considered to allow the F-117 to carry new weapons such as AGM-145 JDAM and AGM-154 JSOW. Further proposed DLIR/FLIR upgrades have been seriously delayed.

Specification: Lockheed F-117A Nighthawk
Origin: USA
Type: single-seat low-observable strike/attack aircraft
Armament: maximum ordnance 5,000 lb (2268 kg); standard ordnance comprises 496-lb (225-kg) GBU-12, 1,984-lb (900-kg) GBU-10 or 2,169 (984-kg) GBU-27A/B LGBs, latter two weapons with either Mk 84 Paveway II or the BLU-109/B Penetrator Paveway III penetration warheads; B61 free-fall thermonuclear weapon; weapons bay may be configured for AAMs, AGM-65 Maverick ASMs, and AGM-88 HARMs
Powerplant: two General Electric F404-GE-F1D2 turbofans each rated at 10,800 lb st (48.04 kN)
Performance: maximum speed 646 mph (1040 km/h) at high altitude; cruising speed 562 mph (904 km/h) at 30,000 ft (9145 m); service ceiling 38,600 ft (11765 m); unrefuelled combat radius about 535 miles (862 km) with a 4,000-lb (1814-kg) warload
Weights: empty about 30,000 lb (13608 kg); maximum take-off 52,500 lb (23814 kg)
Dimensions: wing span 43 ft 4 in (13.20 m); length 65 ft 11 in (20.08 m); height 12 ft 5 in (3.78 m); approximate wing area 1,140.00 sq ft (105.9 m²)

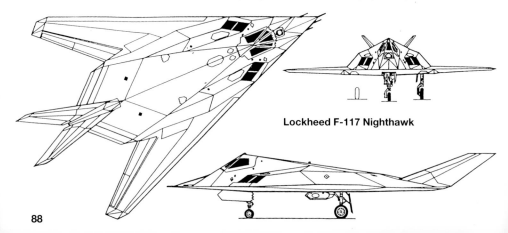

Lockheed F-117 Nighthawk

The F-117 was the world's first operational warplane to employ low observable or 'stealth' technology, and although criticised by some for being old, slow and costly, it remains arguably the USAF's key strike aircraft. The F-117 is configured for just one mission: to attack highly-defended key targets with pinpoint accuracy. Given that this capability is virtually unrivalled, it is likely that USAF will deploy its 'silver bullets' to any overseas situation requiring the ability to deliver two large precision-guided munitions almost undetected by radar.

LOCKHEED P-3 ORION

The US Navy has operated the land-based P-3 Orion maritime patrol aircraft for ASW and anti-shipping, as well as for overland surveillance, reconnaissance, mine-laying, drug interdiction logistic, threat simulation crew training and SAR missions. Although developed to counter the Soviet submarine threat, the maritime patrol force, greatly reduced in size since the end of the Cold War, finds itself in great demand in the littoral warfare environment of the early 21st century. The current front-line version is the P-3C which equips 12 active and seven reserve patrol squadrons The P-3C entered service in 'Baseline' form in 1969 and has been upgraded since through various 'Update' configurations. The P-3C has a sophisticated sensor suite including the UYS-1 acoustic sonobuoy processor and ALR-66 ESM system, plus MAD gear, an IR detection system and a search radar. Some aircraft are equipped with the APS-137 ISAR which can display an image of its target. P-3Cs are currently undergoing several upgrade programmes to extend airframe life until 2015 and to improve their mission suites and armament. The US Navy is gradually upgrading most P-3Cs to an Update III Common Configuration that will be the Fleet standard. The Anti-Surface Improvement Program (AIP) is planned for 146 P-3Cs and includes enhancements in C³I, OTH targeting and survivability. New weapons such as Maverick, SLAM and SLAM-ER give the P-3 a potent stand-off land attack capability. The first AIP P-3C entered service in 1998. Twelve EP-3Es serve in the long-range reconnaissance role, equipped with the Aries II mission avionics suite. US Navy Special Projects Units fly small numbers of modified P-3Bs and P-3Cs for tactical and strategic intelligence collection. P-3A/Bs serve in the maritime patrol role with Argentina, Greece, Norway, Portugal, Spain and Thailand while P-3Cs serve with Australia, Iran, the Netherlands, Norway, Japan, Pakistan and South Korea. Japan operates 110 Kawasaki-built P-3Js while Canada has 18 CP-140 Auroras fitted with different mission avionics to US Navy P-3Cs.

Specification: Lockheed P-3C Orion
Origin: USA
Type: long-range maritime patrol, ASW, ASuV and littoral warfare aircraft
Armament: maximum ordnance load 20,000 lb (9072 kg); 10 weapons include Mk 52/55/56 mines, Mk 54/101 depth bombs, Mk 82/83 series free-fall bombs, Mk 36/38/40 destructors, Mk 46/Mk 50 Barracuda torpedoes; AGM-84D Harpoon AShMs, AGM-84E SLAMs and 2.75-in (70-mm) air-to-surface rockets
Powerplant: four Allison T56-A-14 turboprops each rated at 4,910 ehp (3661 ekW)
Performance: maximum level speed 'clean' at 15,000 ft (4575 m) 473 mph (761 km/h); economical cruising speed at 25,000 ft (7620 m) 378 mph (608 km/h); patrol speed at 1,500 ft (457 m) 237 mph (381 km/h); maximum rate of climb at 1,500 ft (457 m) 1,950 ft (594 m) per minute; service ceiling 28,300 ft (8625 m); radius 1,550 miles (2494 km) with 3 hours on station
Weights: empty 61,491 lb (27890 kg); maximum take-off 142,000 lb (64410 kg)
Dimensions: wing span 99 ft 8 in (30.37 m); length 116 ft 10 in (35.61 m); height 33 ft 8½ in (10.27 m); wing area 1,300.00 sq ft (120.77 m²)

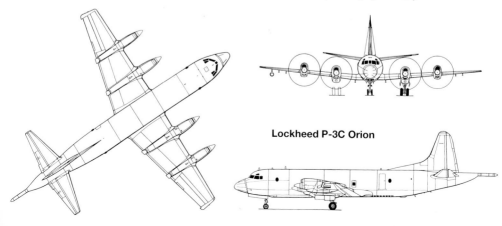

Lockheed P-3C Orion

LOCKHEED S-3 VIKING

The S-3B Viking carries out the US Navy's carrier-based sea control mission. The S-3 was originally designed in the early 1970s with a sophisticated ASW sensor suite. The demise of the Soviet Union and the increasing dominance of littoral warfare led to decreased emphasis on ASW and more emphasis on anti-surface warfare and land-attack missions. The S-3A variant was replaced in the early 1990s by the S-3B. This incorporates upgrades such as the APS-137 inverse synthetic aperture radar and the AGM-84 AShM. Each carrier air wing includes one sea control (VS) squadron equipped with eight S-3Bs. VS squadrons perform anti-submarine, anti-shipping, mine-laying, and surveillance missions for the carrier group. Sixteen S-3A were converted to ES-3A Shadow standard during the early 1990s with a variety of electronic surveillance and intercept equipment to locate and identify hostile emitters and communications stations. In mid-1998, the Navy made the decision to withdraw the ES-3A from service without replacement. The aircraft's mission avionics suite, becoming obsolescent in the age of interconnectivity in the 'electronic battlefield', was deemed as too expensive to upgrade – the ES-3A left service in mid-1999. The S-3B has an important secondary role as an aerial tanker, equipped with D-704 'buddy-buddy' refuelling stores. As the sole carrier aircraft currently capable of this function, the number of S-3Bs per squadron has been increased from six to eight. Several upgrades are being installed on Vikings, including the GPS, carrier aircraft inertial navigation system II, new tactical displays, computer memory, SATCOM equipment and improved radios. Several S-3Bs have been involved in anti-drug trafficking duties, using camera systems, FLIR and hand-held sensors. The S-3B is planned for replacement from 2015 by a variant of the Common Support Aircraft.

Specification: Lockheed S-3B Viking
Origin: USA
Type: four-seat carrier-based ASW/ASuV and littoral warfare aircraft
Armament: maximum load of 7,000 lb (3175 kg); weapons include Mk 82/83 free-fall bombs; Mk 53 mines; Mk 54 depth bombs; Mk 46/53 Barracuda torpedoes, Mk 20 Mod 2 'Rockeye' CBUs, 5-in (127-mm) Zuni and 2.75-in (70-mm) FFAR or Hydra 70 rockets, AGM-84D Harpoon AShMs
Powerplant: two General Electric TF34-GE-2 turbofans each rated at 9,275 lb st (41.26 kN)
Performance: maximum level speed 'clean' at sea level 506 mph (814 km/); patrol speed 184 mph (296 km/); initial rate of climb over 4,200 ft (1280 m) per minute; service ceiling above 35,000 ft (10670 m); radius 530 miles (853 km) with typical weapons load and a loiter of 4 hours 30 minutes
Weights: empty 26,650 lb (12088 kg); maximum take-off 52,540 lb (23832 kg)
Dimensions: wing span 68 ft 8 in (20.93 m); length overall 53 ft 4 in (16.26 m) height overall 22 ft 9 in (6.93 m); wing area 598.00 sq ft (55.56 m²)

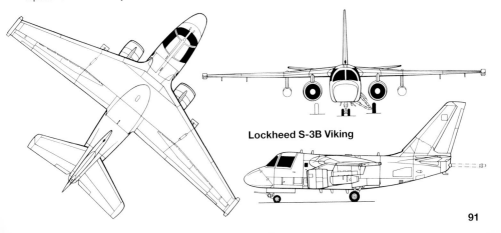

Lockheed S-3B Viking

LOCKHEED U-2

The U-2 is the USAF's principal piloted reconnaissance aircraft, and the service's fleet of about 35 aircraft is thinly spread to meet worldwide contingencies. The U-2 is viewed as both a 'national' and a 'tactical' asset, providing critical intelligence to political decision makers and theatre commanders. It is capable of collecting multi-sensor photo, EO, IR and radar imagery, as well as Sigint. The sensors are carried in the detachable nosecone (with different-shaped cones for different sensor fits), a large 'Q-bay' behind the cockpit for the carriage of large cameras, smaller bays along the lower fuselage and in two removable wing 'super pods'. These sensors include a wide range of recorders for Comint and Elint, imaging radars, ASARS-2 battlefield surveillance, PLSS radar locators and high-resolution cameras. Recorded intelligence can be transmitted via data-link to ground stations, and at least three aircraft are equipped to carry the 'Senior Span' satellite communications antenna in a huge teardrop radome mounted on a dorsal pylon. This allows the transmission of recorded intelligence across global distances in near real-time. From 1994 to 1998 Lockheed re-engined surviving U-2Rs to U-2S standard, the U-2Rs' J75 turbojets being replaced with F118-101 turbofans. Derived from the B-2's F118-GE-100 powerplant, the new engine is more fuel efficient, confers a 15 per cent range increase, restores operational ceiling to a figure above 80,000 ft (24380 m) and improves supportability across USAF bases. All U-2Ss serve with the 9th Reconnaissance Wing headquartered at Beale Air Force Base, California. The primary flying unit is the 99th RS at Beale; its three theatre detachments comprise Det 1 at RAF Akrotiri, Cyprus, OL-FR at Istres AB, France and OL-CH/4402nd Reconnaissance Squadron (Provisional) at Al Kharj AB, Saudi Arabia to provide support for Operation *Southern Watch*. The 5th RS is assigned to Osan AB, South Korea to cover the Far East while the 1st RS undertakes training with two U-2S(T) trainers and T-38A Talons. Progress has been slow in exploring an unmanned replacement for this familiar spyplane.

Specification: Lockheed U-2S
Origin: USA
Type: single-seat high-altitude strategic/tactical reconnaissance aircraft
Payload: up to 3,000 lb (1361 kg) of sensors housed principally in 'superpods' on wings, see main text
Powerplant: one General Electric F101-GE-101 non afterburning turbofan rated at 19,000 lb st (84.50 kN)
Performance: never exceed speed Mach 0.8; maximum cruising speed at 70,000 ft (21335 m) over 430 mph (692 km/); maximum rate of climb at sea level about 5,000 ft (1525 m) per minute; climb to 65,000 ft (19810 m) in 35 minutes; operational ceiling 90,000 ft (27430 m); take-off run about 650 ft (198 m) at maximum take-off weight; maximum range over 3,000 miles (4828 km); maximum endurance 12 hours
Weights: basic empty without engine and equipment pods less than 10,000 lb (4536 kg); operating empty about 15,500 lb (7031 kg); maximum take-off 41,300 lb (18733 kg)
Dimensions: wing span 103 ft 0 in (31.39 m); length 62 ft 9 in (19.13 m); height 16 ft 0 in (4.88 m); wing area about 1,000.00 sq ft (92.90 m²)

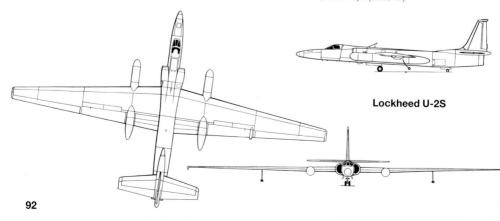

Lockheed U-2S

LOCKHEED MARTIN C-130 HERCULES & C-130J TRANSPORT VARIANTS

First flown in 1954, the C-130 Hercules is the West's most popular and widely used military transport aircraft. The number of military operators now exceeds 60 and for many of these the C-130 is the largest transport type in their inventory. In the airlift role, the Hercules is without peer. Throughout most of its career the basic airframe of the C-130 has changed very little; a stretched-fuselage option is available for operators requiring greater capacity for 'route' work. The two most numerous transport variants are the C-130E (491 built) and C-130H (1,089 built). These remain the workhorses of the USAF's tactical transport fleet. The service is looking to upgrade more than 500 of its surviving C-130E/Hs with a comprehensive avionics package – including a new 'glass' cockpit – to a common C-130X standard. The US Naval Air Reserve has four fleet logistics squadrons equipped with C-130Ts. The Royal Air Force's Lyneham Transport Wing comprises five squadrons equipped with 26 Hercules C.Mk 1 and 29 stretched C.Mk 3s. Most other European air arms operate C-130Hs. Although the USAF has retired all its C-130A/Bs, small numbers have been refurbished for sale to relatively new operators such as Botswana and Romania; the civil L-100 variant is also in limited military service. The latest production variant of the Hercules is the C-130J. This is a much improved, high-technology development powered by AE2100 turboprops that drive six-bladed curved, propellers. Other major changes include a two-crew 'glass' cockpit with four flat-panel liquid crystal displays, modern digital avionics, and a wing with no provision for pylons or external tanks. The type is offered in military C-130J standard-length and C-130J-30 stretched fuselage models, and the civil L-100J. The launch customer was the UK, with orders for the C-130J and C-130J-30 as the Hercules C.Mk 5 and C.Mk 4 respectively. Other customers for C-130J/J-30 transports are Australia, Italy, the USAF and USMC.

Specification: Lockheed Martin C-130J Hercules
Origin: USA
Type: tactical transport
Payload: maximum payload 41,790 lb (18955 kg); accommodation for 92 troops, or 64 paratroops, or 74 litters plus two attendants, (C-130J-30) accommodation for 128 troops, or 92 paratroops, or 97 litters plus four attendants, other loads include light/medium towed artillery pieces, wheeled and tracked vehicles or 436L pallets
Powerplant: four Rolls-Royce Allison AE 2100D3 turboprops each rated at 4,591 shp (3424 kW)
Performance: maximum speed 448 mph (721 km/h); cruising speed 400 mph (644 km/h); climb to 29,000 ft (8839 m) in under 20 minutes; service ceiling 35,000 ft (10668 m); range 3,262 miles (5250 km) with a 40,000-lb (18144-kg) payload
Weights: empty 75,562 lb (34274 kg); maximum take-off 175,000 lb (79380 kg)
Dimensions: wingspan 132 ft 7 in (40.41 m); length 97 ft 9 in (29.79 m); height 38 ft 10 in (11.84 m); wing area 1,745.00 sq ft (162.12 m²)

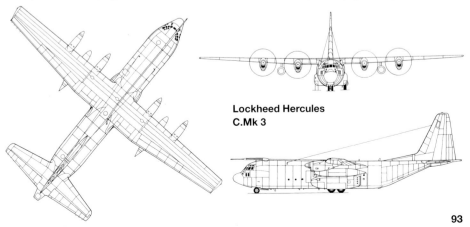

Lockheed Hercules C.Mk 3

LOCKHEED MARTIN C-130 HERCULES SPECIAL VARIANTS

The tremendous versatility of the C-130 has given rise to a host of specialised variants. Aerial refuelling tanker variants are among the most important 'force multipliers'. The USMC operates around 110 KC-130F/R/T models and stretched KC-130T-30 as dual-role tanker/transports. Tanker-configured C–130s are also operated by Brazil, Canada, Saudi Arabia, Singapore and Spain. Malaysia operates two C-130Hs in the maritime patrol role. The USAF is by far the largest operator of other specialised variants. Generic designations include AC-130 (gunship), DC-130 (drone control), EC-130 (EW), HC-130 (long-range SAR), JC-130 (temporary test), KC-130 (tanker), LC-130 (Arctic support) MC-130 (special forces support), NC-130 (permanent special test), RC-130 (reconnaissance), VC-130 (staff/VIP transport) and WC-130 (weather reconnaissance). LC-130H/Rs equipped with ski landing gear are operated by the New York ANG for Arctic/Antarctic support missions. Around 30 aircraft with the general designation EC-130E are configured for a variety of command and control/electronic warfare roles. The EC-130H Compass Call acts as a stand-off communications jammer. About 36 MC-130E/H Combat Talon I/II aircraft support the special forces community. These are used to infiltrate enemy airspace and to drop and, in extreme cases, retrieve special forces troopers. Supporting special operations helicopters are 28 MC-130P and 29 HC-130N/P Combat Shadow aerial tankers which also perform psy operations and leaflet-dropping missions. Ten WC-130H aircraft are dedicated weather reconnaissance aircraft, while a handful of NC-130A/E/Hs is also retained for test and evaluation work. The USAF is slowly introducing specialised variants of the C-130J to replace earlier C-130s while the USMC is receiving KC-130J tanker/transports equipped with underwing-mounted refuelling pods.

Specification: Lockheed Martin EC-130E Hercules
Origin: USA
Type: known EC-130E variants include the ABCCC battlefield airborne control aircraft, EC-130E(RR) Rivet Rider/Commando Solo/ Volant Solo used for propaganda/psy war tasks and EC-130E(CL) Comfy Levi/Senior Hunter jamming and Elint aircraft
Payload: (C-130E) maximum payload 35,700 lb (16194 kg)
Powerplant: four Allison T56-A-7 turboprops each rated at 4,050 shp (3020 kW)
Performance: (C-130E) maximum speed at 30,000 ft (9145 m) 370 mph (595 km/h); maximum initial rate of climb 2,000 ft (610 m) per minute; service ceiling 34,000 ft (10365 m); range 2,356 miles (3791 km) with maximum payload
Weights: empty equipped 69.,300 lb (31434 kg); maximum take-off 135,000 lb (61236 kg)
Dimensions: wing span 132 ft 7 in (40.41 m); length 97 ft 9 in (29.79 m); height 38 ft 3 in (11.66 m); wing area 1,745.00 sq ft (162.12 m²)

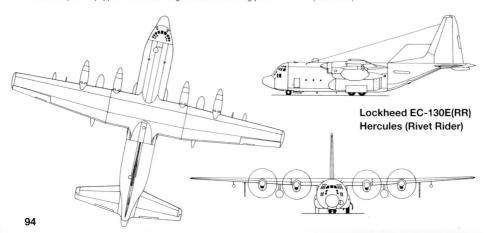

Lockheed EC-130E(RR) Hercules (Rivet Rider)

Although superficially resembling the 'first generation' T56-powered Hercules, the C-130J represents the state-of-the-art in airlifters. Apart from the basic transport, customers such as the USAF have already received several specialised variants for weather reconnaissance (WC-130J) and psychological warfare (EC-130J).

LOCKHEED MARTIN F-16A/B
BLOCKS 1-20

Originally conceived as a lightweight air-combat fighter, the Lockheed Martin (originally General Dynamics) F-16 has evolved into a versatile and effective multi-role workhorse. The type is currently operated by 20 air forces. In the hands of Israeli pilots, F-16s racked up an impressive tally of 44 aerial victories over Syrian MiGs during the 1982 war over the Bekaa Valley. The F-16A/B was built in distinct production blocks numbered 1, 5, 10, and 15. The USAF retired its 296 Block 5/10 F-16s in the early 1990s. Block 15 F-16A/Bs introduced an extended horizontal stabilator and a track-while-scan mode for the radar. Most surviving Block 15 F-16s equip ANG and test units. Of 467 Block 15 F-16As and F-16Bs, 272 were converted to F-16A/B ADF (Air Defense Fighter) standard with upgraded APG-66 radar compatible with AIM-7 Sparrow AAMs, advanced IFF, and improved ECCM and radios. Although most ADFs are in storage three ANG units remain equipped with the type. From 1988 214 new-build F-16As for export were manufactured to Block 15 OCU standard with wide-angle HUD, ring laser INS, increased MTOW capability more reliable Dash 220 engine, compatibility with AIM-9P-4 missiles and provision for ALQ-131 jamming pods. Belgium, Denmark, Norway and the Netherlands bought 521 F-16A/Bs of various Blocks (including OCU) from 1979 to 1992 and are currently upgrading 359 of their aircraft to MLU standard. Dutch and Danish F-16s are equipped with indigenous tactical reconnaissance pods. Taiwan is receiving 120 F-16As and 30 F-16Bs to Block 20 standard (new-build) with an avionics configuration similar to that of the MLU. Other F-16A/B operators are Egypt (40), Indonesia (12), Israel (75, plus 50 ex-USAF examples delivered in 1994-95), Singapore (8), Thailand (36) and Venezuela (24). In 1998 Jordan received 16 surplus ex-USAF F-16A/B ADFs, while Italy is leasing 30 Block 15 F-16ADFs as interim F-104 replacements. Production of F-16A/Bs totals 1,736 aircraft, comprising 1,425 F-16As and 311 F-16Bs.

Specification: Lockheed Martin F-16A Fighting Falcon Block 15 MLU
Origin: USA
Type: single-seat multi-role fighter
Armament: one M61A1 Vulcan 20-mm cannon with 511 rounds; maximum ordnance 12,000 lb (5443 kg), weapons include AIM-120B and AIM-9L/M/P AAMs, AGM-65 Maverick ASMs, Kongsberg Penguin Mk 3 AShMs, DASA DWS 39 gliding submunitions dispenser
Powerplant: one Pratt & Whitney F100-P-220E turbofan rated at 26,660 lb st (118.32 kN) with afterburning
Performance: maximum level speed 'clean' at 40,000 ft (12190 m) over 1,320 mph (2124 km/h) maximum initial rate of climb over 50,000 ft (15240 m) per minute; service ceiling over 50,000 ft (15240 m); combat radius 340 miles (547 km) on a hi-lo-hi mission with six 454-kg (1,000-lb) bombs
Weights: operational empty 14,567 lb (6607 kg); maximum take-off 33,000 lb (14968 kg)
Dimensions: wing span 32 ft 9¾ in (10.01 m) with tip-mounted AAMs; length 49 ft 4 in (15.03 m); height 16 ft 5¼ in (5.01 m); wing area 300.00 sq ft (28.87 m²)

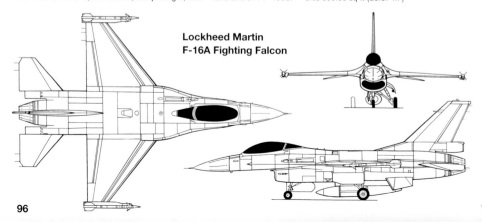

**Lockheed Martin
F-16A Fighting Falcon**

Belgium is one of four NATO start-up operators cycling their F-16s through a comprehensive Mid-Life Update (MLU). This will result in aircraft to virtually the standard of the latest Block 50F-16C/Ds. The MLU introduces APG-66V(2A) radar, GPS, a wide-angle HUD, digital terrain system, colour displays, compatibility with NVGs and a modular mission computer. The first of Belgium's six MLU-equipped F-16AM/BM units became operational in late 1999. Along with new weapons like AIM-120 AMRAAM and Maverick, these customers are also procuring new systems such as Atlantic navigation pods and LANTIRN targeting pods for their F-16s.

LOCKHEED MARTIN F-16C/D
BLOCKS 25–42

The F-16C/D is the most important operational F-16 variant with over1,750 examples in service with nine operators. Compared to the preceding F-16A/B series, the F-16C/D introduced improved ground and all-weather attack capabilities, plus provision for BVR missiles. Major features include a wide-angle HUD, Hughes APG-68 multi-mode radar and a weapons interface for AGM-65D and AMRAAM missiles. The first Block 25 F-16C flew on 19 June 1984. Subsequent models feature a reconfigured engine bay with options for higher-thrust GE F110 (Block 30/40) or P&W F100 (Block 32/42) engines; F-16s with the latter powerplant have enlarged air intakes. Block 30/32 aircraft can carry AGM-88A and AIM-120 weapons. From 1988, Block 40/42 Night Falcons introduced LANTIRN navigation and targeting pods (carried on the sides of the air intake), GPS navigation receiver, AGM-88B HARM II, APG-68V radar, digital flight controls, automatic terrain following and strengthened undercarriage. Block 30-42 F-16C/Ds are operated by Bahrain (22 Blk 40), Egypt (40 Blk 32 and 138 Blk 40), Greece (40 Blk 30), Israel (75 Blk 30 and 60 Blk 40), South Korea (40 Blk 32) and Turkey (43 Blk 30 and 117 Blk 40). Licence manufacture is undertaken in Korea and in Turkey. Many F-16Ds delivered to Israel have been subsequently fitted with a bulged spine, housing unidentified indigenous avionics that are probably associated with a defence suppression role. The USAF received 244 Block 25, 469 Block 30/32 and 462 Block 40/42 F-16C/Ds. These remain the service's primary tactical combat aircraft, the Block 40/42 Night Falcons making up over half of the night/precision strike/attack force. The USAF is purchasing 168 Rafael Litening II navigation/targeting pods for its F-16s. A Block 42 F-16D equipped with AMRAAMs became the first USAF F-16 to score an aerial victory by downing an Iraqi MiG-25 in 1992. The USAF's 40/42 F-16s are unofficially referred to as F-16CGs and F-16DGs.

Specification: Lockheed Martin F-16C Fighting Falcon Block 40/42 – generally similar to the F-16A/B except in the following particulars:
Powerplant: one General Electric F110-GE-100 turbofan rated at 28,984 lb st (128.9 kN) with afterburning (Block 40) or one Pratt & Whitney F100-PW-220 turbofan rated at 23,770 lb st (105.7 kN) with afterburning (Block 42)
Armament: maximum ordnance 6894 kg (15,200 lb), air-to-air weapons include AIM-9L/M/P, Python 3/4, AIM-7 and AIM-120 AAMs, air-to-surface weapons include AGM-65 Maverick ASMs, AGM-88 HARM ARMs, GBU-15 glide bombs, AGM-84D Harpoon AShMs, GBU-10/12/22/24/27 LGBs, Mk 20 Rockeye, CBU-87/89 Gator and CBU-52/58/71 submunitions dispensers,
Dimensions: tailplane span 18 ft 3¾ in (5.58 m); height 16 ft 8½ in (5.09 m)
Weights: (Block 40) empty 19,100 lb (8627 kg); typical combat take-off 23,765 lb (10780 kg); maximum take-off 27,185 lb (12331 kg) for an air-to-air mission without drop tanks or 42,300 lb (19187 kg) with full weapon load

**Lockheed Martin
F-16C Fighting Falcon
Block 30**

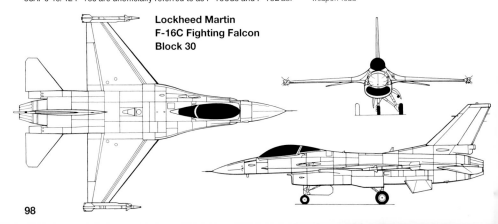

Egypt has built up an impressive force of F-16s and currently deploys eight squadrons from four bases. Under the codename Peace Vector, deliveries comprise 42 Block 15 F-16A/Bs, 40 Block 32 F-16C/Ds and 138 Block 40 F-16C/D Night Falcons, all Block 40 aircraft (illustrated) being powered by F110 engines. A batch of 46 Block 40 aircraft was built under licence by TAI in Turkey.

LOCKHEED MARTIN F-16C/D BLOCKS 50–60

In late 1991 General Dynamics began delivering the latest operational F-16 variants, the Block 50/52 F-16C/D. These feature APG-68(V)5 radar with improved memory and more modes, a new NVG-compatible wide-angle HUD, improved avionics computer, ALE-47 chaff/flare dispenser, ALR-56M RWR, Have Quick IIA radio, Have Sync anti-jam VHF and full HARM integration. These latest F-16 are powered by the IPE (Improved Performance Engine) versions of two standard GE and P&W engines. About 100 of the USAF's 289+ Block 50/52 F-16C/Ds have been raised to Block 50/52D standard with provision for the ASQ-213 HARM Targeting System pod carried under the starboard side of the intake to provide a limited Wild Weasel defence-suppression capability. Smart weapons capability is being applied to this model as well as previous versions. Export operators comprise Greece (40), South Korea (120), Singapore (42) and Turkey (80). Local production is undertaken in both South Korea and Turkey. Singapore operates two-seat F-16Ds fitted with enlarged dorsal spines similar to those of Israeli aircraft. Greece is buying up to 58 F-16s to improved Block 50+ configuration with upgraded radar, a helmet-mounted cueing system, conformal fuel tanks and 'stealthy' nozzles. The latest F-16 development is the Block 60/62 standard that is being developed in response to a requirement from the United Arab Emirates. Changes including agile beam radar, internal FLIR targeting system, an advanced internal ECM system, an advanced cockpit, conformal fuel tanks and an uprated engine. These Desert Falcons are scheduled for delivery between 2004–2007. Israel intends to buy 60 F-16Is that could incorporate some of the features being developed for the UAE. Production of the F-16 remains assured until at least 2009.

Specification: Lockheed Martin F-16C Fighting Falcon Block 50/52 – generally similar to the F-16A/B except in the following particulars:

Armament: future weapons to be integrated onto USAF F-16s are GBU-31/32 JDAM, AGM-154 JSOW, AGM-158 JASSM, CBU-103/104/105 WCMDs and AIM-9X AAMs

Powerplant: one General Electric F110-GE-129 turbofan engine rated at 29,588 lb st (131.48 kN) with afterburning (Block 50) or one Pratt & Whitney F100-PW-229 rated at 29,100 lb st (129.44 kN) with afterburning (Block 52)

Performance: range 2,257 miles (4215 km) with maximum external fuel; radius 923 miles (1485 km) with two 2,000-lb (907-kg) bombs and two AIM-9 Sidewinder AAMs

Weights: empty 18,917 lb (8581 kg); maximum take-off 27,099 lb (12292 kg)

Below: **Known unofficially as F-16CJ/DJs, the USAF's Block 50/52 F-16s are used for defence suppression missions. Although the AGM-88 HARM remains an important weapon, the JDAM bomb is also used to attack enemy radar sites.**

LOCKHEED MARTIN X-35

Lockheed Martin's contender for the JSF programme is the X-35; from 1997 its development has been shared with Northrop Grumman and BAE Systems. The generic X-35 has a configuration similar to that of Lockheed Martin's own F-22 design. Key systems include a multi-function active, electrically-scanned array that combines radar, EW and communications functions and a conformal array imaging IR sensor. Data from the various sensors is fused on the pilot's advanced helmet-mounted display system. The initial layout of the X-35 was frozen in mid-1997 as configuration 220, but further changes are being made before arriving at the definitive JSF design (Configuration 230). Three basic variants are proposed. The X-35A is the conventional land-based model for the USAF, while the STOVL X-35B is being developed for the USMC, RAF and RN. Connected to the engine via a drive shaft, a Rolls-Royce lift fan behind the cockpit provides around half the thrust required for hovering flight. The lift fan results in lower power settings, and cooler exhaust temperatures and velocities. The X-35C is the US Navy's carrier-based CTOL variant. This features a larger wing and control surfaces (fin & elevator) than the other JSF variants. It will be fitted with ailerons, a strengthened landing gear, arrestor hook and a reinforced airframe to absorb catapult launches and arrested landings. Both Royal Navy and US Navy X-35B/Cs will have folding wings. The first X-35A prototype was rolled out in June 2000 and made its maiden flight on 24 October 2000. It was followed on 16 December 2000 by the first X-35C. The X-35B followed in spring 2001. US government down-select of a single contractor or contractor team for the EMD phase is set for autumn 2001, following flight testing which will conclude the same year.

Specification: Lockheed Martin X-35 (provisional)
Type: single-seat multi-role fighter
Origin: USA/UK
Armament: internal Boeing/Mauser 27-mm cannon; maximum load; weapons (carried internally) include two AIM-120 AMRAAMs, 1,000-lb (454-kg) or 2,000-lb (907-kg) GBU-31/32 JDAM bombs
Powerplant: (X-32A/C) one Pratt & Whitney JSF119-PW-611 turbofan with axisymmetric (thrust vectoring) nozzle, rated at c. 40,000 lb st (177.9 kN) with afterburning; (X-32B) one JSF119-611S engine rated at total of 37,000 lb st (164.6 kN) for VTOL, comprising 18,000 lb st (80.1 kN) from Rolls-Royce lift fan, 15,000 lb st (66.7 kN) from main engine's Rolls-Royce swivel-duct nozzle and combined 4,000 lb st (17.8 kN) from two reaction control valves in wingroots
Dimensions: wing span 33 ft 0 in (10.05 m); length 50 ft 9 in (15.47 m); wing area (220A/B) 450.00 sq ft (41.81 m²), (220C) 540.00 sq ft (50.17 m²), 230A/B 460.00 sq ft (42.70 m²), 230C 620 sq ft (57.60 m²)

Lockheed Martin X-35 Configuration 220A

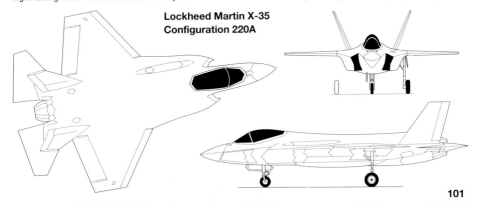

LOCKHEED MARTIN/BOEING
F-22 RAPTOR

Developed to meet the USAF's ATF requirement for an F-15 replacement, the F-22 air dominance fighter will form the core of the USAF's war-fighting capabilities over the forthcoming decades. In 1991 the USAF announced selection of the Pratt & Whitney-powered version of what is now the Lockheed Martin/Boeing F-22 Raptor. Between 1990 to 1997 two YF-22A prototypes evaluated some of the technologies proposed for the production ATF. The F-22's configuration is designed to meet VLO criteria, key features including a trapezoidal wing whose angles are repeated on other surfaces to reduce radar signature, canted fins and internal weapons carriage. The core of the offensive avionics is provided by the APG-77 multi-mode radar with an active electronically scanned array. Provision is made for an IRST and a side-mounted phased-array radar. The highly integrated avionics systems also include a data-link, INS with embedded GPS for high-accuracy navigation, and advanced EW, warning and countermeasures systems. Two central computers manage the automatic switching of the sensors between completely passive and wholly active operation, according to the tactical situation. Artificial intelligence algorithms 'fuse' data from the sensors and present only relevant information to the pilot to reduce workload while at the same time improving tactical awareness. The datalink allows tactical information to be shared with other F-22s. The F119 engines' high military power rating allow the F-22 to supercruise over long ranges while thrust-vectoring nozzles, combined with a triplex FBW FCS, make it exceptionally agile. The EMD contract issued in August 1991 called for 11 (later reduced to nine) F-22s; two were planned as F-22B two-seaters, but this aspect of the programme was cancelled in 1996 as a cost-saving measure. The first EMD F-22A made the type's maiden flight in 1997. By early 2001 the four available EMD aircraft had demonstrated the type's excellent capabilities. However, the US Congress recently called into question the value of such a costly, high-profile programme. Low-rate initial production of the F-22 was finally approved subject to compliance with stringent objectives.

Specification: Lockheed Martin/Boeing F-22A Raptor (provisional)
Origin: USA
Type: single-seat 'stealthy' air dominance fighter
Armament: one internal M61A2 20-mm cannon, three internal weapons bays, underside bay for four AIM-120C AMRAAMs and two lateral intake bays each with two AIM-9M/X Sidewinder AAMs; revised bays for 454-kg (1,000-lb) GBU-32 JDAMs; four underwing stores stations with provision for weapons and/or fuel tanks; planned weapons include BLU-109 Penetrator, WCMD, AGM-88 HARM, 500-lb (207-kg) GBU-22 Paveway III LGB, LOCAAS submunitions dispenser
Powerplant: two Pratt & Whitney F119-P-100 turbofans each rated at about 35,000 lb st (155.69 kN) with afterburning
Performance: (demonstrated by YF-22A) maximum level speed 'clean' Mach 1.58 in supercruise mode at 36,000 ft (10975 m) and Mach 1.70 with afterburning at 30,000 ft (9145 m)
Weights: (estimated) empty 31,670 lb (14365 kg); maximum take-off about 60,000 lb (27216 kg)
Dimensions: wing span 44 ft 6 in (13.56 m); length 62 ft 1 in (18.92 m); height 16 ft 5 in (5.00 m); wing area 840.00 sq ft (78.04 m²)

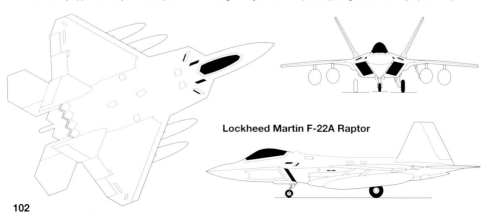

Lockheed Martin F-22A Raptor

Despite the funding of low rate initial production, the future of the F-22 programme remains uncertain: the number to be procured had already been cut from 442 to 339 in 1997. The F-22 remains a high-priority programme for the USAF, and efforts have been made to improve its utility by an expansion of its multi-role capabilities. The USAF hopes to accept the first single-seat F-22A for Air Combat Command by the end of 2005, with initial operating capability in 2006-2007.

McDONNELL DOUGLAS A-4 SKYHAWK

Despite its age, the A-4 Skyhawk is still an agile performer that is cheap to buy and operate. In 2001 the A-4 remains in limited service with the US Navy (two-seat TA-4J aggressors), Indonesia and Israel (where it only equips reserve squadrons). The remaining three major operators have initiated comprehensive upgrades to keep their Skyhawks viable until well into the 21st century. Under Project Kahu, between 1986–1990, New Zealand upgraded 14 A-4Ks with APG-66(NZ) radar and a new nav/attack system for use in the CAS and interdiction roles; they also also have a limited anti-shipping capability. Singapore's air force operates 50 single-seat A-4SU and 18 TA-4SU two-seaters upgraded to 'Super Skyhawk' standard. These are powered by a non-afterburning version of the GE F404-GE-100D turbofan and are equipped with GEC-Marconi Atlantic FLIR pods. The A-4s equip two operational attack units and a training unit at Cazaux in southern France; they also form the mount of the 'Black Knights' national aerobatic team. The most recent and major update has been applied to ex-USMC Skyhawks that were acquired by Argentina in 1997. Under a Lockheed Martin-developed programme, 32 single-seat A-4Ms and four two-seat OA-4Ms were rebuilt to A-4AR/OA-4AR Fightinghawk standard. Modernisation includes a complete overhaul of the airframe; new equipment includes an ARG-1 radar, advanced cockpit displays, HUD, HOTAS controls and AN/ALR-93(V)1 RWR. The ARG-1 is a downgraded version of the F-16 APG-66 radar and allows the use of 'smart' armament. The A-4ARs equip *V Brigada Aérea* at BAM Villa Reynolds. Brazil has recently acquired ex-Kuwaiti A-4KUs and, having acquired the ex-French Navy *Foch* in 2000, is modernising the A-4s for operation once more from an aircraft carrier.

Specification: McDonnell Douglas/Lockheed Martin A-4AR Fightinghawk

Origin: USA

Type: single-seat attack aircraft

Armament: two 20-mm Mk 12 cannon; maximum weapon load 9,155 lb (4153 kg); weapons include US Mk 80 series GP bombs and locally-developed FAS 250-kg, 280-kg and 800-kg GP, fragmentation and sub-munition bombs; provision for LGBs, AGM-65 Maverick ASMs and AIM-9M Sidewinders

Powerplant: one Pratt & Whitney J52-P-408A turbojet engine rated at 11,200 lb st (49.81 kN) thrust

Performance: maximum speed at sea level 685 mph (1102 km/h); initial climb rate 10,300 ft (3140) m per minute; service ceiling 38,700 ft (11795 m); combat radius 340 miles (547) km with a 4,000-lb (1814-kg) warload

Weights: empty 10,465 lb (4747 kg); maximum take-off 24,500 lb (11113 kg)

Dimensions: wing span 27 ft 6 in (8.38 m); length 41 ft 8½ in (12.72 m); height 14 ft 11¾ in (4.57 m); wing area 259.82 sq ft (24.14 m²)

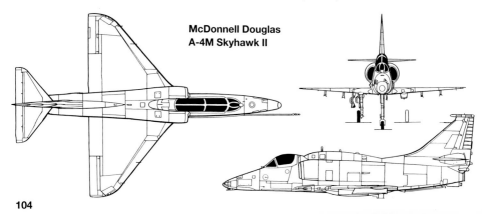

**McDonnell Douglas
A-4M Skyhawk II**

McDONNELL DOUGLAS F-4 PHANTOM II

The F-4 Phantom II is one of the most important warplanes in history. It remains in widespread service in the interceptor, attack and reconnaissance roles. The principal operational variant is the cannon-armed F-4E/F, and this remains sufficiently capable for several operators to have undertaken major upgrade programmes. In Germany severe programme delays with the EF2000 forced the Luftwaffe to execute the Improved Combat Efficiency (ICE) programme for 110 of its F-4Fs. These gained APG-65 radar compatible with AIM-120 AMRAAMs and a new GPS-based navigation suite. The F-4Fs form the backbone of Germany's air defence force and are currently not scheduled to be retired until 2012. Israeli F-4s were upgraded to Kurnass 2000 standard for enhanced ground-attack capability, receiving a modern cockpit with HOTAS controls, multi-mode radar and a wide-angle HUD. The upgraded Israeli F-4Es have been replaced recently by more capable F-15Is in the interdiction role, but remain operational with both frontline and reserve units. Sixty Turkish F-4Es are being upgraded to what is effectively Kurnass 2000 standards, while Greece is updating 39 F-4Es to a standard similar to the German F-4F-ICE. Japan operates 96 F-4EJ Kais modified with APG-66J radar and upgraded avionics. These equip two fighter interceptor squadrons and a fighter support unit. Iran and South Korea operate both F-4Es and the now-ancient F-4D models, while Egypt operates F-4Es only. The RF-4C/E reconnaissance variants serve with Greece, Iran, Israel, Japan, South Korea, Spain and Turkey. Spain has steadily upgraded its 12 RF-4Cs with APQ-172 TFR, laser INS, new ECM systems and EO sensors as well as IFR probes. Japan operates arguably the most capable recce F-4s. Mitsubishi has upgraded the JASDF's RF-4Es to a standard reflecting that of the F-4EJ Kai. Additional capability is provided by the conversion of 17 F-4EJ interceptors to RF-4EJ standard without camera noses but with pod-mounted camera, SLAR or Elint systems.

Specification: McDonnell Douglas F-4E Phantom II

Origin: USA

Type: two-seat interceptor

Armament: one M61 20-mm cannon with 640 rounds, maximum ordnance 7258 kg (16,000 lb); F-4F ICE intercept load comprises four AIM-120 AMRAAMs and four AIM-9L/Ms; F-4EJ Kai configured for maritime attack with ASM-1/2 AShMs plus Mk 82 and JM117 bombs fitted with the GCS-1 IIR-seeker head

Powerplant: two General Electric J79-GE-17A turbojets each rated at 11,810 lb st (52.53 kN) dry and 17,900 lb st (79.62 kN) with afterburning

Performance: maximum level speed 'clean' at 36,000 ft (10975 m) 1,485 mph (2390 km/h); maximum initial climb rate 61,400 ft (18715 m) per minute; service ceiling 62,250 ft (18975 m); area interception combat radius 786 miles (1266 km)

Weights: basic empty 30,328 lb (13757 kg); combat take-off 41,487 lb (18818 kg); maximum take-off 61,795 lb (28030 kg)

Dimensions: wing span 38 ft 5 in (11.71 m); length 63 ft 0 in (19.20 m); height 16 ft 5½ in (5.02 m); wing area 530.00 sq ft (49.24 m²)

**McDonnell Douglas
RF-4E Phantom II**

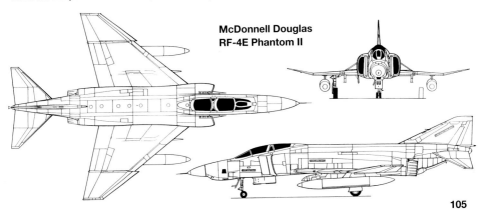

McDONNELL DOUGLAS F-15 EAGLE

The F-15 Eagle remains the world's premier air-to-air fighter. Although now in service for over 20 years, it remains a formidable warplane, as attested by its claim to 36 of the 39 USAF aerial victories in *Desert Storm*, without a single combat loss. The USAF has around 500 F-15s; active-duty units operate F-15C/Ds while ANG squadrons are equipped largely with older F-15A/Bs. The MSIP II upgrade for F-15C/Ds adds APG-70 radar, AIM-120 AMRAAM capability, improved ECM equipment and the JTIDs datalink system. The F-15A/Bs are gaining elements of the MSIP II, as well as improved Dash 220E engines. Their radars are being upgraded to APG-63(V)1 standard that incorporates features of the APG-70. Due to its capabilities the F-15 has only been exported to its most trusted allies. The IDF/AF has three units that are all based at Tel Nof; one unit operates the 13 ex-USAF F-15A/Bs delivered to Israel after *Desert Storm*. Saudi Arabia received 94 F-15C/Ds and equip five squadrons. It is likely that F-15s serving with Israel and Saudi Arabia will receive all or elements of the MSIP II upgrade. Delivered from 1979 to 1996, the JASDF procured a total of 163 F-15Js and 50 F-15DJs, all but 16 of which were manufactured under licence by Mitsubishi Heavy Industries. The F-15J/DJs are almost identical to USAF's F-15C/Ds, but lack the US tactical electronic warfare system and are therefore fitted with indigenous EW equipment. Japanese F-15 improvements include a radar and central computer upgrade, to a standard comparable to the USAF's MSIP II F-15s. Other elements include upgraded ECM systems along with new FLIR and IRST systems. With these modifications, the F-15J will have the capability to carry 'fire-and-forget' BVR AAMs and possess much more resistance to any future EW threat. Production modifications are targeted for FY04, and about 100 F-15Js are planned to be covered by the upgrade. The F-15J/DJs primarily equip eight fighter intercept squadrons – a seven F-15DJs also serve with an aggressor unit.

Specification: McDonnell Douglas F-15C Eagle

Origin: USA

Type: single-seat air superiority fighter

Armament: one M61 20-mm cannon with 940 rounds; maximum ordnance 16,000 lb (7257 kg); USAF air-to-air missiles are AIM-120 AMRAAM, AIM-7M Sparrow and AIM-9M; AA-4 and Python 3/4 within visual range AAMs equip JASDF and IDF/AF F-15s respectively

Powerplant: two Pratt & Whitney F100-P-220 turbofans each rated at 14,670 lb st (65.26 kN) dry and 23,830 lb st (106.0 kN) with afterburning

Performance: maximum level speed 'clean' at 36,000 ft (10975 m) over 1,650 mph (2655 km/h); maximum initial climb rate over 50,000 ft (15240 m) per minute; service ceiling 60,000 ft (18290 m); combat radius 1,222 miles (1967 km) on interception mission

Weights: operating empty 28,600 lb (12793 kg); normal take-off 44,630 lb (20244 kg) on an interception mission

Dimensions: wing span 42 ft 10 in (13.05 m); length 63 ft 9 in (19.43 m); height 18 ft 5½ in (5.63 m); wing area 608.00 sq ft (56.48 m²)

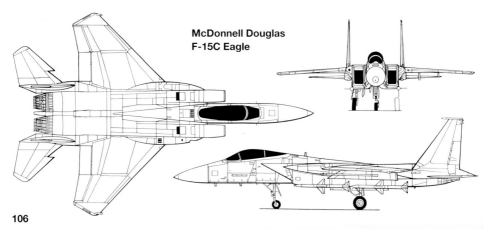

McDonnell Douglas F-15C Eagle

Based at Hickam AFB, the first-stage MISIP
F-15A/Bs of the 199th Fighter Squadron, Air
National Guard, are responsible for the air
defence of the Hawaiian islands. The unit has
pioneered the use of NVGs and datalinks. Note
the drill AIM-7 Sparrow missile round carried
under the port air intake.

McDONNELL DOUGLAS/BRITISH AEROSPACE AV-8B HARRIER II/II PLUS

The AV-8B was developed as a second-generation Harrier, primarily for the US Marine Corps. The Harrier II entered USMC service in 1984 and participated extensively in the 1991 Gulf War; it is routinely deployed onboard amphibious assault ships. The Harrier II fleet, which equips seven operational squadrons, has gone through two avionics upgrades to the baseline version, and is currently going through a re-manufacturing programme. A night-attack sensor upgrade equips four squadrons. The Harrier II+, which incorporates the night-attack upgrades and the APG-65 multi-mode radar, equips two squadrons. A re-manufacture programme for 72 aircraft is underway, involving replacing the Pegasus F402-RR-406 engine with the increased-thrust -408A version. The upgrade includes APG-65 radar, a navigation infra-red set, NVG-compatible cockpit and exterior lighting, and a moving-map display. The USMC has a need for 26 additional re-manufactured aircraft. AV-8Bs are also going through an avionics upgrade with fitment of a GPS, the common missile approach warning system, frequency-agile digital radios, and the digital Advanced Target Hand-off System, and all are gaining the ability to deploy JDAMs. The US is trying to fund an advanced targeting IR set for the Harrier. The two-seat TAV-8B, used by the Harrier training squadron, is also scheduled for upgrade with the F402-RR-408A engine. The first foreign operator was the Spanish navy which received 12 EAV-8Bs, eight AV-8B Plus and a single EV-8B trainer for operation from the carrier *Principe de Asturias*. The *Flotilla de Aeronaves* is having its nine surviving EAV-8Bs converted to the Plus standard. Italy's *Marina Militare* bought 18 AV-8B Harrier II Plus, including two two-seaters, for operation from the carrier *Giuseppe Garibaldi*. The Harriers of both navies are primarily tasked with fleet defence of their respective carriers, and have recently gained AIM-120B AMRAAM missile armament.

Specification: McDonnell Douglas AV-8B Harrier II Plus
Origin: USA/UK
Type: single-seat close support fighter
Armament: one GAU-12A 25-mm cannon (optional) with 300 rounds; maximum ordnance 13,235 lb (6003 kg), weapons include AGM-65 Maverick ASMs, Mk 80 series free-fall GP bombs, Mk 20 Rockeye cluster bombs, AIM-9L/Ms, 2.75-in unguided rockets; Italian and Spanish II+ aircraft have similar weapons options but also gained AIM-120Bs from 1999 and can carry GBU-10/16 LGBs
Powerplant: one Rolls-Royce F402-RR-408 (Pegasus 11-61) turbofan rated at 23,800 lb st (105.87 kN)
Performance: maximum level speed 662 mph (1065 km/h;); maximum rate of climb 14,715 ft (4485 m) per minute; combat radius 103 miles (167 km)
Weights: operating empty 13,968 lb (6336 kg) ; maximum take-off 31,000 lb (14061 kg) with 1,330-ft (405-m) STO or 18,950 lb (8596 kg) for VTO
Dimensions: wing span 30 ft 4 in (9.25 m); length 46 ft 4 in (14.12 m); height 11 ft 8 in (3.55 m); wing area 343.40 sq ft (22.61 m²)

McDonnell Douglas/ British Aerospace AV-8B Harrier II

The AV-8B Harrier II is well suited to the US Marine Corps' requirement for an aircraft that can provide direct fire support for its amphibious landings. The Marine Corps has been by far the largest AV-8B customer, taking delivery of around 270 aircraft. The night attack version (above) is largely comparable to the RAF's GR.Mk 7. Although production of the AV-8B ended in 1997, the USMC is upgrading its fleet through the re-manufacture of some AV-8Bs to II Plus standard.

The Model 500 originated as a civil development of the US Army's 369/OH-6 scout helicopter. Over 25 air arms currently operate small numbers of Model 369/500s in a variety of roles including utility, training, communications and observation. Hughes, and later McDonnell Douglas, developed dedicated military versions, known generically as Defenders, primarily for the scout, light-attack, anti-armour and ASW roles. The basic military version was the MD 500MD/Scout Defender while the MD 500MD/TOW Defender introduced an anti-tank capability with four BGM-71A TOW missiles. Key customers were Israel, Kenya, South Korea (where the type was built under licence in significant numbers). The most significant next-generation military variant is the MD 530MG Defender which introduced a pilot head-up mode called HOLAS (hands on lever and stick) permitting nap-of-earth and all-weather flight. The US Army has operated a variety of converted OH-6s and new-build MD 500s for the special forces role. These comprised MH-6, EH-6 and AH-6 variants for assault, command and control, and as gunships, respectively. The current operational versions comprise around 18 each of the AH-6F and MH-6H. These have modern 'glass' EFIS cockpits, FLIR and improved comm/nav systems. The service tried to incorporate NOTAR technology for greater stealth, but aircraft range was degraded, leading to the return to conventional tail rotor configurations. The fleet was upgraded from 1998 to the Mission Enhanced Little Bird (MELB) configuration that offers improved systems and an increase of over 20 per cent in aircraft payload. The term 'Little Birds' and 'Little Bird Guns' are commonly applied to these rarely seen helicopters. Features include a 'plank' payload beam able to carry armament (AH-6) or personnel (MH-6).

Specification: MD Helicopters MD 530MG Defender
Origin: USA
Type: light multi-role military helicopter
Armament: weapons include BGM-71D/E TOW 2/2A wire-guided ATGMs, 0.50-in or 7.62-mm podded machine-guns, seven- or 12-shot launchers for 2.75-in (70-mm) unguided rockets and Stinger AAMs
Powerplant: one Rolls-Royce Allison 250-C30 turboshaft rated at 375 shp (280 kW)
Performance: maximum speed 150 mph (241 km/h) at sea level; initial climb rate 2,054 ft (626 m) per minute; service ceiling over 16,000 ft (4877 m); range at sea level 202 miles (325 km); endurance at sea level 1 h 56 mins
Weights: empty equipped 1,979 lb (898 kg); maximum take-off 3,100 lb (1406 kg)
Dimensions: rotor diameter 27 ft 4 in (8.33 m); length 32 ft 1¼ in (9.78 m) with rotor turning; height 8 ft 7 in (2.62 m) to top of rotor head; rotor disc area 586.78 sq ft (54.50 m²)

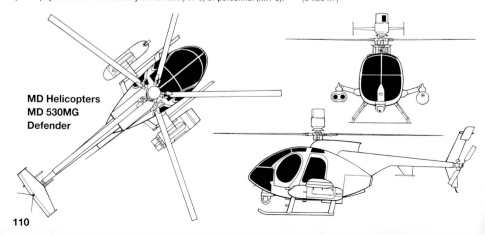

**MD Helicopters
MD 530MG
Defender**

The Philippines Air Force received 33 MD 520MGs for counter-insurgency operations. The MD 520MG is similar to the MD 530MG Defender that has options for a mast-mounted TOW sight, FLIR, RHAW gear, IFF and laser rangefinder. A Nightfox version, with NVG-compatible cockpit and a FLIR is available for low-cost night surveillance and attack missions. The Chilean army operates 24 MD 530Fs as its primary combat helicopter. Other MD 530 military operators include Argentina, Iraq and Mexico.

MIKOYAN-GUREVICH MiG-21 'FISHBED'

The MiG-21 is the world's most widely produced jet fighter and continues to serve in 2001 in significant numbers with at least 37 air arms. The market for upgrades is therefore substantial. Many of the proposed retrofit programmes for the MiG-21, promoted by companies like Elbit, IAI and MiG-MAPO, are applicable mainly to late variants. The most comprehensive recent upgrade that has been applied in quantity concerns Romania's 100 single-seat MiG-21MF and 10 twin-seat MiG-21UM aircraft. These underwent extensive systems and digital avionics modernisation by a combined Aerostar/Elbit team. Procurement comprises Lancer A dedicated ground attack aircraft, two-seat Lancer B conversion trainers and Lancer C dedicated interceptors. New equipment includes Elta EL/M-2032 multi-mode radar for Lancer Cs and EL/M-2001B ranging radar for Lancer A/Bs, DASH helmet sights, Litening targeting pods, advanced cockpit displays and a comprehensive EW suite. Aerostar and Elbit are offering the Lancer III upgrade for MiG-21bis customers. The Indian air force has been by far the largest export MiG-21 customer, receiving nearly 1,000 aircraft – over 700 of which were built under licence by HAL – and has a pressing requirement to upgrade its massive MiG-21bis fleet pending the arrival of the much-delayed indigenously-developed Light Combat Aircraft. India selected MiG MAPO's MiG-21-93 programme in 1994, but this has been experiencing continued delays owing to numerous factors, both Indian and Russian in origin. At the heart of the upgrade is a Kopyo multi-mode radar. Developed from the Zhuk radar installed in the MiG-29M fighter, Kopyo is compatible with BVR weapons including R-27RI semi-active radar and RVV-AE (R-77) active-radar missiles as well as precision-attack weapons such as X-31P and X-25MP high-speed anti-radar missiles, X-31A and X-35 anti-ship missiles and KAB-500 KR television-guided bombs. Several Western avionics systems are to be incorporated on India MiG-21-93s, including a ring laser-gyro inertial navigation system with satellite correction, and a lightweight RWR. The first upgraded aircraft, designated as the MiG-21I, made its maiden flight in October 1998, under the control of the ANPK-MAPO bureau.

Specification: Mikoyan-Gurevich MiG-21MF Lancer A
Origin: USSR (upgrade: Romania/Israel)
Type: single-seat multi-role tactical fighter
Armament: one 23-mm Gryazev-Shipunov GSh-23L two-barrel cannon; maximum weapon load 4,409 lb (2000 kg); weapons include BE100 and BM250 bombs, S-24 240-mm rockets, 57-mm rockets; Lancer also compatible with a range of Israeli supplied Griffin and Lizard LGBs, as well as Opher IR-guided bombs; Lancer C air-to-air weapon options include K-13, R-60, R-73, Magic 2 and Python 3 WVR AAMs
Powerplant: one MNPK 'Soyuz' (Tumanskii/ Gavrilov) R-13-300 turbojet rated at 8,972 lb st (39.92 kN) dry and 14,307 lb st (63.66 kN) with afterburning
Performance: maximum level speed 'clean' at 36,090 ft (11000 m) 1,353 mph (2178 km/h); maximum initial climb rate 23,622 ft (7200 m) per minute; service ceiling 59,711 ft (18200 m); combat radius 230 miles (370 km) on a hi-lo-hi attack mission with four 250-kg (551-lb) bombs and centreline tank
Weights: empty 12,880 lb (5843 kg); maximum take-off 20,723 lb (9400 kg)
Dimensions: wing span 23 ft 5¾ in (7.15 m); length 48 ft 2¾ in (14.70 m); height 13 ft 6¼ in (4.125 m); wing area 247.58 sq ft (23.00 m²)

**Mikoyan-Gurevich
MiG-21UM 'Mongol'**

MIKOYAN-GUREVICH MiG-23M

The 'swing-wing' MiG-23 'Flogger' was developed in the 1960s to replace the MiG-21. It combined greater payload, range and firepower with BVR intercept capability from more powerful onboard sensors. The Model 23-11 prototype first flew in 1967. The production MiG-23M 'Flogger-B' introduced BVR capability with Sapfir-23 ('High Lark') pulse-Doppler radar and R-23 (AA-7 'Apex') semi-active AAMs. Two downgraded export versions of the MiG-23M were produced. The MiG-23MS 'Flogger-E' had the MiG-21's 'Jay Bird' radar in a short radome and therefore no BVR missile capability. The MiG-23MF retained the 'High Lark' radar, AA-7 missile capability and 'Flogger-B' reporting designation. The MiG-23ML 'Flogger-G' was intended to have improved handling especially at high angles of attack, enhanced manoeuvrability and higher 'g' limits. It featured a lightened airframe, more powerful R-35-300 engine, improved, lightweight Sapfir-23L radar adding a new dogfight mode, more capable defensive avionics and a new IRST. It formed the basis for the MiG-23MLD 'Flogger-K' that had a number of aerodynamic modifications to increase high angle-of-attack capability and controlability. By 1999 the MiG-23 had been phased out of front-line service from Russian PVO interceptor and VVS units and now equips reserve and training units only. However, MiG-23 fighters remain in widespread service with export customers. The basic MiG-23M serves with the Turkmenistan PVO while Algeria operates the MiG-23MS. MiG-23MFs serve with Cuba, North Korea, Iraq and Romania. India's surviving MiG-23MFs have been relegated to an air defence training unit. MiG-23MLs serve with Angola and Yemen while a combination of MiG-23MF/ML/MS/MLDs constitute the backbone of the air defence forces of Libya and Syria. Bulgaria operates a mix of MF/ML/MLDs. MiG-23MLDs also equip fighter regiments in Belarus, Kazakhstan and Ukraine. The MiG-23UB 'Flogger-C' is the two-seat trainer and operational conversion variant and remains active with all MiG-23 operators. Phazotron offers a MiG-23 upgrade based around its N019M Topaz multimode radar compatible with R-77 BVR active radar AAMs.

Specification: Mikoyan-Gurevich MiG-23ML 'Flogger-G'
Origin: USSR
Type: single-seat tactical fighter
Armament: one twin-barrelled GSh-23L 23-mm cannon; maximum ordnance 3000 kg (6,614 lb), weapons include R-23R semi-active radar-guided and R-23T IR-guided BVR AAMs, short-range weapons include K-13 (AA-2 'Atoll'), R-60T (AA-8 'Aphid') and R-73E (AA-11 'Archer', MiG-23MLD only)
Powerplant: one MNPK 'Soyuz' (Khachatourov) R-35-300 turbojet rated at 18,849 lb st (83.84 kN) dry and 28,660 lb st (127.49 kN) with afterburning
Performance: maximum level speed 'clean' at 36,090 ft (11000 m) 1,553 mph (2500 km/h); maximum initial climb rate 47,244 ft (14400 m) per minute; service ceiling 60,695 ft (18500 m); combat radius 715 miles (1150 km) with six AAMs
Weights: empty 22,487 lb (10200 kg); normal take-off 32,407 lb (14700 kg); maximum take-off 39,242 lb (17800 kg
Dimensions: wing span 45 ft 9¾ in (13.97 m) spread and 25 ft 6¼ in (7.78 m) swept; length 54 ft 9½ in (16.70 m); height 15 ft 9¾ in (4.82 m); wing area 402.05 sq ft (37.35 m²) spread and 367.71 sq ft (34.16 m²) swept

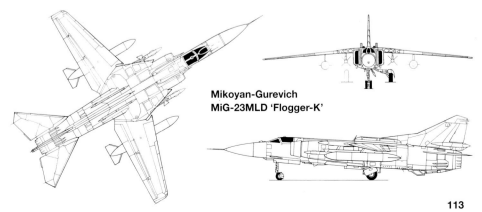

Mikoyan-Gurevich
MiG-23MLD 'Flogger-K'

MIKOYAN MiG-23B/MiG-27

The MiG-23B was developed from the MiG-23 interceptor in the late 1960s to meet a Frontal Aviation requirement for a tactical attack aircraft. The series production MiG-23BN variant proved disappointing in service and was replaced by more capable MiG-27s. The upgraded MiG-23BM/BK variants incorporated the improved avionics of later MiG-27s. Many BM/BKs built for export were described as MiG-23BNs. In 2001 significant operators were Afghanistan, Bulgaria, Cuba, India, Libya and, possibly, Iraq. Algeria's aircraft are receiving an avionics upgrade by a Bulgarian firm. Lesser operators are Angola, Ethiopia and Sudan. During border clashes with Eritrea in 1998 two Ethiopian MiG-23s was lost to ground fire. The MiG-27 was developed as a fully optimised fighter-bomber based on the MiG-23BM. Along with the Su-17, the MiG-27 formed one half of the mainstay of the attack force of Tactical Frontal Aviation armies. Between 1991 to 1994 both types were withdrawn from VVS service. The only current MiG-27 operators are Kazakhstan (with three attack regiments) and India. Both operate the MiG-27M 'Flogger-J' variant fitted with PrNK-23M nav/attack system, 'Pelenga' weapons system giving compatibility with PGMs and guided ASMs and a Klen (maple) laser range-finder/target tracker. The MiG-27s are capable of automatic night or bad weather blind bombing with a very high degree of accuracy. In India HAL has manufactured 165 MiG-27Ms under licence (known by MiG as MiG-27Ls). Although it is giving priority to the MiG-21 upgrade, the Indian air force intends to keep its MiG-27 force viable until 2020, and HAL's Nasik plant is currently investigating a substantial MiG-27 upgrade. This will give the ability to launch stand-off weapons and a night attack capability. New equipment includes two MFDs, updated HUD, HOTAS and a ring laser gyro INS and GPS-based navigation system similar to that fitted to Indian Jaguars. The MiG-27s may also gain an improved EW suite, inflight refuelling capability, FLIR and a Vicon recce pod. MiG-27Ms currently equip nine IAF attack squadrons.

Specification: Mikoyan-Gurevich MiG-27M 'Flogger-J'

Origin: USSR

Type: single-seat strike/attack and close-support aircraft

Armament: one 30-mm GSh-6-30 30-mm six-barrel rotary cannon; maximum weapon load 8,818 lb (4000 kg); weapons include tactical nuclear bombs, Kh-23 (AS-7 'Kerry'), Kh-25ML (AS-10 'Karen') and Kh-25MP (AS-12 'Kegler') ASMs, AS-9 'Kyle' ARM, FAB series free-fall or retarded bombs

Powerplant: one MNPK 'Soyuz' (Tumanskii) R-29B-300 turbojet engine rated at 17,637 lb st (78.45 kN) dry and 25,353 lb st (112.77 kN) with afterburning

Performance: maximum speed 1,170 mph (1885 km/h) or Mach 1.70 at 26,245 ft (8000 m); service ceiling 45,930 ft (14000 m); combat radius 335 miles (540 km) on a lo-lo-lo attack mission with two Kh-29 ASMs and three drop tanks

Weights: empty 26,252 lb (11908 kg); maximum take-off 45,570 lb (20670 kg)

Dimensions: wing span 45 ft 9¾ in (13.97 m) spread and 25 ft 6¼ in (7.78 m) swept; length 56 ft 0¼ in (17.08 m) including probe; height 16 ft 5 in (5.00 m); wing area 402.05 sq ft (37.35 m²) spread and 367.71 sq ft (34.16 m²) swept

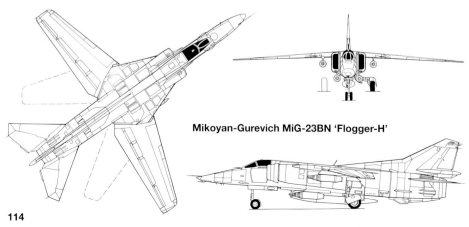

Mikoyan-Gurevich MiG-23BN 'Flogger-H'

MIKOYAN-GUREVICH MiG-25

The Mach 3-capable Mikoyan-Gurevich MiG-25 'Foxbat' was developed in the early 1960s to fulfil the interception and dedicated reconnaissance roles. In 2001 the VVS – Russian air force – operates limited numbers of MiG-25PD/PDS 'Foxbat-E' interceptors. These are found with units that predominantly use the MiG-31. Introduced in 1978, the MiG-25PD was the ultimate 'Foxbat' variant and featured an RP-25 look-down/shoot-down radar, undernose IRST system, R-15BD-300 engines and provision for a huge ventral fuel tank. Elsewhere, MiG-25 interceptors remain in significant use with Libya and Syria, each equipped with three to four units. Algeria has ten MiG-25 interceptors, that are responsible for the air defence of the capital Algiers and the strategic nuclear site near the air base. Iraq is believed to have five MiG-25PDs, while Turkmenistan has two regiments equipped with the earlier MiG-25P model. All MiG-25P/PD/PDS operators also have small numbers of MiG-25PU 'Foxbat-C' two-seat conversion trainers with stepped cockpits. Although use of the fighter variant is diminishing in Russia, reconnaissance variants of the MiG-25 remain important types. Two ORAPs have around 70 MiG-25RBs of various marks; these flew missions during the 1999 campaign in Chechnya. The MiG-25RB 'Foxbat-B' is a dual-role reconnaissance/bomber capable of releasing bombs from altitudes of more than 65,615 ft (20000 m) at supersonic speeds. Subvariants of the MiG-25RB were developed with a variety of systems for Elint and specialised reconnaissance roles. The reconnaissance 'Foxbat' has its own dedicated two-seat trainer, the MiG-25RU. Export MiG-25RB/RUs remain in limited service with Algeria (3) and Syria (8) while India's No. 102 Sqn operates dedicated photo-recce MiG-25R/RUs. MiG-25RBs based in Azerbaijan and Kazakhstan are not thought to be operational. Small numbers of the MiG-25BM 'Foxbat-F' defence suppression variant may remain operational with the Russian air force's research-instructor regiment based at Lipetsk for the development of operational tactics and various research projects.

Specification: Mikoyan-Gurevich MiG-25PDS 'Foxbat-E'

Origin: USSR

Type: single-seat interceptor

Armament: maximum weapon load 8,818 lb (4000 kg); standard intercept load two R-40R/R-46RD radar-guided and two R-40T/R-46TD IR-guided BVR AAMs, plus two R-23R/T or two R-24R/T IR-/radar-guided BVR AAMs or four R-60/60M IR-guided short-range AAMs

Powerplant: two MNPK 'Soyuz' (Tumanskii) R-15BD-300 turbojets each rated at 19,400 lb st (86.30 kN) dry and 24,691 lb st (109.83 kN) with afterburning

Performance: maximum speed 1,864 mph (3000 km/h) or Mach 2.82 at 42,650 ft (13000 m); climb to 65,615 ft (20000 m) in 8 minutes 54 seconds; service ceiling 67,915 ft (20700 m); range 1,075 miles (1730 km) subsonic or 776 miles (1250 km) supersonic with standard fuel; endurance 2 hours 5 minutes

Weights: maximum take-off 80,952 lb (36720 kg) with internal fuel or 90,586 lb (41090 kg) with ventral tank

Dimensions: wing span 45 ft 11¾ in (14.02 m); length 78 ft 1¾ in (23.82 m) height 20 ft 0¼ in (6.10 m); wing area 660.93 sq ft (61.40 m²)

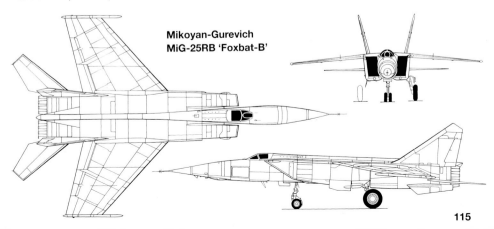

Mikoyan-Gurevich MiG-25RB 'Foxbat-B'

MIKOYAN/ANPK MiG-29 'FULCRUM-A/C'

With its stunning manoeuvrability, the MiG-29 re-established the Soviet Union's reputation as a producer of capable combat aircraft. The MiG-29 was developed to meet a Soviet air forces requirement for a lightweight multi-role fighter. Incorporating an advanced aerodynamic design, the MiG-29 has a N-019 pulse-Doppler radar (NATO 'Slot Back') as its primary sensor; this is allied to an IRST for passive tracking of targets. The 9-12 prototype made its first flight in 1977, and the type entered service with Soviet Frontal Aviation in 1986. Replacing MiG-23s, the MiG-29 was assigned dual air superiority and ground-attack roles. Fighter regiments were also tasked with tactical nuclear strike with 30-kT RN-40 bombs. The basic MiG-29 has proved itself as a formidable close-in dogfighter. The pilot has a helmet-mounted sight to cue missiles onto an off-boresight target. The very agile R-73 remains widely viewed as the best close combat air-to-air weapon. However, the MiG-29's primary BVR weapon, the R-27 (AA-10 'Alamo') is no more than adequate. Furthermore, the RD-33 engines suffer from low maintainability, and the MiG-29 is also handicapped by its lack of range and endurance. The latter parameters were addressed by an improved 9-13 variant allocated the NATO reporting name 'Fulcrum C'. This featured a bulged and extended spine, which houses both fuel and avionics, including an active jammer. Commonly nicknamed 'Gorbatov' (hunchback), this variant was built alongside the standard 9-12 MiG-29s. The MiG-29 was built in substantial numbers and was widely exported. After Russia, Ukraine is the next major operator with six regiments (including 'Fulcrum-Cs'). Other operators are Belarus, Bulgaria, Cuba, Eritrea, Germany, Hungary, India, Iran, Iraq, Kazakhstan, North Korea, Malaysia, Peru, Poland, Romania, Slovakia, Syria, Turkmenistan, Uzbekistan and Yugoslavia. The MiG-29s serve primarily as air defence fighters. All operators have small numbers of MiG-29UB two-seat conversion trainers.

Specification: Mikoyan/ANPK MiG-29 (9-12) 'Fulcrum-A'
Origin: USSR
Type: single-seat tactical fighter
Armament: one GSh-301 30-mm cannon, maximum ordnance 4,409 lb (2000 kg), (intercept) two R-27R/R1 or R-27T/T1IR radar-guided BVR AAMs and four short-range R-60/60M or R-73RM2D IR-homing missiles
Powerplant: two Klimov/Leningrad RD-33 turbofans each rated at 11,111 lb st (49.42 kN) dry and 18,298 lb st (81.39 kN) with afterburning
Performance: maximum level speed 'clean' at 36,090 ft (11000 m) 1,519 mph (2445 km/h) or at sea level 932 mph (1500 km/h); maximum initial climb rate 64,961 ft (19800 m) per minute; service ceiling 55,775 ft (17000 m); ferry range 1,305 miles (2100 km) with three tanks; range 932 miles (1500 km) with internal fuel
Weights: operating empty 24,030 lb (10900 kg); normal take-off 33,598 lb (15240 kg) as an interceptor; maximum take-off 40,785 lb (18500 kg) in strike configuration
Dimensions: wing span 37 ft 3¼ in (11.36 m); length 56 ft 9¾ in (17.32 m); height 15 ft 6¼ in (4.73 m); wing area 409.04 sq ft (38.00 m²)

**Mikoyan MiG-29
'Fulcrum-A' (9-12)**

Russia has some 400 9-12/9-13 MiG-29s assigned to around 10 fighter regiments; five of these are guards units. The shark-mouth, individual markings and non-standard tail codes on these aircraft may indicate an 'aggressor' fighter regiment. Note the single-seater carries R-73 and R-27 missile acquisition rounds. The MiG-29UB trainer in the background lacks radar but features a sophisticated weapons system and emergencies simulator, allowing an instructor to generate appropriate HUD and radar scope symbology in the front cockpit.

To address the shortcomings of the baseline MiG-29 the design bureau developed two radically-improved, multi-role variants. Both the MiG-29M and naval MiG-29K fell victim to fierce spending cuts after the Cold War and their further development was halted. MiG MAPO chose to pursue more limited upgrade programmes for more immediate application to Russian and export baseline MiG-29s. The MiG-29S upgrade was applied to a limited number of Russian 9-13 MiG-29s, the first phase introducing provision for underwing fuel tanks. It remains unclear if further phased improvements were applied. These included a doubling of the warload, provision for IFR and an upgraded N019MP Topaz radar with simultaneous dual target engagement capability. The radar would have given compatibility with R-77 BVR AAMs. Such features were subsequently offered for export MiG-29s, along with Western navigation and communications equipment as well as a bolt-on retractable IFR probe. The standard export MiG-29S was known as the MiG-29SD for 9-12 airframes and as the MiG-29SE when based on the 9-13 airframe. Malaysia's MiG-29Ns are effectively MiG-29SDs. While these versions were marketed as air superiority fighters, the MiG-29SM stressed its multi-role capability with TV- and laser-guided air-to-surface weapons. Pending the production of a fifth-generation fighter, the Russian air force is upgrading over 150 9-13 MiG-29s to a standard comparable to the MiG-29SMT (9-17); this first full-standard prototype flew in 1998. The upgrade will include an N-019ME or MP radar, a modern 'glass' cockpit, greatly increased internal fuel capacity, RD-43 engines, improved serviceability, addition of an IFR system, and increased combat load; not all of the features mentioned will be incorporated in the first phase of the upgrade. India's acquisition and upgrade of the former RNS carrier *Admiral Gorshkov* has attracted renewed interest in the MiG-29K. DASA, Aerostar and Elbit offer the Sniper upgrade that incorporates elements from the MiG-21 Lancer.

Specification: Mikoyan/ANPK MiG-29SMT – generally similar to 9-12 MiG-29 except for the following details:

Type: single-seat multi-role fighter

Armament: maximum ordnance 11,025 lb (5000 kg); air-to-air weapons comprise R-77 (AA-12 'Adder') active radar-guided BVR AAMs, R-27R1/T1 medium-range and R-27RE1/TE1 long-range IR/radar-guided BVR AAMs, R-73E close combat AAMs; air-to-ground weapons include Kh-31A and Kh-35 AShMs, Kh-31P and Kh-25MP ARMs, TV-guided Kh-29T missiles and KAB-500Kr bombs, Kh-29L and Kh-25ML laser-guided missiles and KAB-500L LGBs; Phase II MiG-29SMT will be compatible with new K-30, K-37M and K-77M AAMs, and with Kh-25MPU, Kh-29L, Kh-35, Kh-36 and Kh-38 air-to-surface missiles

Powerplant: two RD-43 turbofans each rated at 22,058 lb st (98.1 kN) with afterburning, possibly later with thrust-vectoring nozzles

Performance: combat radius 963 miles (1550 km) in air superiority role and 683 miles (1100 km) in air-to-ground role; unrefuelled range 2,714 miles (3500 km)

Weights: maximum take-off 46,297 lb (21000 kg)

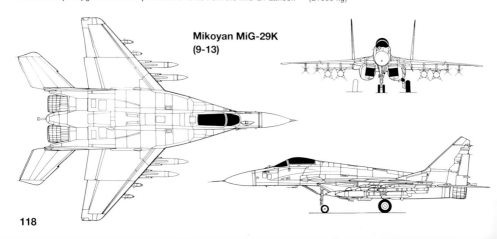

Mikoyan MiG-29K (9-13)

A MiG-29SE demonstrator shows off the range of air-to-air weapons it can carry. In the foreground are (from left to right) R-77, R-27T, R-27R and R-73E. R-60Ms are carried under the outermost wing pylons. Malaysia's MiG-29Ns were effectively built to MiG-29 SD standards. These are receiving a Topaz M radar upgrade that gives compatibility with the R-77. This missile is easily identifiable by its 'potato masher' rear fins.

The MiG-31 (NATO 'Foxhound-A') was developed as part of an overall programme to provide the Soviet air defences with the ability to meet the threat posed by NATO low-level strike aircraft and cruise missiles. The prototype Ye-155MP first flew 1975; production of the MiG-31 began in 1979 and the type entered service in 1982. The MiG-31's N-007 Zaslon radar was the world's first phased-array unit; it can track 10 targets simultaneously, and control the engagement of four of them at once. Operational experience showed that the MiG-31 was deficient in range and some 40-45 aircraft were fitted with semi-retractable IFR probes. Introduced in 1990, the MiG-31B gained an improved radar with better ECCM capability, upgraded R-33S AAM armament and improved avionics, including new digital processors. Existing MiG-31s were upgraded to the same standard as the MiG-31BS. MiG-31s continue to form the backbone of Russia's air defences. At least 300 are in service, equipping around 15 fighter regiments. Kazakhstan is the only former Soviet republic to operate the MiG-31, with a regiment (the 356th IAP) based at Semipalatinsk. The MiG-31M remains the most advanced version of the 'Foxhound' yet seen. It was designed to exploit the longer-range R-37 (with a claimed reach of up to 186 miles/300 km) as well as the R-77 AAM. It featured Zaslon-M radar, plus a range of new avionics systems, an extensively redesigned rear cockpit with new displays and uprated D-30F-6M engines. The first of seven flying MiG-31M prototypes made its maiden flight in 1985. The MiG-31M had the misfortune of being born at the wrong time, when defence budgets were being slashed. Today, the programme seems to be 'dead in the water'. MiG MAPO has proposed several MiG-31 variants for a variety of roles including defence suppression and long-range interdiction, as well as an export MiG-31E interceptor with downgraded radar. The latest version is the MiG-31BM; this is billed as a true multi-role 'Foxhound', able to undertake long-range interception, precision strike and defence suppression tasks. Both cockpits feature advanced displays allowing the crew to deploy PGMs.

Specification: Mikoyan/ANPK MiG-31B 'Foxhound-A'
Origin: USSR
Type: two-seat long-range interceptor
Armament: one GSh-6-23 23-mm cannon with 260 rounds, maximum intercept load of four long-range R-33 (AA-9 'Amos') semi-active radar-homing AAMs plus two medium-range R-40T (AA-6 'Acrid') IR-homing AAMs or four short-range R-60T (AA-8 'Aphid') AAMs; MiG-31BM weapons include R-33S, R-37 (AA-X-13) and R-77 BVR AAMs, plus Kh-58E (AS-11 'Kilter') and Kh-31P (AS–17 'Krypton') ARMs
Powerplant: two PNPP Aviadvigatel (Soloviev) D-30F6 turbofans each rated at 20,944 lb st (93.19 kN) dry and 34,171 lb st (152.06 kN) with afterburning
Performance: maximum speed 1,865 mph (3000 km/h) or Mach 2.83 at 57,400 ft (17500 m); climb to 32,810 ft (10000 m) in 3 minutes; service ceiling 67,585 ft (20600 m); range 2,050 miles (3300 km) with external fuel; combat radius 447 miles (720 km) with standard fuel
Weights: empty 48,115 lb (21825 kg); maximum take-off 91,851 lb (46200 kg)
Dimensions: wing span 44 ft 2 in (13.46 m); length 74 ft 6 in (22.69 m); height 20 ft 2¼ in (6.15 m); wing area 663.08 sq ft (61.6 m²)

Mikoyan MiG-31B 'Foxhound'-A

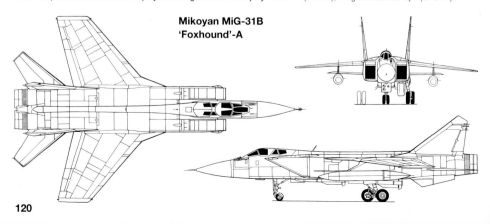

MIKOYAN/ANPK MiG I.42 (I.44) MFI

During the mid to late 1990s the aviation community was tantalised by the impending debut of Russia's first 'fifth-generation' fighter, the Mikoyan MFI. The MFI was developed to counter the threat posed by the ATF programme under which the F-22 was created. Mikoyan claims that the MFI's combination of aerodynamic properties, armament and avionics render it superior to any contemporary fighter, including the F-22A. The aircraft rolled out in 1999 is apparently designated MiG 1.44 and is understood to be a demonstrator only. The planned production MFI is referred to as the 1.42. and will have a slightly different air intake design, an internal weapons bay (faired over on the 1.44) and, possibly, cranked-delta wings. The 1.44/1.42 is the first Russian fighter to employ a 'tail-first' configuration. Weapons are mostly carried in an internal bay in the centre fuselage (faired over on the 1.44). The MFI is (or will be) equipped with a pulse-Doppler fire control radar persistently referred to as NO-14. This phased-array unit is designed for BVR combat and has the ability to attack six targets at a time. Prototype construction began in 1989, and after lengthy ground tests, the 1.44 made its first high-speed run in late 1994. Unfortunately, the programme had to be suspended before the 1.44 could become airborne due to ANPK MiG's dire financial problems. The 1.44 remained classified by the Russian Defence Ministry until it was finally publicly unveiled in January 1999. After great delay, the 1.44 finally made its brief but important first flight in January 2001. The future of the MFI remains unclear, and the line between it and the 1.44 remains equally blurred. Even though the MiG 1.42 is the Russian air force's officially selected 'fifth-generation' fighter, Russia's current economic situation precludes the construction of new combat aircraft for the Russian Air Force in the next few years. The MFI's projected unit price of $70 million – two to three times as much as the current 'fourth-generation' fighters – is almost certainly unsupportable in today's Russia.

Specification: Mikoyan/ANPK MIG 1.44 (estimated)

Origin: Russia

Type: single-seat demonstrator for 1.42 MFI multi-role tactical fighter

Armament: principal armament will consist of unidentified 'fifth-generation', long-range 'fire-and-forget' air-to-air (possibly folding fin variant of R-77/AA-12 'Adder') and air-to-surface missiles reportedly developed specially for the MFI

Powerplant: two Saturn Lyul'ka AL-41F turbojets each rated at approx. 39,350 lb st (175.0 kN) with afterburning

Performance: maximum speed Mach 2.6 at altitude; maximum 'supercruise' capability in region of Mach 1.6 -1.8; service ceiling 65,620 ft (20000 m); range 2,796 miles (4500 km)

Weights: normal take-off 66,138 lb (30000 kg); maximum take-off 77,161 lb (35000 kg)

Dimensions: wing span 55 ft 10½ in (17.03 m); length 74 ft 10¾ in (22.83 m); height 18 ft 9¼ in (5.72 m); wing area (including canard foreplanes) 1090.00 sq ft (101.20 m²)

Mikoyan/ANPK MiG 1.44

MIKOYAN/ANPK MiG AT (ADVANCED TRAINER)

MiG and Yakovlev are battling for a potential advanced trainer contract to replace up to 1,000 Aero L-29 and L-39 trainers in CIS air force service. There is also wider interest in their designs in the export market. MiG MAPO's contender is the MiG AT (Advanced Trainer). Although relatively orthodox, the straight-wing design is claimed to have the same high-Alpha handling as the MiG-29. The MiG AT is being developed as a joint venture with Turbomeca and SNECMA for the Larzac engine and Sextant Avionique for the avionics. Mikoyan has built three flying prototypes for the initial fly-off evaluation. The first prototype represents the ATF basic trainer version for the export market, with a modified version of Sextant's Topflight modular avionics suite. The second is to MiG ATR trainer standards, with Russian avionics. The third is the prototype for the MiG ATS combat-capable trainer. It has a helmet-mounted target designation system, provision for seven external hardpoints (in place of the basic trainer's three) and a variety of centreline targeting pods. The as-yet unbuilt MiG AS will be a single-seater, described as being analogous to the BAE Hawk 200. Mikoyan is also offering any MiG AT variant with folding wings, arrestor hook, and strengthened landing gear. All variants use a high proportion of Russian systems and equipment. The first prototype made its maiden flight in March 1996. By 2001 all three prototypes had flown and initial series production of a further 16 aircraft was well under way. The future of the MiG AT remains uncertain, with much still to be decided. However, Mikoyan has marketed the aircraft aggressively. The MiG AT lost out to the BAE Systems Hawk in its first competition in South Africa, but this decision may yet be reversed.

Specification: Mikoyan/ANPK MiG MiG-ATF
Origin: Russia
Type: two-seat basic and advanced jet trainer and light attack aircraft
Armament: (MiG AS) maximum weapon load 4,409 lb (2000 kg); weapons include Kh-29TD or Kh-31AS/PE ASMs, 57-mm or 80-mm unguided rockets, 100-500 kg GP bombs, 23-mm gun pods and 9M120 Vikhr/Ataka ATGMs, AAMs include R-73E, R-77, AIM-9L and Magic 2
Powerplant: two SNECMA Larzac 04R20 turbofans each rated at 3,175 lb st (14.12 kN)
Performance: maximum level speed at 8,200 ft (2500 m) 621 mph (1000 km/h); maximum initial climb rate 5,510 ft (1680 m) per minute; service ceiling 50,860 ft (15500 m)
Weights: normal take-off (training) 10,163 lb (4610 kg); maximum take-off (training) 12,544 lb (5690 kg); maximum take-off (combat) 15,430 lb (7000 kg)
Dimensions: wing span 33 ft 4 in (10.16 m); length 39 ft 4¾ in (12.01 m); height 14 ft 6 in (4.42 m); wing area 190.2 sq ft (17.67 m²)

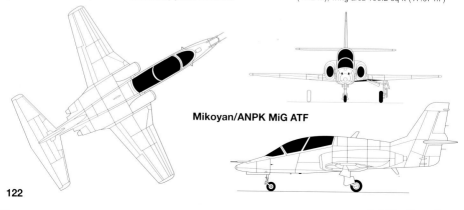

Mikoyan/ANPK MiG ATF

MIL Mi-8/-17 'HIP' SERIES & Mi-14 'HAZE'

The Mil Mi-8 (NATO 'Hip') is one of the most prolific utility helicopters ever built with over 7,300 examples manufactured since 1961. The combat proven Mi-8 is rugged and dependable, and large numbers remain in widespread use. The Mi-8 and improved Mi-17 variant continue to form the backbone of the Russian army aviation's combat transport force; they also serve with over 70 other air arms worldwide. The most widely built version for military customers is the Mi-8T 'Hip-C', the standard utility transport. The Mi-8TB "Hip-E" armed derivative packs a heavy punch with a trainable machine-gun, bombs, rockets and ATGMs. To improve performance, the Mi-8 was re-engined with 1,874-shp (1397-kW) TV3-117MT engines to produce the Mi-17 (NATO 'Hip-H'). This variant was introduced in 1975. Export customers often use the civil Mi-17 designation, but the CIS air forces use the Mi-8MT designation. 'Hip-H' helicopters in CIS service are often fitted with extra cockpit armour, IR jammers and chaff/flare dispensers. The same basic helicopter without armament is the Mi-8AMT. The Mi-8/17 have given rise to a bewildering range of versions that fulfil a wide variety of specialised roles. Dedicated combat support variants include airborne reserve command post, ECM (with onboard jammers), Comint and command relay. Other versions carry out delivery of fuel to front-line units, photo-reconnaissance, artillery fire-correction, reconnaissance, VIP transport, minelaying and mineclearing. These specialised variants mostly serve with the Russian forces, but are also found with other CIS operators including Belarus and Ukraine. Recent combat experience in Chechnya has led to a development with a night attack capability. This is equipped with an NVG-compatible cockpit, FLIR, LLLV and laser rangefinder. Mil has also produced a shore-based Mi-8 derivative as the Mi-14 'Haze' for a variety of naval roles including ASW, SAR and mine countermeasures. The most significant current operator is the A-VMF (Russian naval aviation).

Specification: Mil Mi-8T 'Hip-C'
Origin: USSR
Type: medium utility helicopter
Payload: maximum internal payload 8,818 lb (4000 kg); maximum external payload 6,614 lb (3000 kg) carried externally; standard accommodation for 24 troops
Armament: (dedicated armed variants) 7.62-mm and 12.7-mm trainable machine-guns; 57-mm and 80-mm rockets, 551-lb (250-kg) bombs grenade launchers, current ATGM options include 9M17P Skorpion, 9M114 Shturm and 9M120 Vikhr, plus Igla-V AAMs
Powerplant: two Klimov (Isotov) TV2-117A turboshaft engines each rated at 1,677 shp (1250 kW)
Performance: maximum speed 155 mph (250 km/h) at sea level; cruising speed 140 mph (225 km/h) at optimum altitude; initial climb rate 886 ft (270 m) per minute; service ceiling 14,765 ft (4500 m); combat radius 217 miles (350 km)
Weights: empty 15,784 lb (7160 kg); maximum take-off 26,455 lb (12000 kg)
Dimensions: main rotor diameter 69 ft 10¼ in (21.29 m); length 82 ft 9¾ in (25.24 m) with rotors turning; height 18 ft 6½ in (5.65 m); main rotor disc area 3,832.08 sq ft (356.00 m²)

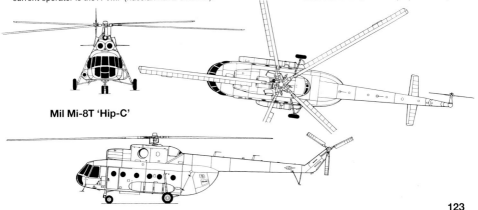

Mil Mi-8T 'Hip-C'

MIL Mi-24 'HIND'

The Mi-24 'Hind' is one of the most widely-known assault helicopter gunships in the world, and remains in service with over 35 air arms. The Mi-24 was developed from the tried and tested Mi-8 assault transport and was first flown in V-24 prototype form in 1969. The definitive initial production variant was the Mi-24D 'Hind-D' (Mi-25 for export). This introduced heavily-armoured, stepped cockpits and an undernose gun turret. From 1976 to 1978, the 'Hind-D' was joined in service by the up-engined Mi-24V 'Hind-E' (export Mi-35), which also featured improved armament of tube-launched 9M114 Shturm (AT-6 'Spiral') ATGMs. Combat experience in Afghanistan led to the development of the Mi-24P 'Hind-F' with a 30-mm GSh-30K twin-barrel cannon mounted on the forward fuselage. Later specialised 'Hind' variants include the Mi-24RKR 'Hind-G1' NBC reconnaissance helicopter; Mi-24K 'Hind-G2' for artillery fire correction; Mi-24BMT minesweeper conversion and Mi-24PS for paramilitary use. In 2001 Mi-24s remain in widespread service, the Russian army being the most significant operator with around 700. Other major users include Algeria, Angola, Belarus, Czech Republic, Hungary, India, Kazakhstan, Libya and Poland. The market for upgrades is substantial, with an estimated 1,600 'Hinds' remaining in service. A number of programmes are available. The Mi-24M (export Mi-35M) is available from Mil as a staged upgrade that includes a refurbished airframe for prolonged service, Mi-28 dynamic systems, upgraded 2,194-shp (1,636-kW) TV3-117VMA engines, an MFD-equipped cockpit compatible with NVGs, pilot's HUD, FLIR, a nose turret carrying a GSh-231 23-mm two-barrel cannon, 9M120 (AT-12 'Swinger') ATGMs, and compatibility with 9M39 Igla (SA-18 'Grouse') AAMs. Mil proposes to upgrade around 200 Russian Federation 'Hinds' to these standards as Mi-24VMs. The Mi-24 has seen widespread combat action, fighting in Afghanistan, Chad, Angola, Sri Lanka and, most recently, in the wars in Chechnya in 1995 and 1999.

Specification: Mil Mi-24D 'Hind-D'
Origin: Russia
Type: two-seat gunship helicopter
Armament: one four-barrelled JakB 0.5-in (12.7-mm) gun, maximum ordnance of 5,291 lb (2400 kg); weapons include 9M17P Skorpion (AT-2 'Swatter') radio-guided ATGMs, 57-mm, 80-mm, 130-mm and 240-mm rockets, UPK-23-250 23-mm cannon pods and 30-mm AGS-17 grenade launchers
Powerplant: two Klimov (Isotov) TV3-117 Series III turboshafts each rated at 2,200 shp (1640 kW)
Performance: maximum level speed 'clean' at optimum altitude 192 mph (310 km/h); maximum rate of climb at sea level 2,461 ft (750 m) per minute; service ceiling 14,765 ft (4500 m); combat radius 99 miles (160 km) with maximum military load
Weights: empty 18,519 lb (8400 kg); normal take-off 24,250 lb (11000 kg); maximum take-off 27,557 lb (12500 kg)
Dimensions: main rotor diameter 56 ft 9 in (17.30 m); wing span 21 ft 5½ in (6.54 m); length overall, rotors turning 64 ft 11 in (19.79 m); height overall 21 ft 4 in (6.50 m) with rotors turning; main rotor disc area 2,529 sq ft (235.00 m²)

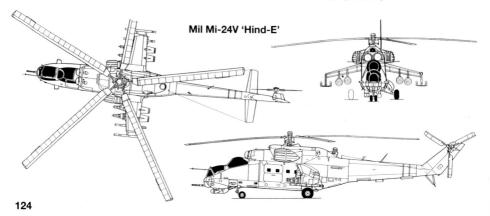

Mil Mi-24V 'Hind-E'

'Hinds' pack a formidable punch while retaining the capability to drop a squad of troops directly onto the battlefield. This Mi-35P (export variant of Mi-24P) totes a fixed 30-mm cannon, 57-mm rocket launcher pods and 9M114 tube-launched anti-tank missiles. The various upgrades on offer concentrate on improving the night attack capability of the 'Hind' via digital avionics, NVGs and FLIR, as well as introducing newer weapons with greater stand-off range such as the Ataka (AT-12) ATGM.

MIL Mi-28 'HAVOC'

Despite its reported defeat by the Ka-50 'Hokum', Mil claims to have received an order for the Mi-28 'Havoc' combat helicopter from the Russian armed forces and continues to actively market the type. The first of four prototypes made its maiden flight on 10 November 1982. The third and fourth prototypes were completed to Mi-28A standard with uprated engines exhausting via downward-inclined diffusers. The fourth production-standard prototype also had a moving, gyro-stabilised, undernose EO sensor turret and wing-tip pods carrying ECM and chaff dispensers. The Mi-28 has a conventional helicopter gunship layout with the pilot in the rear and gunner in front. It is armed with a 30-mm trainable cannon housed in a turret under the nose. Twin 150-round ammunition boxes are co-mounted to traverse, elevate and depress with the gun itself. The gun is identical to that of Russian BMP-3 IFVs and uses the same ammunition. The Mi-28's cockpit is NVG compatible; the pilot has a HUD and one CRT on which TV imaging can be displayed. The primary sensor package comprises the optical sights and laser rangefinder in an undernose turret. The crew are protected by energy-absorbing seats and an emergency escape system allows the crew to escape safely by parachute. A hatch in the port side, to the rear of the wing, gives access to the avionics compartment and a space large enough to accommodate two or three passengers during a combat rescue. In 1994 Russian army funding allowed modification of the first Mi-28A prototype to Mi-28N configuration. This introduced a mast-mounted MMW Kinzhal V or Arbalet radar, composite rotor blades, FLIR, an EFIS cockpit, improved armament options including Igla AAMs and uprated TV3-117VK engines. The Mi-28N made its first flight in April 1997. Mil also proposes a variant of the Mi-28 for support of amphibious naval assaults.

Specification: Mil Mi-28N 'Havoc'
Origin: Russia
Type: two-crew anti-tank, close support and air combat helicopter
Armament: one 30-mm 2A42 cannon; maximum weapon load of 3,572 lb (1920 kg); weapons include 9M114 Shturm C, 9M120/9M121F Vikhr or 9A-2200 ATGMs
Powerplant: two Klimov TV3-117VK turboshaft engines each rated at 2,466 shp (1839 kW)
Performance: maximum level speed 199 mph (320 km/h); maximum cruising speed 168 mph (270 km/h); maximum climb rate 2,677 ft (816 m) per minute; hovering ceiling 11,820 ft (3600 m) out of ground effect; range 285 miles (460 km) with maximum standard fuel
Weights: empty equipped 18,938 lb (8590 kg); maximum take-off 25,353 lb (11500 kg)
Dimensions: main rotor diameter 56 ft 5 in (17.20 m); span 16 ft ¼ in (4.88 m); length 55 ft 9¾ in (17.01 m) including cannon but excluding rotors; height to top of rotor head 12 ft 6½ in (3.82 m); main rotor disc area 2,501 sq ft (232.35 m²)

Mil Mi-28A 'Havoc'

MITSUBISHI F-1 & T-2

The Mitsubishi T-2 was Japan's first indigenously-produced military supersonic aircraft. Developed to replace the T-33 and F-86 as an advanced trainer for the JASDF, the T-2 is remarkably similar to the SEPECAT Jaguar. The first XT-2 prototype flew in 1971 and production deliveries began in 1976, the JASDF receiving 28 T-2(Z) advanced trainers and 62 T-2(K) combat trainers fitted with J/AWG-11 radar and 20-mm cannon. Two T-2s served as prototypes for a single-seat fighter support derivative, designated F-1. The T-2's rear cockpit, is occupied by an INS, bombing computer, radar warning avionics (with fin-mounted aerials) and other EW system in the F-1. The F-1 is primarily assigned an anti-shipping role, and from 1982 it was fitted with the Mitsubishi J/AWG-12 multimode radar for compatibility with the ASM-1 radar-guided weapon. The F-1 probably relies on the Orions of the JMSDF for third party targeting of the missiles since the range of its own radar is limited. The original JASDF requirement for 160 F-1s was reduced by budgetary constraints to 77 examples, the last of which was delivered in 1987. The F-1 equipped a peak of three fighter support units, but this has now been reduced to two, based respectively at Misawa and Tsuiki. In the late 1990s, the F-1 gained a new air-to-surface weapon, the ASM-2 imaging-infra-red missile, with a reported range of c. 62 miles (100 km). The F-1 is now nearing the end of its useful operational life and is scheduled to be replaced by the Mitsubishi F-2, with the 3rd *Koku-dan* at Misawa being the first unit scheduled to convert to the new type. In 2001 the T-2 remains an integral part of the JASDF's Air Training Command, equipping two squadrons of the 4th Air Wing at Matsushima; pilots accrue 140 hours on the type before progressing to a front-line posting. However, it has already been partially replaced by the Kawasaki T-4 and will finally give way to the two-seat F-2B. The T-2 also serves in small numbers as a hack for the two JASDF F-1 squadrons.

Specification: Mitsubishi F-1
Origin: Japan
Type: single-seat anti-ship, attack and close-support aircraft
Armament: one JM61 Vulcan 20-mm rotary cannon; maximum ordnance 6,000 lb (2721 kg) including ASM-1/S AShMs, AIM-9L AAMs; 500-lb (227-kg) Mk 82 or 750-lb (340-kg) bombs, bombs fitted with the GCS-1 IIR-seeker head (optimised for anti-shipping roles) and 2.75-in (70-mm) JLAU-3A, or RL-7, or 5-in (125-mm) RL-4 rocket pods
Powerplant: two Ishikawajima-Harima TF40-IHI-801 (Rolls-Royce/Turboméca Adour Mk 801A) turbofans each rated at 7,305 lb st (32.49 kN) with afterburning
Performance: maximum level speed 'clean' at 36,000 ft (10975 m) 1,056 mph (1700 km/h); maximum rate of climb at sea level 35,000 ft (10670 m) per minute; combat radius 345 miles (555 km) on a hi-lo-hi attack mission with two AShMs and two tanks
Weights: operating empty 14,017 lb (6358 kg); maximum take-off 30,203 lb (13700 kg)
Dimensions: wing span 25 ft 10¼ in (7.88 m); length 58 ft 7 in (17.86 m) including probe; height 14 ft 5 in (4.39 m); wing area 227.88 sq ft (21.17 m²)

Mitsubishi F-1

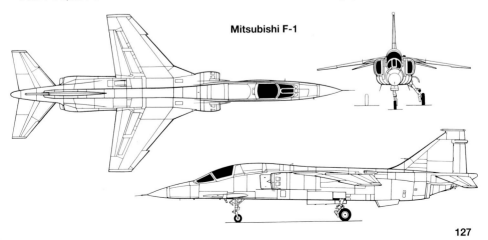

MITSUBISHI F-2

In October 1987, Japan selected the F-16C Fighting Falcon as the basis for a much developed version to replace the Mitsubishi F-1, primarily in the fighter support role. Although a costly and controversial programme – one F-2 costs at least the same as four Block 52/52 F-16Cs – the F-2 illustrates Japan's commitment to maintaining its high-technology aerospace industry. The F-2 features a new wing of 25 per cent greater-area and co-cured, all-composite construction, with radar absorbent material on the leading edges. In order to house additional mission avionics that include an integrated EW system, the F-2's fuselage has a lengthened forward section when compared to the F-16C. Other features include a longer nose to accommodate an active phased-array radar, a larger tailplane, a brake chute and a strengthened canopy. Mitsubishi is the prime contractor responsible for airframe assembly as well as manufacture of the forward fuselage section, while the other major assemblies are produced by Lockheed Martin, Kawasaki and Fuji. With either wing tip-mounted AIM-9 or Mitsubishi AAM-3 AAMs, the F-2 still has 11 hardpoints available for other stores, including the ASM-2 anti-ship missile as one of the principal weapons. The F-2 programme has suffered long delays, cost escalation and a number of structural problems including wing cracking and severe flutter. Four prototypes have been built comprising two single-seat XF-2As and a pair of two-seat XF-2B. The first XF-2A recorded the type's maiden flight on 7 October 1995. In late 1995 the Japanese government approved a programme for the manufacture of 130 aircraft with an entry into service scheduled for 1999. Delays resulting from modifications to cure structural problems delayed the F-2's entry into operational service until 2001. The current production programme calls for production of 83 F-2A single-seaters and 47 F-2B two-seaters. Retaining full combat capability, these have a fuel capacity reduced by 685 litres. The F-2Bs will be used for conversion and proficiency training, replacing Mitsubishi T-2s.

Specification: Mitsubishi F-2A

Origin: Japan/USA

Type: single-seat, close-support and anti-ship fighter with secondary defensive counter-air role

Armament: one 20-mm JM61A1 cannon, maximum weapon load of 17,824 lb (8085 kg); weapons include ASM-1/2 AShMs, AIM-7F/AIM-7M+ Sparrow AAMs, AIM-9L or AA-3+ AAMs, 500-lb (227-kg) Mk 82 and 750-lb (340-kg) JM117 free-fall bombs with GCS-1 IIR seeker heads, 1,000-lb (454-kg) bombs, CBU-87/B cluster bombs, JLAU-3/A and RL-4 rocket launchers

Powerplant: one General Electric F110-GE-129 turbofan engine rated at 17,000 lb st (75.62 kN) dry and 29,500 lb st (131.22 kN) with afterburning

Performance: maximum speed 1,321 mph (2125 km/h) or Mach 2.0 at altitude; combat radius more than 518 miles (834 km) on an anti-ship mission

Weights: empty 21,003 lb (9527 kg); maximum take-off 48,721 lb (22100 kg)

Dimensions: wing span 36 ft 6 in (11.13 m) with tip-mounted missile launchers; length 50 ft 11 in (15.52 m); height 15 ft 4⅔ in (4.69 m); wing area 375.03 sq ft (34.84 m²)

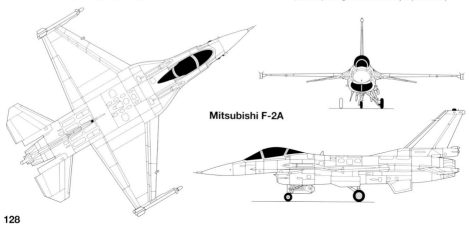

Mitsubishi F-2A

NAMC Q-5 'FANTAN'

The Q-5 attack aircraft is a purely Chinese design derived from the J-6 (itself a licence-built MiG-19) but markedly increased in effectiveness by an increase in the dimensions and, in its early form, by the presence of an internal bomb bay. The engine inlet duct is bifurcated and served by plain lateral inlets, leaving the extended nose available for sensors. The original Q-5 (Qiangjiji-5, Attack aircraft 5) first flew in 1969 and production examples were delivered to the PLAAF from 1970. The subsequent Q-5 I featured a bomb bay sealed off and used to house additional fuel – entered production in 1981. Q-5 I aircraft in service with the Chinese navy are reportedly equipped with a pulse-Doppler type radar and can carry two torpedoes and launch the C-801 AShM. From 1983 Pakistan received 52 A-5Cs (Q-5 IIIs). These aircraft featured upgraded avionics, Martin-Baker Mk 10 ejection seats and hardpoints compatible with Western weapons, including Sidewider AAMs, and currently equip two squadrons. Similar aircraft were exported to Bangladesh (24) and Myanmar (24). The Q-5 IA added two additional hardpoints beneath the wings, as well as defensive systems and many features from the A-5C. The Q-5A remains in service in substantial numbers with various components of the Chinese armed forces. It is estimated that there are some 500 examples equipping 12 PLAAF regiments, while a further 100 Q-5s serve with four PLANAF regiments. In addition 40 Q-5 1As were exported to North Korea. The Q-5 II designation applies to aircraft similar in standard to the Q-5 IA, but built with, or retrofitted with RWR. Recent upgrade programmes to fit French (Q-5K Kong Yun), Italian (A-5M) or Russian avionics have all been abandoned. In excess of 1000 examples of all variants of the Q-5/A-5 have been built. It is likely that any continued production, now by Hongdu Aviation Industry Group, is for attrition replacement purposes only.

Specification: Nanchang Q-5 IA 'Fantan'
Origin: China
Type: single-seat close-support and attack aircraft with secondary air-to-air capability
Armament: two internal 23-mm cannon with 100 rpg; maximum ordnance 4,410 lb (2000 kg) including 551-lb (250-kg), 1,102-lb (500-kg) bombs, practice bombs and rocket pods, plus PL-5 AAMs
Powerplant: two Liming (LM) (previously Shenyang) Wopen-6A turbojets each rated at 6,614 lb st (29.42 kN) dry and 8,267 lb st (36.78 kN) with afterburning
Performance: maximum level speed at 36,000 ft (11000 m) 740 mph (1190 km/h); maximum rate of climb at 16,400 ft (5000 m) 20,275 ft (6180 m) per minute; service ceiling 52,000 ft (15850 m); combat radius with maximum external stores, afterburners off lo-lo-lo 248 miles (400 km)
Weights: empty 14,054 lb (6375 kg); maximum take-off 26,080 lb (11830 kg)
Dimensions: wing span 31 ft 9 in (9.68 m); length 51 ft 4¼ in (15.65 m) including probe; height 14 ft 2¾ in (4.33 m); wing area 300.86 sq ft (27.95 m²)

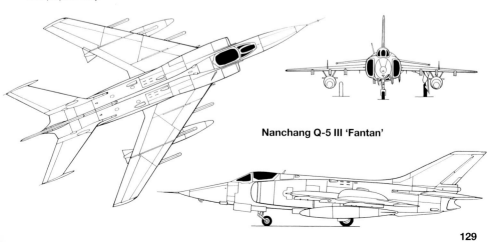

Nanchang Q-5 III 'Fantan'

NH INDUSTRIES NH 90

In 1985 five European nations signed a memorandum of understanding covering a 'NATO helicopter for the '90s', or NH 90. The UK dropped out of the programme in 1987, leaving France, Germany, Italy and the Netherlands in the project by means of NH Industries. This was established in France in 1992 to control a collaborative programme involving Eurocopter France (with NFT [Norway] as a risk-sharing partner from 1994), Agusta, Eurocopter Deutschland and Fokker. Stated requirements were 220 helicopters for France, 214 for Italy, 272 for Germany and 20 for the Netherlands, and it was anticipated that a first flight in 1995 would pave the way for deliveries from 1999. The two initial versions are the NH 90 NFH (NATO Frigate Helicopter) for the autonomous ASW and AShW roles, and the NH 90 TTH (Tactical Transport Helicopter) for assault transport, rescue, EW and VIP transport duties. The NFH variant is being developed under Agusta leadership and its advanced mission suite includes a 360° search radar, dipping sonar, FLIR, MAD, and ESM and ECM systems. The TTH variant is being developed under Eurocopter Deutschland leadership, with a cabin for 20 troops or one 4,409-lb (2000-kg) vehicle. It can carry area-suppression and self-defence weapons. A FLIR is standard on the TTH to provide a night and adverse-weather NOE flight capability, and both models are controlled via a quadruplex fly-by-wire control system. Two engine types are available to increase the NH 90's export potential. The first of five flying and one ground-test prototypes was the French-assembled PT 1 that first flew on 18 December 1995 with RTM 322 engines. The partner nations have now identified home requirements for 642 NH 90s, with 244 helicopters placed on firm order in March 2000.

Specification: NH Industries NH 90
Origin: France/Germany/Italy/Netherlands
Type: three/four-crew shipborne ASW/ASuV or two-crew land-based tactical helicopter
Armament: maximum load 3,086 lb (1400 kg); NFH weapons include homing torpedoes and Marte Mk 2/S AShMs (Italian model)
Powerplant: two RTM 322-01/9 turboshaft engines each rated at 2,100 shp (1566 kW) or two General Electric/Alfa Romeo T700-T6E turboshaft engines each rated at 2,040 shp (1521 kW)
Performance: (estimated) maximum cruising speed (NFH) 181 mph (291 km/h), (TTH) 185 mph (298 km/h); range, both models (maximum fuel), 748 miles (1204 km)
Weights: empty (TTH) 11,905 lb (5400 kg), (NFH) 14,171 lb (6428 kg); maximum take-off 22,046 lb (10000 kg)
Dimensions: main rotor diameter 53 ft 5½ in (16.30 m); length 64 ft 2 in (19.56 m) with the rotors turning; height 17 ft 10 in (5.44 m) with the rotors turning; main rotor disc area 2,246.18 sq ft (208.67 m²)

NH Industries NH 90

NORTHROP F-5E TIGER II

The first F-5A Freedom Fighter single-seat light-fighter prototype flew in May 1963 and went on to form the basis of a major warplane family. Canadair built the CF-5A/Ds and NF-5A/Bs for the Canadian and Dutch air force respectively; the survivors of these fleets are finding a ready resale market to countries including Botswana, Turkey and Venezuela. In addition, South Korea, Brazil, Greece, Iran, Morocco, Norway, Philippines, Saudi Arabia, Spain, Taiwan, Thailand, Turkey, Venezuela and Yemen all currently operate first generation F-5s. Venezuela's VF-5A/Ds have received a limited upgrade by Singapore Technologies Aerospace. The improved F-5E/F Tiger II was developed from the F-5A/B as an International Fighter Aircraft for sale to US allies. The F-5E prototype first flew in August 1972 and was followed by some 1,300 production F-5Es and two-seat F-5Fs for sale to 20 air forces. The F-5E was also assembled under licence in Taiwan and South Korea. Tiger IIs remain in widespread service with Bahrain, Brazil, Chile, Honduras, Indonesia, Iran, Jordan, Kenya, Malaysia, Mexico, Saudi Arabia, Singapore, Switzerland, Taiwan, Thailand, Tunisia, US Marine Corps and US Navy and Yemen. Reconnaissance F-5E variants are operated by Malaysia (RF-5E Tigereye), Singapore (RF-5S) and Taiwan (RF-5E Tigergazer). Numerous update programmes are available to keep this important warplane viable until well into the 21st century. These upgrades offer a mix of new avionics and structural refurbishment of the airframe. Chile operates F-5Es upgraded with Israeli assistance to Tiger III standard; their advanced avionics – including Elta 2032 radar and HOTAS controls – give a level of combat capability matching that of the F-16. The FIAR Grifo F/X Plus multi-mode radar has been fitted to Singaporean F-5S aircraft and has also been selected for Brazil's F-5Es. US-based TCA is offering to re-manufacture existing single-seat F-5s to two-seat F-5F configuration in order to meet a projected demand for cost-effective lead-in fighter trainers.

Specification: Northrop F-5E Tiger III
Origin: USA
Type: single-seat lightweight tactical fighter
Armament: one 20-mm Ford M39A2 fixed cannon; maximum weapon load 7,000 lb (3175 kg); weapons include AIM-9P Sidewinder and Python 3/4 AAMs; other weapons carried by F-5Es include AGM-65G Maverick ASMs (Switzerland), GPU-5 30-mm cannon pods (Thailand), AGM-45 Shrike ARM, GBU-10/12 LGBs, Rockeye CBU and R550 Magic AAMs (Saudi Arabia)
Powerplant: two General Electric J85-GE-21B turbojet engines each rated at 3,500 lb st (15.57 kN) dry and 5,000 lb st (22.24 kN) with afterburning
Performance: maximum speed 1,056 mph (1700 km/h) at 36,000 ft (10975 m); initial climb rate 34,300 ft (10455 m) per minute; service ceiling 51,800 ft (15550 m); combat radius 875 miles (1405 km) with two AIM-9 AAMs and maximum fuel
Weights: empty 9,558 lb (4349 kg); maximum take-off 24,664 lb (11187 kg)
Dimensions: wing span 26 ft 8 in (8.13 m) without tip-mounted AAMs; length 47 ft 4¾ in (14.45 m) including probe; height 13 ft 4½ in (4.08 m); wing area 186.00 sq ft (17.28 m²)

Northrop RF-5E Tigereye

NORTHROP GRUMMAN B-2 SPIRIT

The black, bat-like B-2A Spirit is the 'silver bullet' of US policy, reserved for use against targets of the highest priority. The B-2 is the costliest warplane ever built (around $900 million per copy), is difficult to maintain and is prone to trouble with the coating that provides much of its 'stealth'. The B-2 Spirit was developed as a low observable strategic bomber for the Cold War mission of attacking Soviet strategic targets. Composites are extensively used to provide a radar-absorbent honeycomb structure; the bomber has a minimal IR signature, does not contrail and uses its shielded APQ-181 radar only momentarily to identify a target just before attacking. The 'glass' cockpit is usually flown by a crew of two. The aircraft has a quadruplex-redundant digital fly-by-wire system and highly advanced, classified EW system. Six prototypes were funded and the first was rolled out on 22 November 1988. The B-2's first flight took place on 17 July 1990, when this machine (also known as AV-1/Air Vehicle One) was delivered to the USAF at Edwards AFB for the start of the test programme. In July 1991 the USAF implemented a 'set of treatments' to rectify a shortfall in the B-2A's 'stealth' capabilities. The USAF had originally wanted 132 aircraft, but funding restrictions have seen the fleet completed with just 21 aircraft. The last of these was delivered on 14 July 2000 and is the AV-1 prototype upgraded to Block 30 standard. The first operational B-2A was delivered to the 509th Bomb Wing on 17 December 1993 and full IOC came in April 1997. Having progressed through the Block 10 and 20 standards of 'stealth', systems and weapons capability, the entire B-2A fleet will be brought to Block 30 standard with full weapons and stealth capabilities. The B-2A made its combat debut over Kosovo in 1999, employing the Joint Direct Attack Munition (JDAM) and other weapons to great effect. Although the USAF's B-2 force is garrisoned at Whiteman AFB, Missouri, the service has ambitious plans to operate the aircraft temporarily from forward bases like Guam and Diego Garcia.

Specification: Northrop Grumman B-2A Spirit
Origin: USA
Type: two/three-crew long-range low-observable strategic bomber
Armament: maximum load of 40,000 lb (18144 kg) carried in two internal bays; strategic strike weapons carried on rotary launchers include 16 AGM-129 ACMs, 16 B61 or 16 B83 thermonuclear free-fall bombs; other weapons include GBU-32 JDAMs, JASSM, AGM-154C JSOW, BLU-109/A Penetrators, 4,700-lb GAM-113 (GPS-guided version of CALCM), GAM-84 (GPS-guided version of Mk 84 free-fall bomb)
Powerplant: four General Electric F118-GE-100 turbofan engines each rated at 19,000 lb st (84.52 kN)
Performance: maximum speed c. 475 mph (764 km/h) at high altitude; range 7,595 miles (12223 km) with eight AGM-129s and eight B61 bombs on a hi-hi-hi mission; endurance more than 36 hours
Weights: empty 153,700 lb (69717 kg); typical take-off 336,500 lb (152635 kg)
Dimensions: wing span 172 ft (52.43 m); length 69 ft (21.03 m); height 17 ft (5.18 m); wing area about 5,275.00 sq ft (490.05 m²)

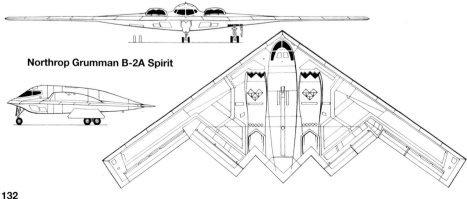

Northrop Grumman B-2A Spirit

The USAF's small force of 'flying wings' is charged with flying nuclear and conventional missions to targets as far as 6,000 miles (9655 km) away. The much-publicised 'global reach' was demonstrated during Operation *Allied Force* in March-April 1999 when B-2s flew nonstop from the centre of the US to strike targets in Belgrade.

NORTHROP GRUMMAN E-8 J-STARS

The E-8 Joint Surveillance Target Attack System (J-STARS) was developed by prime contractor Grumman (now Northrop Grumman) and made a 'star' debut in 1991 during Operation *Desert Storm* long before it was considered operational. Based on the airframe of a Boeing 707-300 airliner, the E-8 provides the kind of capability for monitoring and controlling the land battle that the E-3 provides for the air battle. The E-8's primary mission system is the AN/APY-3 multi-mode side-looking radar whose antenna is housed in a large ventral canoe fairing. The radar allows the onboard controllers to monitor the positions and movements of all ground vehicles, as well as serving other functions. It can also differentiate between wheeled and tracked vehicles. The two E-8A prototypes were deployed during *Desert Storm*, but now serve purely in the training role. The USAF's operational variant is the E-8C and this is responsible for ground surveillance, targeting, attack and battlefield management as well as bomb damage assessment. The E-8's communications and electronics systems also have a role in SEAD and the detection of elusive ground targets such as mobile missile launchers. The USAF's E-8Cs are being progressively improved through staged upgrades; by 2006 the Block 50 upgrade is projected to add a new AN/APY-X radar. This adds new capabilities such as automatic target recognition, helicopter detection and tracking, Elint gathering, and maritime detection. By Fiscal Year 2000 the USAF had ordered a total of 14 E-8Cs and ultimately intends to procure 19 aircraft. The eight operational examples serve with 93rd Air Control Wing at Robins AFB, Georgia. The USAF is considering the re-engining of its E-8C fleet with CFM56 powerplants. In 1999 a team of Raytheon and Bombardier was chosen to provide the systems and platform to fulfil the RAF's ASTOR (Airborne Stand-Off Radar) requirement. ASTOR is similar to J-STARS and has an in-service date set for 2004. ASTOR will reportedly incorporate certain features destined for future J-STARS use that will make it more capable than the contemporary standard US E-8s.

Specification: Northrop Grumman E-8C J-STARS

Origin: USA

Type: long-range/high-endurance ground surveillance and land battle management system aircraft

Accommodation: normal flight crew of three, plus up to 18 systems operators; an entire replacement crew can be carried for long-endurance missions

Radar performance: area of coverage approx. 19,305 sq miles (50,000 km²); target detection range 30-155 miles (50-250 km) with E-8C flying at altitude of 30,000-40,000 ft (9144-12192 m)

Powerplant: four Pratt & Whitney TF33-P-102B turbofans each rated at 18,000 lb st (80.10 kN) but being upgraded to TF33-P-102C turbofans each rated at 19,200 lb st (85.40 kN)

Performance: maximum operating speed 555 mph (892 km/h); service ceiling 42,000 ft (12800 m); maximum endurance with one inflight refuelling 20 hours

Weights: empty 171,000 lb (77564 kg); maximum take-off 331,000 lb (150139 kg)

Dimensions: wing span 145 ft 9 in (44.42 m); length 152 ft 11 in (46.61 m); height 42 ft 6 in (12.95 m); wing area 3,050 sq ft (283.35 m²)

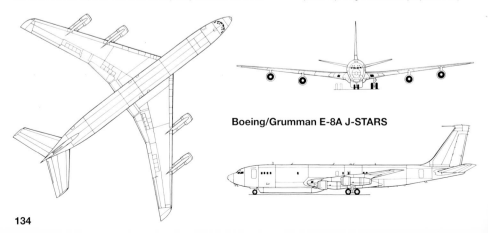

Boeing/Grumman E-8A J-STARS

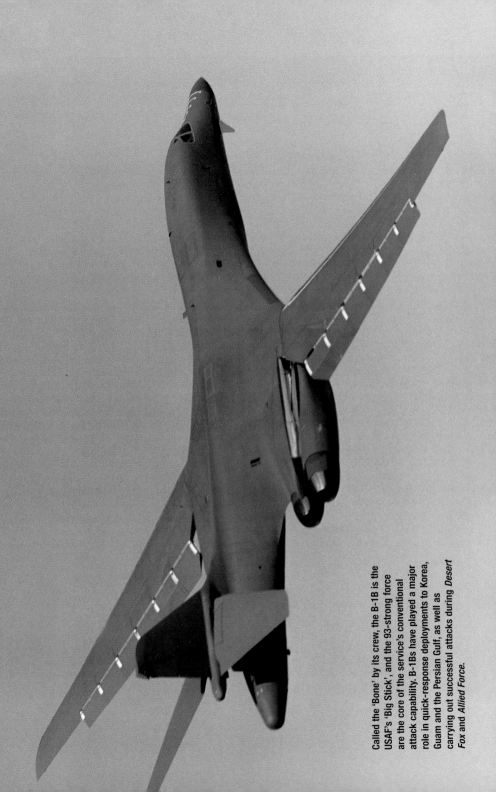

Called the 'Bone' by its crew, the B-1B is the USAF's 'Big Stick', and the 93-strong force are the core of the service's conventional attack capability. B-1Bs have played a major role in quick-response deployments to Korea, Guam and the Persian Gulf, as well as carrying out successful attacks during *Desert Fox* and *Allied Force*.

SAAB 37 VIGGEN

Designed to meet exacting Swedish requirements, the innovative Saab 37 Viggen (thunderbolt) multi-role fighter was for many years the backbone of Sweden's air defence, and today five of the *Flygvapnet's* front-line *Flottiljer* continue to fly the type. The first Viggen prototype made its maiden flight in 1967, and the initial production AJ 37 attack fighter (108 built) flew in 1971. The other major variants comprised 27 SF 37s for all-weather overland reconnaissance, 28 SH 37s for maritime reconnaissance and 17 Sk 37 operational conversion trainers. Between 1979 and 1990 the *Flygvapnet* received 149 second-generation JA 37s for the interception role. During 1993-1997 Saab converted 48 AJ 37, 25 SF 37 and 25 SH 37s to AJS 37 standard to provide integrated attack, fighter and reconnaissance capabilities. Funding problems restricted the upgrade and a common standard was not achieved. Despite this programme, the attack/recce Viggens were rapidly replaced by JAS 39 Gripens and only one wing (F21) operate these AJS 37s in 2001. Meanwhile the JA 37 has been kept continually up-to-date, with the most recent programme referred to as the Mod D standard. This adds an updated PS46A radar and a new weapons interface and stores management computer that enables the use of AIM-120 AMRAAMs. The first upgraded JA 37 was re-delivered in 1998. The JA 37 currently equips four wings, each with two *Divisionen* (squadrons). Ten of the *Flygvapnet's* 14 surviving Sk 37 trainers have been converted into SK 37E Stör-Viggens (jammer Viggens). These will be tasked with EW training for Sweden's armed forces and operational EW support for *Flygvapnet* combat units as well as type conversion for all future Viggen pilots. EW equipment comprises various systems installed in the airframe, as well as advanced U95 active jammer pods, U22/A jammer pods and KB chaff and flare dispenser pods. The Viggen will be finally replaced by the Gripen in 2006.

Specification: Saab JA 37 Viggen Mod D
Origin: Sweden
Type: single-seat interceptor and attack aircraft
Armament: one ventral 30-mm Oerlikon KCA cannon; primary armament of up to six Rb 71 (Sky Flash) or Rb 99 (AIM-120 AMRAAM) and Rb 24 J (AIM-9J) or Rb 74 (AIM-9L) AAMs; maximum ordnance 13,000 lb (5897 kg) for secondary air-to-surface role, AJS 37 weapons include Rb 04E and Rb 15F AShMs, AGM-65 Maverick ASMs, DWS 39 Mjölner SMDs and M70 135-mm rockets
Powerplant: one Volvo Flygmotor RM8B turbofan (P&W JT8D-22) rated at 28,110 lb st (125.04 kN) with afterburning
Performance: maximum level speed 'clean' at 36,000 ft (10975 m) more than 1,321 mph (2126 km/h); combat radius more than 622 miles (1000 km) on hi-lo-hi profile
Weights: normal take-off 33,069 lb (15000 kg); maximum take-off 37,478 lb (17000 kg) for intercept
Dimensions: wing span 34 ft 9¼ in (10.60 m); canard foreplane span length 53 ft 9¾ in (16.40 m) including probe; height 19 ft 4¼ in (5.90 m); wing area 495.16 sq ft (46.00 m²)

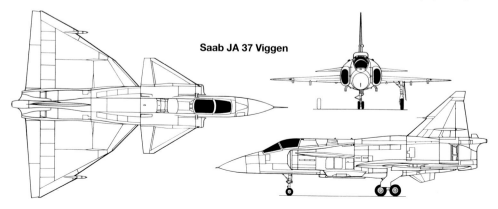

Saab JA 37 Viggen

SAAB JAS 39 GRIPEN

Designed to replace the Viggen in a variety of roles, the JAS 39 Gripen (griffin) will form the core of Swedish air power well into the 21st century. Developed by Saab Military Aircraft and marketed jointly by Saab and BAE Systems, the Gripen is a fourth-generation lightweight multi-role combat aircraft that features a delta-canard configuration coupled with a digital fly-by-wire control system. Power is provided by a modified version of the proven F404J turbofan, developed and produced by Volvo Flygmotor and fitted with a new afterburner. Unlike the Viggen, the JAS 39A lacks a thrust reverser but still possess excellent short-field capability. Ericsson developed the JAS 39's advanced multi-mode, pulse-Doppler PS-05/A radar. Gripen also features a wide-angle holographic HUD and a podded FLIR for attack and recce missions. Five prototypes and 30 production aircraft were initially ordered, the first prototype making its maiden flight in 1988. In June 1992 a second batch of 110 aircraft, including 14 JAS 39B two-seaters, was ordered. Problems with the flight control software resulted in the loss of two prototypes and the first production JAS 39A, with consequent delays to in-service date while software upgrades were developed. Eventually, 2 *Divisionen* of F7 at Såtenäs was declared combat-ready on the JAS 39A in late 1997. Swedish defence cuts in 2000 have reduced the final number of Gripen *Divisionen* (squadrons) to eight, distributed with four wings. All will have partially re-equipped with the Gripen by 2004. To date, *Flygvapnet* has a total of 204 Gripens on order, comprising 176 single-seaters and 28 fully combat-capable two-seaters. *Flygvapnet* has already announced that the third production batch will be to JAS 39C and JAS 39D standard, with features including helmet-mounted sights, IR-OTIS IRST and improved EW systems. These planned improvements are also being retrofitted to earlier JAS 39A/Bs. The sole export order to date is for 28 Gripens for South Africa; these will have a carry a range of indigenous weapons.

Specification: Saab JAS 39A Gripen
Origin: Sweden
Type: single-seat all-weather fighter, attack and reconnaissance aircraft
Armament: one 27-mm Mauser BK27 cannon, plus maximum weapon load of 14,330 lb (6500 kg); (air-to-air) Rb 74 (AIM-9L), Rb 99 (AIM-120) and IRIS-T (from 2004) missiles; (air-to-ground) Rb 75 (AGM-65 Maverick) ASM, Rbs 15F AShM, DWS 39 anti-armour dispenser weapon, KEPD 150 Taurus SOMs; proposed air-to-air weapons for South African Gripens include V-3E A-Darter agile dogfight and A-Darter active-radar BVR AAMs
Powerplant: one Volvo Aero RM-12 turbofan engine rated at 12,140 lb st (54.00 kN) dry and 18,100 lb (80.51 kN) with afterburning
Performance: maximum speed Mach 1.8 at altitude; service ceiling 65,615 ft (20000 m); range 1,864 miles (3000 km) with drop tanks
Weights: empty 14,599 lb (6622 kg); maximum take-off about 28,660 lb (13000 kg)
Dimensions: wing span 27 ft 6¾ in (8.40 m); length 46 ft 3 in (14.10 m); height 14 ft 9 in (4.50 m)

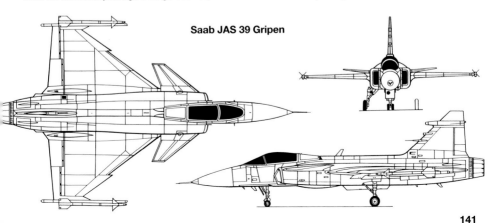

Saab JAS 39 Gripen

SAC J-8 'FINBACK'

Built only in small numbers up to 1987, the J-8 resembled little more than a scaled-up twin-engined MiG-21 and had only a limited combat capability. Revealed in 1984, the J-8 I 'Finback-A' was an all-weather development with a basic fire-control radar, 23-mm cannon and missile armament. The J-8 I first flew in prototype form in 1981 and was followed by around 100 production aircraft (including J-8s upgraded as J-8 Is). In 1981 work began on the much revised J-8 II 'Finback-B' with uprated engines, replacement of the nose inlet by two lateral inlets, and the addition of a monopulse search radar. The first of four J-8 II prototypes made its maiden flight in 1984 and these have been followed by at least 24 production J-8 IIs. SAC and Grumman co-operated to develop an improved J-8 II with modernised avionics, radar and weapons systems but this programme was terminated by the USA in 1989. Despite this setback, SAC has developed the upgraded F-8 IIM that represents a major advance. Installation of a Phazotron Zhuk-8 II multi-mode pulse-Doppler radar gives compatibility with R-27/AA-10 'Alamo' AAMs – the first BVR weapons to be associated publicly with a Chinese combat aircraft. Other possible AAMs may include an air-launched variant of the LY-60 SAM (itself a weapon that uses technology from the Italian Aspide) and the Russian Vympel R-77/AA-12 'Adder'. The F-8 IIM also features a HOTAS-equipped cockpit and uprated engines. Other proposed indigenously-developed improvements include low-altitude navigation and FLIR/targeting pods, integral jamming system, a digital FBW FCS and helmet-mounted sight. The first rebuilt F-8 IIM made its maiden flight in 1996 and an unknown number have been built to date. The F-8 IIM may have been developed for export, as an upgrade for the PLAAF's J-8s, or simply as a testbed to integrate technologies already in place on Chinese Su-27s on an indigenous airframe. Around 100 J-8 I/IIs currently serve with four PLAAF regiments; the type may also serve with the PLAN-AF.

Specification: Shenyang J-8 IIM 'Finback-B'
Origin: China
Type: single-seat air-superiority fighter with secondary ground attack capability
Armament: one 23-mm Type 23-3 cannon with 200 rounds; maximum weapons load of 9,259 lb (4500 kg); weapons include PL-2/3/5/7/9 indigenous short-range AAMs, or R-27R1 BVR AAMs; air-to-ground weapons include NORINCO 250-kg, 500-kg and 1,000-kg free-fall bombs, 57-mm rockets, and possibly C-801 AShMs
Powerplant: two Liyang (LMC) Wopen-13B II turbojet engines each rated at 10,582 lb st (47.10 kN) dry and 15,432 lb st (68.70 kN) with afterburning
Performance: maximum speed 1,452 mph (2337 km/h) at altitude; maximum climb rate 44,094 ft (13440 m) per minute; service ceiling 59,060 ft (18000 m); radius 372 miles (600 km) on a typical CAP mission
Weights: empty 22,864 lb (10371 kg); normal take-off 33,704 lb (15288 kg); maximum take-off 41,621 lb (18879 kg)
Dimensions: wing span 30 ft 7⅞ in (9.34 m); length 70 ft 10 in (21.59 m) including probe; height 17 ft 9 in (5.41 m); wing area 454.25 sq ft (42.20 m²)

Shenyang J-8II 'Finback-B'

SEPECAT JAGUAR

Resulting from an Anglo-French specification of 1965 for a STOL advanced/operational trainer and tactical support aircraft, the SEPECAT Jaguar first flew in prototype form on 8 September 1968. The RAF bought 165 GR.Mk 1 single-seat and 35 T.Mk 2 two-seat aircraft. Some 14 of the latter were upgraded to Jaguar T.Mk 2A standard with the FIN1064 nav/attack unit and Adour Mk 104 engines, while the GR.Mk 1 also received the Mk 104 engines and was subsequently modified to Jaguar GR.Mk 1A standard with FIN1064 and provision for AIM-9 AAMs on underwing (later overwing) pylons. The Jaguar fleet has since undergone a series of major upgrades which now make the aircraft one of the most useful in RAF service. These updates, prompted by the type's stunning performance during *Desert Storm*, have resulted in the GR.Mk 3A single-seater with TERPROM terrain-reference navigation system, a helmet-mounted sight, a glass cockpit, and full TIALD and ASRAAM capability. Some 40 single-seaters and seven two-seaters will be brought to full GR.Mk 3A/T.Mk 4A standard, and all will feature Adour Mk 106 engines offering 10 per cent more thrust but reduced operating cost. The RAF's Jaguar force remains centred on Nos 6, 41 and 54 Sqns at RAF Coltishall, Norfolk. France bought 160 single-seat Jaguar As and 40 two-seat Jaguar Bs. A far more austere warplane in French service, the Jaguar is in the twilight of its career with the country, but did fight in the 1991 Gulf War. Jaguar exports have been of the Jaguar International which is similar to the Jaguar GR.Mk 1/T.Mk 2. Ecuador, Oman and Nigeria all fly Jaguars as front-line equipment, while India remains by far the largest Jaguar operator and continues to build the type under licence. Indeed, HAL has built the Jaguar IM with Agave radar and Sea Eagle missiles specifically for Indian use. Oman is upgrading six of its Jaguars to a standard similar to GR.Mk 3A.

Specification: SEPECAT Jaguar A
Origin: UK/France
Type: single-seat attack and tactical reconnaissance aircraft
Armament: two DEFA 553 30-mm cannon; maximum ordnance 10,000 lb (4536 kg) weapons include AS30L laser-guided ASMs, AS37 Martel ARMs; free-fall bombs and LGBs; Belouga cluster bombs; rocket pods; BAP-100 anti-runway and BAT-120 area-denial bomblets; and R550 Magic 2 self-defence AAMs
Powerplant: two Rolls-Royce/Turboméca Adour Mk 102 turbofans each rated at 7,305 lb st (32.49 kN) with afterburning
Performance: maximum level speed 'clean' at 36,000 ft (10975 m) 1,056 mph (1699 km/h); combat radius 530 miles (852 km) on a hi-lo-hi attack mission with internal fuel
Weights: empty equipped 15,432 lb (7000 kg); maximum take-off 34,612 lb (15700 kg)
Dimensions: wing span 28 ft 6 in (8.69 m); length 57 ft 6¼ in (17.53 m) including probe; height 16 ft ½ in (4.89 m); wing area 260.27 sq ft (24.18 m²)

SEPECAT Jaguar International IM

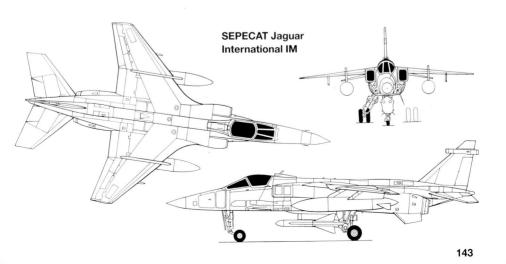

SIKORSKY S-61/H-3/SH-3 SEA KING

The S-61/H-3 was developed in the late 1950s primarily for the carrier-based ASW role. Improved ASW, SAR and transport models followed, culminating in the multi-role SH-3H that was phased out of front-line US Navy service in 1995. The USMC continues to operate the VH-3D as a presidential transport. Sikorsky licensed H-3 production to Agusta (Italy), Mitsubishi (Japan) and Westland (UK). These remain in widespread service in a variety of roles. Current significant operators of ASW-roled S-61/SH-3s include Brazil, Canada, Spain, Iran and Peru. They serve primarily in the SAR role in Denmark and Japan, and in the transport/utility role in Australia and Venezuela. Italian Agusta-Sikorsky AS-61Rs are carry machine-guns for a combat SAR role, while Malaysia operates 40 ageing S-61A-4 Nuris as assault transports. The most important current operator is the UK's Fleet Air Arm that has around 90 Westland-built Sea Kings in the ASW, AEW and assault transport roles. The Royal Navy's three carriers embark the Sea King HAS.Mk 6 for SAR and the FAA is upgrading its AEW.Mk 2/2As to AEW.7 standard. The latter carry side-mounted Searchwater radar to provide crucial airborne early warning for the fleet. Spain upgraded three of its SH-3Ds to a similar standard. The RAF operates the Sea King HAR.Mk 3A for SAR role and the FAA has Sea King HC.Mk 4 for assault transport. The latter have been used intensively in support of UK operations in former Yugoslavia. Egypt, India, Pakistan and Qatar operate Westland-built Sea Kings primarily in the ASW and assault transport roles; the latter three operators also have helicopters armed with Sea Eagle or Exocet missiles for anti-shipping duties. Belgium and Norway operate recently-upgraded Sea Kings for SAR missions. Norway's aircraft received FLIR, Sea Searcher radar and advanced avionics. Westland built the last Sea King in 1997.

Specification: Westland Advanced Sea King
Origin: UK/USA
Type: two/four-crew shipborne and land-based anti-submarine and general-purpose medium helicopter
Armament: maximum weapon load 2,500 lb (1134 kg); weapons include Mk 46 or Stingray torpedoes, Mk 11 depth charges, or Sea Eagle (India Sea King) or AM.39 Exocet (Pakistani Sea King, Qatari Commando) AShMs
Powerplant: two Rolls-Royce Gnome H.1400-1T turboshaft engines each rated at 1,660 shp (1238 kW) for take-off and 1,465 shp (1092 kW) for continuous running
Performance: maximum cruising speed 126 mph (204 km/h) at sea level; maximum initial climb rate 2,030 ft (619 m) per minute; range 921 miles (1482 km) with standard fuel
Weights: empty equipped 16,377 lb (7428 kg) in the ASW role; maximum take-off 21,500 lb (9752 kg) (all versions)
Dimensions: main rotor diameter 62 ft 0 in (18.90 m); length 72 ft 8 in (22.15 m) with the rotors turning; height 16 ft 10 in (5.13 m) with the rotors turning; main rotor disc area 3,019.07 sq ft (280.47 m²)

**Sikorsky SH-3H
Sea King**

SIKORSKY S-65/H-53

The S-65/H-53 Sea Stallion was designed to meet a USMC requirement for a heavy-lift troop transport helicopter. The twin-engined CH-53D has been in service since 1968 and currently equips four heavylift units. The CH-53D can carry 37 troops or 8,000-12,000 lb (3628-5443 kg) of cargo. The three-engined CH-53E Super Stallion equips six USMC units and can transport 55 troops or 16 tons of cargo internally; it can can carry the 26,000-lb (11794-kg) Light Armored Vehicle externally. It is armed with two 0.50-in machine-guns for self-defence, and can be refuelled in flight from a KC-130. The CH-53E is expected to remain in service until 2025, the USMC plans a two-phase service-life extension programme that will comprise an airframe overhaul followed by an avionics upgrade with new cockpit systems compatible for night operations. The US Navy operates a derivative of in the mine countermeasures (MCM) role. The three-engined MH-53E Sea Dragon tows a variety of MCM and side-scan sonars and equips two joint active/ reserve HM squadrons, plus an HC squadron in the vertical onboard delivery role The USAF has operated a variety of twin-engined MH-53 variants in the combat SAR and special operations roles. The current MH-53J Pave Low III variant is comprehensively equipped for low-level night/all-weather insertion of special forces troops in a hostile air defence environment. The major non-US S-65 operator is the *Heeresflieger* (German army) with around 96 licence-built CH-53Gs. These are receiving three major upgrades: new missile warning and self-protection systems; provision for two external fuel tanks allowing range to be increased to 1,118 miles (1800 km) when carrying 36 armed soldiers or a 5500-kg (12,125-lb) payload; and addition of an NVG-compatible cockpit for night low-level flying capabilities. All CH-53Gs had been upgraded by Eurocopter Germany by early 2001. Other lesser operators are Israeli air force which has two squadrons of upgraded CH-53D Yasur-2000 transports and the Iranian navy which operates five former MCM-tasked RH-53Ds as logistical transports.

Specification: Sikorsky MH-53J Pave Low III Enhanced
Origin: USA
Type: all-weather special operations and CSAR helicopter
Payload: maximum payload 20,000 lb (9072 kg); standard crew comprises two pilots and two para-rescuemen (PJs)
Armament: provision for one 0.5-in (12.7-mm) machine-gun on rear ramp and two 7.62-mm Miniguns in forward windows
Powerplant: two General Electric T64-GE-7A turboshafts each rated at 3,936 shp (2935 kW)
Performance: maximum level speed 'clean' at sea level 196 mph (315 km/h); maximum cruising speed 173 mph (278 km/h); maximum initial climb rate 2,070 ft (631 m) per minute; service ceiling 20,400 ft (6220 m); unrefuelled range 540 miles (868 km); endurance 5 hours
Weights: empty 23,569 lb (10691 kg); mission take-off 38,238 lb (17344 kg); maximum take-off 42,000 lb (19051 kg)
Dimensions: main rotor diameter 72 ft 3 in (22.02 m); fuselage length 67 ft 2 in (20.47 m) excluding IFR probe; height overall 24 ft 11 in (7.60 m) and to top of rotor head 17 ft 1½ in (5.22 m); main rotor disc area 4,099.82 sq ft (380.87 m²)

**Sikorsky MH-53E
Sea Dragon**

SIKORSKY S-70A/UH-60 BLACKHAWK

The Blackhawk has been the US Army's standard assault transport since 1979. It is the only rotary-wing aircraft to be operated by all five US armed forces and is also in widespread military service worldwide. Sikorsky built over 1,000 of the initial UH-60A model for the US Army before switching production from 1989 to the up-engined UH-60L variant; UH-60A/Ls equip both regular and reserve units. The US Army fields several specialised versions. The MH-60L 'Crash Hawk' and MH-60K 'Velcro Hawk' serve today as the primary SOA assault platforms. MH-60Ls have been modified into a direct action penetrator for service with the 160th SOAR as gunships. The Army operates around 60 EH-60Cs outfitted with a command and control Sigint (Comint) jamming system known in the latest field version as the Quick Fix IIB. The Army is fielding the latest upgraded variant known as EH-60L with the Advanced Quick Fix (AQF) system. The Army plans to upgrade around 350 UH-60A to UH-60Q Dustoff configuration for the medical evacuation role and around 600 UH-60As to a common UH-60L+ configuration to standardise equipment. The ultimate UH-60X standard is being studied; this will incorporate the dynamic systems developed for the S-92 with a new more powerful engine. The Oregon ARNG operates UH-60L Firehawk as firefighting helicopters. The USAF has around 90 HH-60G Pave Hawks for combat rescue/SAR and seven MH-60Gs to support special operations forces. The US Marine Corps operates nine VH-60N 'White Hawks' as presidential VIP transports. Over 350 S-70As have been exported; significant operators are Australia, Colombia, Japan (aircraft for the JGSDF licence-built by Mitsubishi) South Korea, Saudi Arabia, Turkey. Lesser users are Argentina, Brunei, Chile, Egypt, the Hong Kong Government Flying Service, Israel, Jordan, Mexico, Morocco, Philippines and Thailand.

Specification: Sikorsky UH-60L Blackhawk
Origin: USA
Type: assault and utility transport helicopter
Payload: maximum payload 2,640 lb (1197 kg) carried internally and 9,000 lb (4082 kg) underslung; standard accommodation for two pilots, crew chief and 11 troops
Armament: usually none, but provision is made for AGM-114A Hellfire ATMs, Stinger AAMs, M56 mine dispensing pods, plus machine-gun and rocket pods, all weapons carried on ESSS
Powerplant: two General Electric T700-GE-701C turboshafts each rated at 1,800 shp (1342 kW) for continuous running
Performance: maximum sea level cruising speed 183 mph (294 km/h); service ceiling 19,140 ft (5835 m); range 363 miles (584 km) with max. internal fuel; endurance 2 hours
Weights: empty 11,516 lb (5224 kg); maximum take-off 24,500 lb (11113 kg)
Dimensions: main rotor diameter 53 ft 8 in (16.36 m); length overall, rotors turning 64 ft 10 in (19.76 m); height overall 16 ft 10 in (5.13 m) with rotors turning; main rotor disc area 2,262 sq ft (210.15 m²)

Sikorsky HH-60G Pave Hawk

The US Navy's CH-60S Knighthawk will replace UH-1, H-3 and H-46 variants in the vertical replenishment, utility and executive transport roles as well as HH-60Hs in the strike rescue role. The CH-60's advantages over the HH-60H include the ability to carry a rigid inflatable boat internally and the Black Hawk's versatile external stores support system. The CH-60 has dual large cargo doors, a cabin able to handle palletised cargo and an external cargo hook. This is the trials YCH-60S that flew in 1997.

SIKORSKY S-70B/SH-60B SEAHAWK

Versions of the Sikorsky H-60 Seahawk dominate US naval aviation. The three types currently in service will be replaced by two follow-on types under development. The SH-60B Seahawk deploys the LAMPS III ASW system and functions as an extension of the shipboard weapon system of the warship on which it is deployed. With radar, ESM, MAD, IR, and sonobuoy sensors, the SH-60B can detect and track submarines and surface ships and attack with torpedoes and missiles. The Navy is receiving 93 SH-60Bs upgraded to Block I standard with expanded weapons capability. SH-60F Ocean Hawk ASW helicopters are embarked on US Navy supercarriers to provide inner-zone defence of a carrier battle group; they also serve in plane guard, rescue, and logistics roles. The HH-60H Ocean Hawk has the primary role of conducting combat SAR, and insertion and extraction of special warfare forces. The Navy is currently developing the SH-60R Strikehawk to replace both the SH-60B and SH-60F as well as the HH-60H. The SH-60R will lose the MAD but will feature many improvements, including an increase in gross operating weight; two additional stores stations; an AYK-14 mission computer; improved cockpit displays; an AQS-22 dipping sonar; a UYS-2 acoustic processor; a multi-mode radar; an upgraded ESM system; an IR red sensor; and an integrated self-defence system. The SH-60R is scheduled to enter service in 2002, and the re-manufacture programme is to continue through 2010. The CH-60S Knighthawk is being developed for the vertical replenishment role. This combines the rotor, engines, tail pylon, gear box, and rescue hoist of a Black Hawk with the automatic FCS of a Seahawk. The prototype CH-60S Knighthawk was flown in 1997 and was approved in 1998 for low-rate initial production. The YCH-60 is also undergoing development as a mine-warfare platform to replace the MH-53E. Export operators of SH-60B, SH-60Fs and hybrid SH-60B/Fs comprise Australia, Greece, Japan Spain, Thailand and Turkey. The US Coast Guard flies the HH-60J Jayhawk in the SAR role.

Specification: Sikorsky SH-60B Seahawk
Origin: USA
Type: multi-role shipborne naval helicopter
Payload: (HH-60H) 4,100 lb (1860 kg) carried internally'
Armament: (SH-60B) one pintle-mounted 7.62-mm machine-gun, Block I upgrade adds Mk 50 torpedoes and AGM-119B Mod 7 Penguin Penguin AShM; (HH-60H) 7.62-mm machine-guns and AGM-114 Hellfire anti-armour missiles; SH-60R will retain 7.62-mm machine-gun, Penguin and Hellfire missiles, plus Mk 46 and Mk 50 advanced torpedoes
Powerplant: two General Electric T700-GE-401C turboshafts each rated at 1,900 shp (1417 kW) for continuous running
Performance: dash speed at 5,000 ft (1525 m) 145 mph (234 km/h); vertical climb rate 700 ft (213 m) per minute; operational radius 58 miles (93 km) for a 3-hour loiter
Weights: (SH-60B) empty 13,648 lb (6191 kg); mission take-off 20,244 lb (9182 kg) for the ASW mission; (HH-60R) maximum take-off 23,500 lb (10659 kg)
Dimensions: main rotor diameter 53 ft 8 in (16.36 m); fuselage length 50 ft 0¾ in (15.26 m); height overall, rotor turning 17 ft (5.18 m); main rotor disc area 2,262 sq ft (210.15 m²)

Sikorsky HH-60H Rescue Hawk

SIKORSKY S-92A HELIBUS

The S-92 was originally conceived as an enlarged derivative of the S-70, and was even dubbed 'Growth Hawk'. The S-92 is a medium-lift helicopter that is being developed primarily for a variety of military roles such as transport, SAR, AEW, but also has some potential for civil sales. Launched in 1995, the S-92 programme is led by Sikorsky, but includes participation by a number of risk-sharing overseas partners, including Mitsubishi, AIDC, EMBRAER, Gamesa and Jingdezhen. The S-92 uses many of the proven dynamic systems from (or derived from) those used on the S-70 and is of broadly similar configuration to the earlier S-65. Extensive use is made of composites (about 40 per cent by weight). Powered by CT7-6D engines, the first of four flying S-92 prototypes made its maiden flight on 23 December 1998. The next three prototypes have CT7-8s. This engine is offered for production S-92s, with Rolls-Royce/Turbomeca RTM 322 as an alternative choice. All S-92s have a crashworthy fuel system, while military aircraft have provision for an optional IFR probe. The basic S-92 military version is equipped with a rear loading ramp, sliding cabin windows, a cargo hook, provision for pintle-mounted 7.62-mm machine-guns and folding seats for 22 fully-equipped troops. This is a considerably smaller payload than that of the rival EHI EH 101 and has prompted Sikorsky to develop a stretched S-92 derivative. This is being offered to meet a joint Scandinavian requirement for 40–50 helicopters for the SAR, ASW and transport roles, as well as a Canadian Forces replacement for the CH-124 Sea King.

Specification: Sikorsky S-92A Helibus
Origin: USA
Type: medium-lift transport helicopter
Payload and accommodation: maximum underslung payload 10,000 lb (4536 kg); standard accommodation for 22 fully-equipped troops or a light vehicle
Powerplant: two General Electric CT7-8 turboshafts each rated at 2,050 shp (1529 kW) for continuous running
Performance: maximum cruising speed 178 mph (287km/h); range 553 miles (890 km) with normal fuel load
Weights: empty 15,200 lb (6895 kg); maximum take-off with internal load 25,200 lb (11430 kg) and 26,500 lb (12020 kg) with external load
Dimensions: main rotor diameter 56 ft 4 in (17.71 m); length overall, rotors turning 68 ft 5 in (20.85 m); height overall, rotors turning 21 ft 2 in (6.45 m); main rotor disc area 2,492.40 sq ft (231.55 m²)

Sikorsky S-92

SUKHOI S-37 BERKUT

On 25 September 1997 the S-37 Berkut (royal eagle) made its maiden flight from the LII flight test centre airfield at Zhukhovskii. The S-37 is being developed by Sukhoi to explore the post-stall manoeuvrabilty and superma-noeuvrability. Although very much a research aircraft and concept demonstrator in its present form, it may yet form the basis of a fifth generation Russian fighter. It is of similar size to the MiG 1.44, and could be offered to meet the Russian air force's MFI ('heavy fighter') requirement. The most radical aspect of the Berkut is its forward swept wing, 90 per cent of which is of composites construction to ensure adequate torsional stiffness. The very advanced aerodynamic configuration includes strakes, canards, wing LERXes, tailplanes and twin fins. Combined with extensive use of radar absorbent materials, these are carefully shaped to minimise radar cross section. The S-37 shares many components with the Su-27, including the strengthened undercarriage developed for the naval Su-33, tailfins and canopy. It is reported to be fitted with the quadruplex FBW system of the Su-35/Su-37. Little hard information regarding the S-37's present or future capabilities has been revealed. Almost certainly, it is not flying with engines representative of a production fighter derivative. It further lacks radar, mission systems or weapons but clearly has provision for their installation, as evidenced by the various dielectric panels, and radomes around the airframe as well as mock-up IRST and exhaust vent for an internal gun. Weapons carriage is said to be either on conventional pylons or in a semi-conformal arrangement to minimise radar cross-section. The type may also have an internal weapons bay. Berkut testing continues at the slow pace allowed by the limited funding available.

Specification: Sukhoi S-37 Berkut
Origin: Russia
Type: single-seat research and technology demonstrator aircraft
Armament: none; likely provision for an internal GSh-301 30-mm cannon, possible internal weapons bay, likely AAM to be folding fin variant of R-77 active-radar BVR missile
Powerplant: two Aviadigital D-30F6 turbofans each rated at 20,930 lb st (93.10 kN) dry and 34,392 lb st (153 kN) with afterburning
Performance: (estimated) maximum speed at altitude 1,367 mph (2200 km/h) and at sea level 870 mph (1400 km/h); service ceiling 59,060 ft (18000 m); range 2,050 miles (3300 km)
Weights: normal take-off approximately 56,592 lb (25670 kg); maximum take-off 74,957 lb (34000 kg)
Dimensions: wing span 55 ft 0 in (16.70 m); length overall 74 ft 0 in (22.60 m); height overall 21 ft 0 in (6.40 m); wing area approximately 600 sq ft (56 m²)

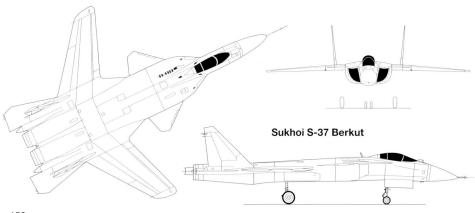

Sukhoi S-37 Berkut

SUKHOI Su-17 'FITTER

A swing-wing development of the Su-7 'Fitter' tactical attack aircraft was first flown in 1966. Derivatives of the production Su-17 remain in widespread service in 2001. The basic Su-17M 'Fitter-C' (export Su-20) survives in surprising numbers; major operators are Afghanistan, Egypt, Turkmenistan and Vietnam. Entering production in 1974, the Su-17M-2D 'Fitter-D' introduced a revised avionics suite and a Klem laser rangefinder. A slightly sanitised version was built for export under the designation Su-17M-2K 'Fitter-F'. Current operators are Libya, Yemen and Peru (aircraft of the latter are fitted with IFR probes). The Su-17M-3 'Fitter-H' (export Su-22M-3) had increased fuel capacity (using the deeper fuselage of the related Su-17UM-3 trainer) and improved self-defence capability. It is operational Afghanistan, Iraq, Peru, Syria and Uzbekistan. Nine M3s equip an A-VMF maritime attack squadron. The ultimate single-seat attack variant, the Su-17M4 'Fitter-K' (export Su-22M-4), introduced compatibility with a wide range of new Soviet PGMs. New avionics included a PrNK-54 navigation system which reduced pilot workload and improved navigational and weapons delivery accuracy. The M4 was optimised for high speed at low level and dispensed with variable geometry inlets of earlier versions; its top speed is limited to Mach 1.3. The 'Fitter-K' is externally identifiable by a prominent ram-air inlet at the base of the vertical fin. Su-17M4s currently serve with Angola, Bulgaria, the Czech Republic, Iraq, Poland, Syria, Vietnam, Slovakia and Ukraine. Of these, Poland is by far the biggest operator with three regiments. These also constitute Poland's sole aerial reconnaissance assets, using KKR-1 recce pods adopted from Su-20s retired in 1997. Poland's 'Fitter' fleet has also been fitted with Western-style navigation aids and identification equipment. The Su-17M4 had been largely retired from Russian Frontal Aviation by 1994. Limited numbers equip an air force training academy. All operators have small number of 'Fitter' trainers, the most common model is Su-17UM-3D 'Fitter-G' (export Su-22UM-3K); interestingly this is the fastest 'Fitter' variant with a top speed of Mach 2.1.

Specification: Sukhoi Su-17M-4 'Fitter-K'
Origin: USSR
Type: single-seat ground attack fighter
Armament: two NR-30 30-mm cannon, each with 80 rounds; maximum weapon load 9,369 lb (4250 kg); weapons include radio or TV command-guided, laser-homing or anti-radiation Kh-23, Kh-25, Kh-29 and Kh-58E ASMs, R-60 AAMs for self-defence, unguided rockets from 57 to 330 mm calibre, GSh-23L 23-mm cannon pods, FAB series GP bombs
Powerplant: one NPO Saturn (Lyul'ka) AL-21F-3 turbojet rated at 17,196 lb st (76.49 kN) dry and 24,802 lb st (110.32 kN) with afterburning
Performance: maximum level speed 'clean' at sea level 870 mph (1400 km/h); maximum initial climb rate 45,276 ft (13800 m) per minute; service ceiling 49,870 ft (15200 m); combat radius 715 miles (1150 km) on a hi-lo-hi attack mission with a 4,409 lb (2000-kg) warload
Weights: normal take-off 36,155 lb (16400 kg) maximum take-off 42,989 lb (19500 kg)
Dimensions: wing span 45 ft 3 in (13.80 m) spread and 32 ft 10 in (10.00m) swept; length 61 ft 6¼ in (18.75m) including probes; height 16 ft 5 in (5.00m); wing area 430.57 sq ft (40 m²) spread and 398.28 sq ft (37 m²) swept

Sukhoi Su-17M4 'Fitter-K'

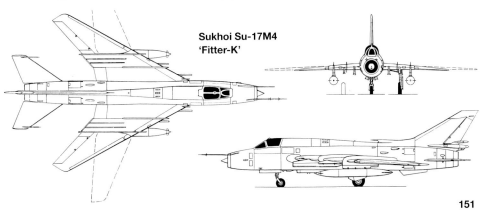

SUKHOI Su-24 'FENCER'

Developed to replace the Yak-28 'Brewer' in the tactical bomber, reconnaissance and EW roles, the Su-24 entered Frontal Aviation service in 1973 and with the Group of Soviet Forces in Germany in 1979; from 1984 the Su-24 saw active service in Afghanistan. The Su-24 is fast and stable at low level, and can carry an impressive warload, albeit at the expense of an appreciable reduction in range. Early versions were hampered by poor quality, unreliable avionics and these shortcomings were addressed by the Su-24M 'Fencer-D'. Effectively a second-generation 'Fencer', it featured a new Orion forward-looking attack radar, an IFR probe and a new PNS-24M nav/attack system. The Kaira laser rangefinder and target designator gave compatibility with a new range of PGMs. The Su-24 was used intensively during the two major Russian interventions in Chechnya. The Su-24M formed the basis of two specialised EW/reconnaissance variants. The highly versatile reconnaissance-configured Su-24MR 'Fencer-E' has a comprehensive IR, optical and EO sensor suite. Podded Elint and SLAR systems provide radiation and electronic intelligence, or laser imagery. It lacks any offensive capability other than self-defence R-60 AAMs. The Su-24MP 'Fencer-F' is a dedicated tactical EW/ECM aircraft and serves in limited numbers. The A-VMF has around 70 Su-24/Su-24M assigned to maritime attack plus 12 recce Su-24MRs. Sukhoi is proposing a range of several Su-24 upgrades. After Russia, Ukraine is the next most significant operator with six Su-24 attack regiments, plus two regiments with Su-24MR/MPs. Ukraine has two independent reconnaissance regiments of Su-24MRs, one of which also operates small number of Su-24MPs. Belarus retains one regiment equipped with Su-24Ms. Other CIS operators are Azerbaijan, Kazakhstan and Uzbekistan (which has Su-24MRs). The Su-24MK 'Fencer-D (Mod)' is a downgraded export version of the Su-24M. A total of about 70 have been exported to Algeria, Iran, Iraq, Libya and Syria. Iraq's 24 aircraft all sought refuge in Iran after *Desert Storm* and have been absorbed into the IRIAF; these are operated alongside 12 Su-24MKs acquired from Russia.

Specification: Sukhoi Su-24M 'Fencer-D'
Origin: USSR
Type: two-seat interdiction and strike/attack aircraft
Armament: one GSh-6-23M 23-mm cannon; maximum ordnance 17,637 lb (8000 kg); weapons include TN-1000 and TN-1200 free-fall nuclear weapons; comprehensive range of Russian semi-active laser and TV-guided PGMs includes Kh-23, Kh-25ML, Kh-29L/T and Kh-59 Ovod ASMs; Kh-25MP, Kh-31P, Kh-29MP and Kh-58 ARMs; Kh-31A and Kh-35 AShMs, KAB-500Kr LGBs, R-60 AAMs
Powerplant: two Perm/Soloviev (Lyul'ka) AL-21F-3A turbojets each rated at 24,691 lb st (109.83 kN) with afterburning
Performance: maximum level speed 'clean' at 36,089 ft (11000m) Mach 1.35 and at low-level 820 mph (1320 km/h); service ceiling 55,775 ft (17000 m); combat radius at sea level with 5,500-lb (2500-kg) warload 348 miles (560 km) and with external tanks 777 miles (1250 km)
Weights: empty 49,162 lb (22300 kg); normal take-off 79,365 lb (36000 kg)
Dimensions: wing span 57 ft 10½ in (17.64 m) spread and 34 ft (10.37 m) swept; length 74 ft 1½ in (22.59 m); height 20 ft 4 in (6.19 m); wing area 594 sq ft (55.17 m²) spread and 549 sq ft (51.02 m²) swept

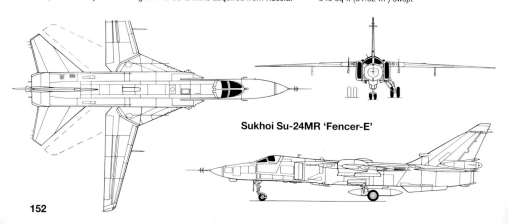

Sukhoi Su-24MR 'Fencer-E'

The Islamic Republic of Iran Air Force operates more than 30 Su-24MKs, split between 12 aircraft purchased new from Russia and 24 aircraft which flew to safety from Iraq during the 1991 Gulf War. In Iranian service the Su-24MK fulfils a number of attack roles; in addition to overland attack, they are also tasked with maritime attack. Some of the latter are reported to have a maritime blue camouflage. The already impressive range of Iran's Su-24s can be further extended by UPAZ 'buddy' refuelling pods, as displayed by the furthest aircraft.

SUKHOI Su-25 'FROGFOOT'

The Sukhoi Su-25 'Frogfoot' remains the mainstay of Russian *shturmovoy* (ground-attack) regiments. The type is broadly analogous to the US A-10 but has been matured into a more sophisticated warplane. The T-8 prototype made its first flight on 22 February 1975, but type was comprehensively redesigned before series production was authorised. Su-25s flew some 60,000 combat sorties in Afghanistan and this experience led to a range of modifications applied to production aircraft from 1987. Su-25s were also heavily committed to support Russian interventions in Chechnya. The need for an all-weather and night capable Su-25 with increased range/endurance and survivability led to the Su-25T. This is based on the airframe of the Su-25UB two-seat trainer version with the humped rear cockpit faired over. An early batch of 20 Su-25Ts was built during 1990–1991 in Tbilisi (Georgia). Production was subsequently transferred to Ulan-Ude (Russia). The first Russian-built Su-25T flew in 1995; the variant has since been redesignated Su-25TM or Su-39. Unusually, the TM carries its Kopyo-25 radar externally in a pod under the fuselage. The 20 Georgian-built Su-25Ts have been upgraded at Ulan Ude to Su-25TMs. Su-25UBs are similarly being upgraded as Su-25UBMs. The Russian air force currently operates about 250 Su-25s and is upgrading around 80 to Su-25SM standard using some of the systems developed for the Su-25TM. These will have nose-mounted Kopyo radars. The Su-25 will reportedly play a major role in the rapid-deployment groups that are being formed in each of the Russian Federation's six military districts. These units will have four Su-25TMs and 12 Su-25SMs. The Su-25TM is offered for export as the Su-25TK. Many former Soviet republics gained the Su-25 regiments stationed on their territory on break up of the Soviet Union. Such operators comprise Armenia, Azerbaijan, Belarus, Georgia, Georgia (Abkhazia), Kazakhstan, Turkmenistan (in storage) and Uzbekistan. Export Su-25K operators are Angola, Bulgaria, Czech Republic Iraq, North Korea, Peru and Slovakia.

Specification: Sukhoi Su-25TM (Su-39)
Origin: Russia
Type: single-seat all-weather, anti-armour/ close support aircraft
Armament: one 30-mm NNPU-8M cannon with 200 rounds; maximum ordnance load 11,023 lb (5000 kg); primary weapons comprise Vikhr M ATGMs; other weapons include TV-guided Kh-29T, laser-guided Kh–25ML and Kh-29L ASMs, Kh-35 AShM, Kh-58U and Kh-31P ARMs, KAB-500Kr LGBs, KMGU-2 submunitions dispensers, 250-kg and 500-kg RBK series cluster bombs and 50- to 500-kg FAB series GP bombs, plus R-27R, R-77 and R-73 AAMs
Powerplant: two MNPK Soyuz/Gavrilov R-195Sh turbojets each rated at 9,921 lb st (44.13 kN)
Performance: maximum level speed 'clean' at sea level 590 mph (950 km/h); maximum initial climb rate 11,415 ft (3480 m) per minute; service ceiling 32,800 ft (10000 m); combat radius 248 miles (400 km) on a lo-lo-lo profile with 4,409-lb (2000-kg) warload
Weights: maximum take-off 45,194 lb (20000 kg)
Dimensions: wing span 47 ft 7¾ in (14.52 m); length 50 ft 4½ in (15.35 m); height 17 ft 0¾ in (5.20 m); wing area 324.00 sq ft (30.10 m²)

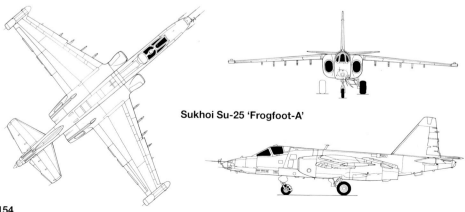

Sukhoi Su-25 'Frogfoot-A'

Featuring folding wings and an arrestor hook, the UTG is a navalised derivative of the two-seat Su-25UB. The batch of 12 production aircraft was split between Russia (seven) and Ukraine. The Su-25UTG/UBPs are embarked upon the carrier 'Kuznetsov' to support Su-27K naval fighters (above left).

SUKHOI Su-27/Su-33/Su-37

The Su-27 was developed primarily for Russia's PVO interceptor forces. Work on the T-10 design that led to the Su-27 began in 1969. The requirement was for a highly manoeuvrable fighter with very long range, heavy armament and modern sensors, capable of meeting the F-15 on equal terms. The first prototype T-10 'Flanker-A' flew in 1977. The early flight development programme revealed serious problems that led to a total redesign; the resulting T-10S-1 flew in 1981. The single-seat Su-27 'Flanker-B' eventually entered operational service in 1985 and remains a formidable interceptor. Its heavy armament of up to 10 AAMs radar gives excellent combat persistence; outstanding manoeuvrability, coupled with a helmet sight to cue agile R-73 missiles also make it a potent close combat fighter, and its large internal fuel capacity confers a very long range that allows the Su-27 to escort Su-24 interdictors. All operators also use Su-27UB 'Flanker-C' two-seat trainers. This retains full combat capability and has been developed further (described separately). The Su-27K is a naval fighter variant that has the A-VMF service designation Su-33. A total of 24 production aircraft has been built to date; the type made its first deployment on carrier Kuznetsov in 1995. Sukhoi is developing variants for the reconnaissance and EW/command post roles. In 1988 Sukhoi flew a significantly developed single-seat version of the 'Flanker-B' as the Su-27M. This was proposed as a 'super agile' Su-27 primarily for counter-air missions, but also with a greatly expanded air-to-surface capability. The Su-27M was later redesignated Su-35 by Sukhoi and offered as a MiG-29/Su-27 replacement. Its development was halted after 11 prototype and pre-series/technology demonstrator aircraft had been built. The last Su-35 ('711') was fitted with thrust-vectoring nozzles to confer even higher levels of manoeuvrability. This aircraft is now known as the Su-37 and is being actively proposed for the Russian air force.

Specification: Sukhoi Su-27 'Flanker-B'
Origin: Russia
Type: single-seat air superiority fighter
Armament: one 30-mm GSh-30-1 cannon with 150 rounds; maximum ordnance 13,228 lb (6000 kg); weapons include up to six medium-range R-27 (AA-10 'Alamo') and four short-range R-73 (AA-11 'Archer') AAMs
Powerplant: two NPO Saturn (Lyul'ka) Al-31F turbofans each rated at 17,857 lb st (79.4 kN) dry and 27,557 lb st (122.6 kN) afterburning
Performance: maximum level speed 'clean' at 36,090 ft (11000 m) 1417 mph (2280 km/h); maximum rate of climb at sea level 64,960 ft (19800 m) per minute; service ceiling 58,071 ft (17700 m); range at high altitude 2,287 miles (3680 km)
Weights: empty 39,021 lb (17700 kg); maximum take-off 72,751 lb (33000 kg)
Dimensions: wing span 48 ft 2¼ in (14.70 m); length length 71 ft 11½ in (21.94 m) excluding probe; height 19 ft 5½ in (5.93 m), wing area 500.54 sq ft (46.50 m²)

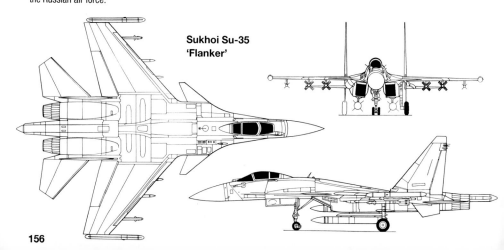

Sukhoi Su-35 'Flanker'

'711' was the final Su-35 aircraft fitted with thrust-vectoring nozzles and now designated Su-37. Key features include a 'glass' cockpit with advanced MFDs, quadruplex digital FBW FCS, canard fore-planes, 31,970 lb-st (142.2-kN) AL-37FU engines (under develop-ment) and provision for inflight refuelling. The Su-37 also features two radars: an advanced N011M electronically-scanned phased-array radar in the nose and a smaller rearward-facing unit in the tail-cone to cue rearward-firing AAMs.

SUKHOI Su-27IB/Su-30/Su-32

Sukhoi has developed and is proposing several two-seat variants and derivatives of the 'Flanker' that could form the core of Russian air power well into the 21st century. Development has followed several major strands. The combat capability of the two-seat Su-27UB was exploited further to produce the Su-27PU (Sukhoi designation Su-30, Su-30K for export). Intended for long-range/extended endurance interception missions, it features provision for inflight refuelling that allows missions of up to 10 hours duration. Only 21 production Su-27PUs have been built; the type entered service in 1996 with a Russian PVO operational training regiment and may still be undergoing operational evaluation in 2001. Sukhoi is also offering the multi-role Su-30KM as an upgrade for Russian Su-27UB/Su-30s. The Su-30KM features a high degree of commonality with the MiG 29SMT. The Su-30M (Su-30MK for export) was the first true multi-role two-seater and is broadly analogous to the F-15E. As ordered by India, the Su-30MKI will be the definitive standard with canard foreplanes, thrust vectoring and with option of Western avionics, displays and defensive systems. The more radical of two-seat Su-27 developments adds an entirely new forward fuselage section ahead of the wing, featuring side-by-side seating for a crew of two. The resulting Su-27IB (Sukhoi designation Su-34) was developed primarily as tactical strike/attack Su-24 replacement but is also being offered for other combat support roles. The Su-32FN/Su-32MF is a long-range land-based maritime attack/ ASW Su-27IB version. Funding for both versions remains scarce in Russia and only four prototype/pre-series Su-27IBs and one 'Su-32' (essentially a repainted Su-27IB) had been flown by 1997. The latest side-by-side variant is the Su-27KUB (Su-33B). First flown in 1999, it will serve primarily as a trainer for Su-27K pilots, but will also have a combat role. The Su-27KUB has a similar cockpit to the Su-27IB, but features a new N014 radar in conical nose radome.

Specification: Sukhoi Su-34
Origin: Russia
Type: two-seat long-range interdictor
Armament: one 30-mm GSh-301 cannon; maximum weapon load 17,636 lb (8000 kg); weapons include Kh-25M (AS-10 'Karen'), Kh-29 (AS-14 'Kedge'), Kh-31 A/P (AS-17 'Krypton'), Kh-59M (AS-18 'Kazoo'), Kh-35 (AS-20 'Kayak') and Kh-41 Moskit ASMs
Powerplant: two NPO Saturn (Lyul'ka) AL-31F turbofans each rated at 16,755 lb st (74.5 kN) dry and 27,557 lb st (122.6 kN) with afterburning
Performance: maximum speed at sea level 870 mph (1400 km/h); maximum level speed at height 1,553 mph (2500 km/h); service ceiling 65,000 ft (19800 m); range with maximum internal fuel 2,485 miles (4000 km)
Weights: empty 39,022 lb (17700 kg) maximum take-off 97,800 lb (44360 kg)
Dimensions: wing span 48 ft 2¾ in (14.70 m); length 76 ft 5¼ in (23.30 m); height 21 ft 4 in (6.50 m); wing area 667.40 sq ft (62 m²)

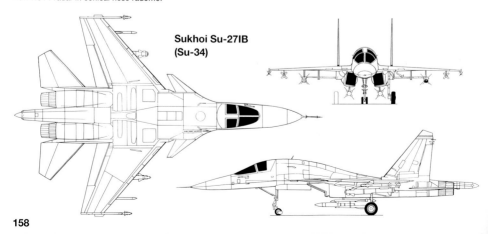

Sukhoi Su-27IB (Su-34)

First flown in 1990, the Su-27IB (Su-34) is easily distinguished by its side-by-side cockpit and 'Platypus' nose. It was developed primarily for the strike/attack role to replace the Su-24. It is also being proposed for the Russian air force to serve in the heavy interceptor, reconnaissance, EW and defence suppression roles. The Su-32FN is a related naval attack variant fitted with Leninetz mission avionics, a powerful maritime search radar and a tail-mounted MAD for submarine detection. Sukhoi is offering a multi-role export derivative as the Su-32MF.

TUPOLEV Tu-22M 'BACKFIRE'

The Tu-22M was developed from the earlier Tu-22 design, incorporating variable-geometry outer wing panels. The first Tu-22M-0 prototype flew in 1969. Powered by a military derivative of the engine originally designed for the Tu-144 supersonic airliner, the 'Backfire' is extremely fast, even at low level. The Tu-22M lacks sufficient range for truly strategic missions and is classified as a medium bomber. The first series production model was the Tu-22M-2 'Backfire-B' (211 built) for the VVS and the AV-MF. Normally armed with a single Kh-22 stand-off missile, this variant became operational with 185 GvTBAP at Poltava in 1978, and also served in Afghanistan. The ultimate bomber/missile carrying variant is the Tu-22M-3 'Backfire-C', (268 built). The M-3 features strengthened wings, raked rectangular intakes serving more powerful engines. It also had a greatly increased weapons load (see specification). The Tu-22M3 remains numerically the most important bomber in the Russian air force's Long-Range Air Army inventory, and serves with seven regiments (one of which also operates Tu-22M-2s). The A-VMF has about 80 Tu-22Ms, mostly M-3 models, split equally between divisions subordinated to the Northern and Pacific Fleets. The AV-MF has 12 M-3s converted as Tu-22MR reconnaissance aircraft, and reportedly also operates limited numbers of recce-configured Tu-22M2Rs. Because of delays in the development of the Sukhoi T-60, the intended replacement of the Tu-22M3, it has been decided to embark on a major upgrade of the 'Backfire'. The Tu-22M-2/M-3s of both the Air Force and Naval Aviation will be upgraded to Tu-245 standard, with a new radar, new missile systems and an automatic terrain-following capability. Russia is also trialling small numbers of redundant Tu-22M-3 airframes converted as Tu-22MP prototypes of a planned EW/escort jammer variant. The sole non-Russian operator of the potent 'Backfire' is Ukraine, which gained former Black Sea Fleet A-VMF regiments of Tu-22M-2/M-3s. About 50 bombers equip three air force heavy bomber regiments.

Specification: Tupolev Tu-22M-3 'Backfire-C'

Origin: Russia

Type: twin-engined medium-range bomber/maritime attack and reconnaissance aircraft

Armament: defensive armament of one GSh-23 23-mm cannon in remotely-operated tail turret; maximum weapon load 52,910 lb (24000 kg); primary weapon Kh-22 (AS-4 'Kitchen') nuclear or conventional stand-off missile, internal rotary launcher for six Kh-15 (AS-16 'Kickback') SRAMs or Kh-15P ARMs; maximum internal load 26,014 lb (11800 kg) of free-fall FAB series bombs up to 3000 kg, other weapons include Kh-31A/P (AS-17 'Krypton' and Kh-35 (AS-20 'Kayak' ASMs

Powerplant: two Samara/Kuznetsov NK-25 turbofans each rated at 55,115 lb st (245.20 kN) with afterburning

Performance: maximum level speed 'clean' at 36,090 ft (11000m) 1,242 mph (2000 km/h); unrefuelled combat radius with 12-tonne payload up to 1,150 miles (1850 km)

Weights: basic empty 119,048 lb (54000 kg); maximum take-off 286,596 lb (130000 kg)

Dimensions: wing span 112 ft 6½ in (34.30 m) spread; length 129 ft 11 in (39.60 m); height 35 ft 5¼ in (10.80 m); wing area 1,829.92 sq ft (170.0 m²) spread

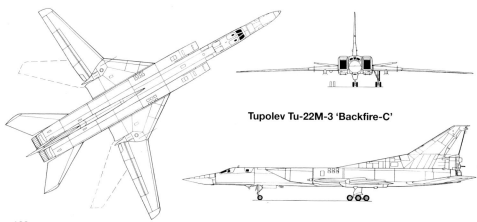

Tupolev Tu-22M-3 'Backfire-C'

TUPOLEV Tu-95/Tu-142 'BEAR'

The turboprop-powered Tu-95 'Bear' strategic bomber entered service in 1956 and remains an important part of Russia's long range air power. The current bomber/missile carrier version is the Tu-95MS 'Bear-H'. This entered service in 1984 and was manufactured until 1992. There are two sub-variants, both based on the maritime Tu-142 (see below). The Tu-95MS16 'Bear-H16' carries 16 long-range ALCMs (six internally and ten externally). The Tu-95MS6 'Bear-H6' is the more numerous version, with provision for external missile carriage deleted in accordance with the SALT/START Treaties. About 60 Tu-95s of both variants are based with heavy bomber regiments at Engels and Ukrainka. This total includes three aircraft formerly held in Ukraine. Russia plans to add the Kh-101 ALCM and Kh-SD ASM to the inventory of the Tu-95MS to improve their conventional long-range precision strike capability. The air force also operates 11 earlier-model Tu-95KUs as trainers. The Tu-142 'Bear-F' was designed primarily for ASW and a variety of naval roles. Around 40 examples equip a single A-VMF (Russian naval aviation) regiment at Kipelovo, assigned to the Northern Fleet. The major ASW variants are the Tu-142MK 'Bear-F' Mod 3 and improved Tu-142M-Z 'Bear-F' Mod 4, the last of which was completed in 1994. The Tu-142MR 'Bear-J' is a command post/communications relay platform for communicating with sub-merged nuclear-missile armed submarines. Such is the importance of the Tu-142 in Russian service, that surviving 'Bear-F' Mod 4 airframes are likely to be updated with Leninets Sea Dragon system, which includes a new radar, LLLTV, FLIR, new sonobuoys, revised ESM and MAD systems, and an armament of up to eight Kh-35 (AS-20 'Kayak') AShMs for an extended ASV/ASW role. The only Tu-142 export operator is the Indian navy which has seven Tu-142MK-Es at Arrakonam. These are broadly similar to the 'Bear-F' Mod 3, but have certain downgraded systems.

Specification: Tupolev Tu-9MS6 'Bear-H6'
Origin: Russia
Type: four-turboprop strategic bomber
Armament: two NR-23 23-mm twin-barrel cannons in tail turret (some MS6s have a single gun); MKU-6 internal rotary launcher for six Kh-55/AS-15 'Kent-A' or Kh-55SM/AS-15 'Kent-B' long-range ALCMs, with range of 1,491 - 1,864 miles (2400 - 3000 km); Kh-35/AS-20 'Kayak' AShMs of Tu-142MZ have range of 81 miles (130 km)
Powerplant: four KKBM (Kuznetsov) NK-12MA turboprops each rated at 14,795 ehp (11033 ekW)
Performance: maximum level speed 'clean' at 25,000 ft (7620 m) 575 mph (925 km/h); cruising speed at optimum altitude 442 mph (711 km/h); service ceiling 39,380 ft (12000m); unrefuelled operational radius 3,977 miles (6400 km) with 25,000-lb/11340-kg weapon load
Weights: empty 202,380 lb (91800 kg); maximum take-off 407,850 lb (185000 kg)
Dimensions: wing span 164 ft 2 in (50.04 m); length 161 ft 2¼ in (49.13 m); height 43 ft 7¾ in (13.30 m); wing area 3,120.50 sq ft (289.90 m²)

Tupolev Tu-95MS 'Bear-H'

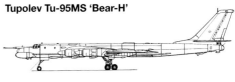

TUPOLEV Tu-160 'BLACKJACK'

The Tu-160 'Blackjack' is the world's largest operational bomber. Dwarfing the similar-looking B-1B, it is the heaviest combat aircraft ever built. Unlike the B-1B, the Tu-160 remains committed to both low-level penetration (at transonic speeds) and high-level penetration at speeds of about Mach 1.9. Although the aircraft has a FBW control system all cockpit displays are conventional analogue instruments, with no MFDs, CRTs and no HUD. The long pointed radome houses a terrain following and attack radar. Below this is a fairing for a forward-looking TV camera used for visual weapon aiming. The development programme of the Tu-160 was extremely protracted; the prototype Tu-160 first flew in 1981 and the second aircraft was lost in 1987. Series production was at Kazan and continued until January 1992, when President Yeltsin announced that no further strategic bombers would be built. It is believed that production totalled no more than 39 'Blackjacks'. Even after the aircraft entered service, problems continued to severely restrict operations and production began before a common standard and configuration was agreed. Thus wingspans, equipment fit, and intake configurations differ from aircraft to aircraft. Nineteen Tu-160s were delivered to the 184th Guards TBAP at Priluki beginning in May 1987. These were left at the Ukrainian base after the break up of the USSR in 1991 and, after protracted discussions between Ukraine and the Russian Federation, eight were returned to Russia in 1999. Scrapping of the remaining Tu-160s held in Ukraine began in late 1998 under a contract issued by the US government. In early 2001, Russia declares six operational Tu-160s as ALCM carriers under the START treaty. These are assigned to the 121st Guards HBAR at Engels and were joined in 2001 by the first of the eight refurbished aircraft formerly held in Ukraine. Although perhaps up to a dozen further airframes are nominally serviceable it seems unlikely that Russia has sufficient funds to rework these aircraft. US-based Platforms International Corp. has acquired three demilitarised ex-Ukrainian Tu-160s which it is converting as Tu-160SK launchers for space vehicles.

Specification: Tupolev Tu-160 'Blackjack-A'
Origin: Russia
Type: long-range strategic bomber
Armament: maximum weapon load 88,815 lb (40000 kg); two tandem fuselage weapons bays, each normally equipped with rotary launcher for six Kh-55/AS-15 'Kent-A' or Kh-55SM/ AS-15 'Kent-B' ALCMs with ranges between 1,491 - 1,864 miles (2400 - 3000 km), 12 Kh-15P (AS-16 'Kickback') 'SRAMskis' or free-fall bombs; future planned weapons include Kh-101 precision-attack ALCMs with conventional warheads
Powerplant: four SSPE Trud (Kuznetsov) NK-321 turbofans each rated at 30,843 lb st (137.20 kN) dry and 55,115 lb st (245.16 kN) with afterburning
Performance: maximum level speed 'clean' at 40,000 ft (12200 m) 1,380 mph (2220 km/h); service ceiling 49,200 ft (15500 m); maximum unrefuelled range 7,640 miles (12300 km)
Weights: empty equipped 260,140 lb (118000 kg); normal take-off 589,947 lb (267600 kg); maximum take-off 606,261 lb (275000 kg)
Dimensions: wing span 182 ft 9 in (55.70 m) spread and 116 ft 9¾ in (35.60 m) swept; length 177 ft 6 in (54.10 m); height 43 ft 0 in (13.10 m); wing area 3,875.13 sq ft (360 m²)

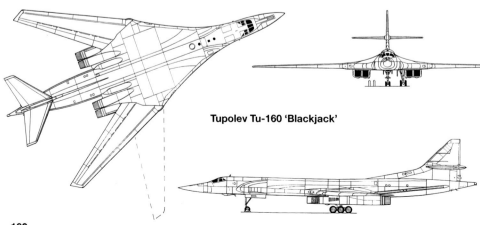

Tupolev Tu-160 'Blackjack'

WESTLAND/GKN WESTLAND LYNX

The Lynx is arguably the most capable and versatile helicopter in its class. Launched as part of the Anglo-French helicopter agreement of 1967, the Lynx design is wholly of Westland origin, but production of the type is shared in the ratio of 70:30 between GKN Westland in the UK and Eurocopter France. All versions of the Lynx have advanced digital flight controls plus all-weather avionics. The four-bladed semi-rigid main rotor confers a level of agility matched by no other helicopter of its generation. The first Lynx prototype flew in 1971 and production has been predominantly for use by UK armed forces. The type entered service in 1977 as the Lynx AH.Mk 1 battlefield helicopter for the British Army and Royal Marines. Some 103 examples were upgraded to the Lynx AH.Mk 7 standard and these remain the Army Air Corps' primary anti-armour type, equipping 11 operational squadrons. The upgraded Lynx AH.Mk 9 includes a nosewheel undercarriage and advanced BERP main rotor blades. Procurement comprises eight converted AH.Mk 7s and 16 new-builds. The other major operator is the Royal Navy; the Lynx is its primary shipbased helicopter and fulfils ASW, ASV, SAR, OTH targeting for SSNs and communications duties. From 1994 the RN began to receive the latest version, the Lynx HMA.Mk 8. A total of 38 previous versions is being upgraded to this standard. The equivalent export version is known as the Super Lynx and orders for new-build helicopters have come from Portugal, Brazil, South Korea. The latter two customers, plus Denmark, have also had previous Lynx versions upgraded to Super Lynx standard. Operators of earlier naval Lynx variants comprise France, Germany, the Netherlands, Nigeria, Norway and Pakistan. The Marineflieger has overhauled the airframes and rotor systems of 17 of its older Lynx Mk 88s for service beyond 2010, and is also adding FLIR and GPS.

Specification: Westland Lynx AH.Mk 7
Origin: UK/France
Type: anti-tank and transport helicopter
Payload: maximum payload 3,000 lb (1361 kg); 12 troops
Armament: maximum ordnance about 1,210 lb (550 kg), standard anti-armour load comprises eight BGM-71 TOW wire-guided anti-tank missiles
Powerplant: two Rolls-Royce Gem 42-1 turboshafts each rated at 1,135 shp (846 kW)
Performance: maximum continuous cruising speed at optimum altitude 159 mph (256 km/h); maximum rate of climb at sea level 2,480 ft (756 m) per minute; hovering ceiling 10,600 ft (3230 m); combat radius 29 miles (46 km) for a 2-hour patrol on an anti-tank mission
Weights: operating empty 6,772 lb (3072 kg) in the anti-tank role; maximum take-off 10,750 lb (4876 kg)
Dimensions: main rotor diameter 42 ft (12.80 m); length overall, rotors turning 49 ft 9 in (15.16 m); height overall 12 ft (3.73 m) with rotors stationary; main rotor disc area 1,385.44 sq ft (128.71 m2)

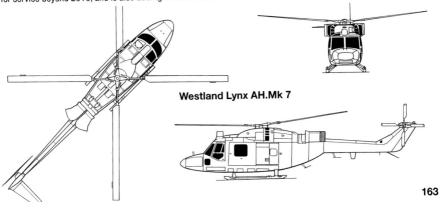

Westland Lynx AH.Mk 7

XAC JH-7/FBC-1 FLYING LEOPARD

The JH-7 has been in development since the mid-1970s to meet a requirement from the Chinese PLAAF and PLAN-AF for an all-weather interdictor. In design, the JH-7 resembles a scaled-up SEPECAT Jaguar. Its projected performance approaches that of the Tornado IDS, albeit with a reduced payload, but with a longer unrefuelled range. The JH-7 features a wide range of indigenously-developed systems and equipment; these include the JL-10A multi-mode radar, Blue Sky low-altitude radar/FLIR navigation pods and inertial/GPS navigation systems. The Xian WS-9 engines are licence-manufactured Rolls-Royce Spey turbofans. Although the prototype reportedly first flew in 1988, the programme was troubled by technical problems throughout the 1990s, leading China to consider alternative combat aircraft from Russia in the form of Sukhoi Su-27s and two-seat Su-30s. Surprisingly, the acquisition of the Sukhois has not ended the JH-7 programme. It is likely that the JH-7's revival has stemmed from the PLA's desire to modernise its air forces, and for the need of the Chinese aerospace industry to be able to offer more modern fighters for export. The decision to feature the JH-7 prominently at the Zhuhai airshow in 1998 was accompanied by a modest order for the type. With the PLAAF's acquisition of Su-30 for the long-range strike role, the JH-7 is being acquired for the PLAN-AF, with a reported figure of between 25 to 32 aircraft for a single regiment. The service is gaining a potent long-range maritime attack capability. Armed with the indigenous C-802 or supersonic KR-1 missiles (the latter a version of the Russian Kh-31P/AS-17 'Krypton'), the JH-7 will markedly effect the balance of power in the Taiwan Straits, and beyond into the South China Sea. During China's 1995/96 'exercises' near Taiwan, Chinese television briefly showed a JH-7 dropping a clutch of free-fall GP bombs. The JH-7 is being promoted actively for export as the FBC-1 Flying Leopard. It was recently offered – unsuccessfully – to Iran.

Specification: XAC JH-7/FBC-1 Flying Leopard
Origin: People's Republic of China
Type: two-seat all-weather interdictor and maritime attack aircraft
Armament: one twin-barrelled 23-mm cannon; maximum ordnance 14,330 lb (6500 kg); weapons include C-701, C-801 and C-802K AShMs; KR-1 (version of Russian Zvezda Kh-31 co-produced in China) Mach 2.5-capable ARM; 500-lb (227-kg) LGBs and short-range PL-5 or PL-9 AAMs (latter cued by a CLETRI version of Ukrainian Arsenel helmet sight)
Powerplant: two Xian WS9 (Rolls-Royce Spey Mk 202) turbofans each rated at 20,515 lb st (91.20 kN) with afterburning
Performance: maximum level speed 'clean' at 36,080 ft (11000 m) 1,122 mph (1808 km/h); service ceiling 'clean' 51,180 ft (15600 m); combat radius 1,025 miles (1650 km)
Weights: maximum take-off 62,776 lb (28475 kg); maximum landing 46,583 lb (21,130 kg)
Dimensions: wing span 41 ft 8¼ in (12.71 m); length including probe 73 ft 3 in (22.33 m) including probe; height 21 ft 6¾ in (6.58 m); wing area 563 sq ft (52.30 m²)

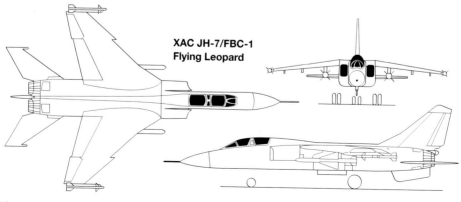

**XAC JH-7/FBC-1
Flying Leopard**

YAKOVLEV/AERMACCHI YAK-130

The Yak-130 was designed to meet the same Russian air force instructional trainer system requirement as the MiG AT. This specified an aircraft with simulators and ground-based training aids, like the US Navy's T-45TS system. The Yak-130 has a less conventional configuration than its MiG competitor, featuring swept wings with winglets. On take-off, the engines are fed with air by auxiliary overwing air intakes and by the main intakes, which feature swing-down intake doors, much like those fitted to MiG-29 and Su-27. In 1992, Yakovlev teamed with Aermacchi to develop the Yak-130. Like the MiG AT, it features a reprogrammable flight control system that can be used to simulate the handling of a variety of front-line types. The current Yak/AEM-130 export version includes avionics and systems sourced from BAE Systems and Honeywell. The first of three Yak-130D demonstrators made its maiden flight in 1996; these have reportedly been followed by a further pre-series batch of seven for evaluation. The intended production configuration of the Yak-130 will differ in important aspects, notably a shorter and shallower fuselage with a more downswept nose, and a 'dog-tooth' on the tailplane leading edge to enhance effectiveness at high angles of attack. Yakovlev plans to develop a family of Yak-130 variants. These include a combat-capable two-seater and a single-seat combat version with seven hardpoints; a hooked carrier-capable aircraft; and a two-seat side-by-side trainer optimised for training bomber and transport pilots. By 2001, the Russian requirement for its new trainer remained vague, with no service entry planned until at least 2003/4. Strong interest in the Yak-130 as a subsonic multi-role fighter is currently being expressed by Slovakia.

Specification: Yakovlev Yak-130
Origin: Russia
Type: two-seat basic and advanced jet trainer
Armament: maximum ordnance 6,614 lb (3000 kg); proposed weapons include AGM-65 Maverick or Kh-25ML and ASM-1 ASMs, or AIM-9L, Magic 2 or R-73 (AA-11 'Archer') AAMs
Powerplant: two Povazské Strojàrne ZMK DV-2S (Klimov RD-35) turbofans each rated at 4,852 lb st (21.58 kN)
Performance: maximum level speed at 15,000 ft (4570 m) 644 mph (1037 km/h); maximum rate of climb at sea level 10,000 ft (3048 m) per minute; service ceiling 42,660 ft (13000 m); combat radius 345 miles (555 km) configured for CAP
Weights: empty 10,141 lb (4600 kg); maximum take-off as a trainer 14,330 lb (6500 kg); maximum take-off for an attack mission 20,943 lb (9500 kg)
Dimensions: wing span 31 ft 10¾ in (9.72 m); length 37 ft 8¼ in (11.49 m); height 15 ft 7½ in (4.76 m); wing area 253.20 sq ft (23.52 m²)

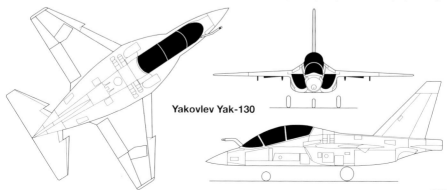

Yakovlev Yak-130

Major air arms of the world

Algeria

Established in 1962 after independence from France, the *al-Quwwat al-Jawwiya al-Jaza'eriya* (QJA – Algerian air force) now relies heavily on equipment of Russian origin. The most numerous types are the MiG-21, MiG-23 and Su-7/20, although the fighter force is spearheaded by a small number of MiG-25s. A recent addition, greatly enhancing the attack capability, is the Sukhoi Su-24 'Fencer'. The helicopter force includes large numbers of Mi-8/17s for assault and Mi-24s for attack duties.

Main types in inventory
Fighter/attack: MiG-21, MiG-23,
 MiG-25, Su-7, Su-20, Su-24
Transports: C-130, An-12, Il-76
Helicopters: Mi-8, Mi-17, Mi-24
Trainers: L-39, Beech 24,
 T-34 Mentor, Mi-2, Zlin 142

Training is undertaken on a mixture of Soviet, Czech and Western types.

Argentina

The *Fuerza Aérea Argentina* (Argentine air force) has recently acquired 32 A-4AR/OA-4AR Fightinghawk aircraft to revitalise the fast-jet fleet. This aircraft is a modified A-4 Skyhawk but has a new avionics system based on that of the F-16. The Skyhawks serve alongside an elderly Mirage and Finger fleet, the latter being upgraded versions of the IAI Dagger (Mirage 5 copy).

Since 1997 the *Comando de la Aviación Naval* (COAN) has been without a carrier, although the Super Etendard strike force remains. Ex-US Navy Orions have assumed the patrol role from Electras, although one of the latter is used for Sigint work.

The *Comando de Aviación del Ejército* (army aviation) is largely helicopter-equipped, but includes a number of fixed-wing types, notably the Grumman Mohawk, used for battlefield observation duties.

Main types in air force inventory
Fighter/attack: A-4AR
 Fightinghawk, Mirage III/5,
 IAI Finger, IA-58 Pucará
Transports: C-130, Boeing 707,
 Fokker F27, Fokker F28
Helicopters: MD 500/530,
 UH-1H, Bell 212, CH-47 Chinook
Trainers: Beech Mentor, EMB-312 Tucano,
 IA-63 Pampa, MS.760 Paris
Main types in navy inventory
Fixed-wing: Super Etendard, T-34, MB.326, P-3
 Orion, L-188 Electra, King Air 200, S-2T Tracker
Rotary-wing: AS-61, UH-1H, Alouette III, Fennec
Main types in army inventory
Fixed-wing: OV-1 Mohawk, G222
Rotary-wing: Bell 205/UH-1H, A.109, AS 332

Australia

The teeth of the Royal Australian Air Force is 82 Wing at Amberley, which operates two squadrons of F-111C/Gs in the attack role (along with four RF-111Cs for reconnaissance). This fleet has considerable long-range strike power, including anti-ship capability through the Harpoon missile and precision attack capability with Paveway bombs and AGM-142. Three squadrons (plus an OCU) fly the Hornet on multi-role tasks. The fleet is undergoing a modification programme which upgrades the radar and adds new weapons. The transport fleet is based around the Hercules, although the Caribou is available for operations in the Australian interior. Orions provide a vital patrol function around the long coastline and over the surrounding seas. Training is mostly handled by the PC-9, which also forms the equipment of the 'Roulettes' national aerobatic display team.

The Royal Australian Navy is now primarily an ASW helicopter operator, having not possessed an aircraft carrier

Main types in RAAF inventory
Fighter/attack: F/A-18, F-111
Transports: C-130H/J,
 Boeing 707, DHC-4 Caribou,
 Falcon 900
Patrol: AP-3C Orion
Trainers: PC-9, MB.326, CT-4
 Airtrainer, King Air 200
Main types in RAN inventory
S-70B Seahawk, AS 350 Ecureuil, Sea King,
 Bell 206
Main types in AAAC inventory
Bell 206, Bell UH-1H, S-70A Black Hawk,
 CH-47D Chinook, DHC-6, King Air 200

since 1982. The Australian Army Aviation Corps supports the army, and operates a mix of types, including the Chinook.

Aircraft from all three services took part in the United Nations operation to restore peace in East Timor.

Austria

Austria maintains one of the smallest air arms in Europe, and its posture is strictly defensive. Two squadrons fly elderly Drakens, armed with AIM-9 Sidewinder missiles. A cheap replacement is being sought. The only other combat aircraft is the Saab 105, which is mainly used for training but can also be employed on light attack and reconnaissance duties. The transport fleet consists of two Skyvans and a few Turbo-Porters, the latter appreciated

Main types in inventory
Fixed-wing: Saab J35 Draken, Saab 105, Pc-6, PC-7, Skyvan
Rotary-wing: AB 206/OH-58B, AB 204, AB 212, Alouette III

for their STOL capabilities. The helicopter fleet is tailored to troop transport and rescue work in the mountains.

Bahrain

Since independence in 1971, the island Gulf state of Bahrain has enjoyed considerable wealth from its oil deposits. The Bahrain Amiri Air Force, though small, is well-equipped. The force centres around the 22 F-16C/D Block 40s operated by the 1st Fighter Wing at Shaikh Isa air base, augmented by a squadron of F-5Es. Fourteen AH-1E Cobras equip an attack helicopter squadron. The remainder of the fleet consists of transports, including

Main types in inventory
Fighters: F-16, F-5
Transports: Gulfstream II/III, Boeing 727
Helicopters: AH-1 Cobra, UH-60L, Bell 412, BO 105

those of the Bahrain Royal Flight, and helicopters of the Public Security Wing.

Bangladesh

The *Bangladesh Biman Bahini* (Bangladesh air force) acquired the MiG-29 in 1999, adding to a fleet of fighter/attack aircraft of Chinese origin. The BBB also acquired US aid in the form of Cessna T-37 trainers. The Mi-17 and Bell 212 helicopters are regularly called upon during the monsoon season to aid in flood relief work. The army has a tiny air element with Cessna lightplanes.

Main types in inventory
Fighter/attack: MiG-29, Chengdu F-7, Nanchang A-5
Transport: An-32
Trainers: Guizhou FT-7, Shenyang FT-6, Nanchang PT-6, T-37, L-39 Albatros
Helicopters: Bell 206, Bell 212, Mi-17

Belgium

Belgium's shrinking defence budget has reduced the air force to six squadrons with 90 F-16s, although all have undergone the Mid-Life Update programme. Working alongside the Dutch, Belgian F-16s saw action during the 1999 Allied Force operation over Kosovo. There is a small transport element which includes Airbus A310s. A squadron of Sea Kings provides a North Sea SAR capability. The Belgian army operates Agusta A.109s in both scout and attack roles, armed with TOW for the latter,

Main types in inventory
Fighter/reconnaissance: F-16
Transports: C-130, A310, HS748, Merlin, Falcon 20/900, BN-2
Trainers: Alpha Jet, SF.260
Helicopters: A.109, Sea King, Alouette II/III

while the small naval flight has Alouette IIIs for logistics supply flights to Belgian naval vessels.

Bolivia

The *Fuerza Aérea Boliviana* is starved of cash, and its only true combat aircraft are elderly Lockheed T-33s, augmented by PC-7s converted for counter-insurgency duties. As well as the air force, Bolivia has a small naval air arm (for patrolling Lake Titicaca) equipped with a single Cessna 402, and an army aviation component with a CASA 212 and light aircraft. The police air wing operates a single Cessna 421.

Main types in inventory
Fighter/attack: Lockheed T-33, PC-7
Transports: C-130, Basler Turbo 67, Convair 580, Fokker F27, Pilatus PC-6, Arava
Helicopters: UH-1, SA 315 Lama
Trainers: Cessna 152/172, Lancair 320, A-122 Uiraparu, A-132 Tangara

Brazil

The fifth largest nation in the world, Brazil covers a huge area, including the vast, impenetrable tracts of the Amazon basin. The air force has a relatively small fighter force based on the F-5, Mirage III and AMX, while seeking new equipment which may result in the purchase of an aircraft in the class of the Gripen to replace the air defence-orientated F-5 and Mirage. A large patrol force based on variants of the locally-produced EMB-110/111 Bandeirante provides rescue cover and surveillance in many of the remote areas, as well as coastal patrol. In the latter role the P-3 Orion has been acquired. To provide an effective counter to drug smugglers, polluters and illegal logging, Brazil has instigated the SIVAM (Sistema de Vigilancia da Amazonia) project, which has resulted in the procurement of two special surveillance versions (one for AEW and one for multi-sensor surveillance) of the EMB-145 and a large fleet of EMB-314 Super Tucano (ALX) aircraft, the latter being armed to counter illegal activities across the Amazon basin.

Main types in inventory
Fighter/attack: F-5E, Mirage III, AMX, EMB-312/314 Tucano, A-4 Skyhawk
Transport/reconnaissance: EMB-110/111, C/KC-130, P-3, DHC-5, KC-137, HS748, Learjet, Cessna 208, EMB-145
Trainers: EMB-326 Xavante, EMB-312 Tucano, Regente, Universal
Helicopters: HB 350/355 Esquilo, AS 565 Panther, Lynx, ASH-3, Bell 206, AS 332

The sizeable Brazilian naval air arm is largely helicopter-based, although it has acquired ex-Kuwaiti Skyhawks which will operate from a new aircraft-carrier which replaces the *Minas Gerais*. The new carrier is the ex-French *Foch*, acquired in 2000. There is also a small army air element, based on the Fennec (and similar licence-built Esquilo) and Panther.

Bulgaria

Bulgaria's air arm has struggled with shrinking budgets and the desire to 'Westernise'. The MiG-29 is its most capable fighter, although the MiG-21 is more numerous. An upgrade programme for the MiG-21s is under review as the most likely way forward, as funds will not permit purchase of Western types. The small naval air arm operates the Mi-14 on Black Sea patrol duties.

Main types in inventory
Fighter/attack: MiG-21, MiG-23, MiG-29, Su-22, Su-25
Transports: An-2, An-24, An-26, An-30, LET 410, Tu-134, Yak-40
Trainers: L-29, L-39
Helicopters: Mi-8, Mi-14, Mi-17, Mi-24

Canada

Canada's unified forces (Canadian Armed Forces) no longer maintain a permanent presence in Europe, but still participate in UN- or NATO-led operations. In recent years Canadian aircraft have played a significant part in Operations Desert Storm and Allied Force. The sole combat jet type is the CF-18 Hornet, which equips four front-line squadrons and a training unit. The Hornet force is ably supported by Hercules tankers, while Hercules and Airbus A310s provide strategic transport. Canada also takes electronic warfare training seriously, with dedicated T-33 and Challenger aircraft supporting air defence and maritime training. A significant portion of the air force provides transport and SAR assets throughout Canada's northern regions, using STOL transports and SAR helicopters. The AW520 Cormorant has been chosen to replace the elderly Labrador in the latter role.

The maritime force uses the CP-140 Aurora for ASW and general patrol duties, the latter including sovereignty, fishery and ice reconnaissance missions. The elderly Sea King helicopters are due for imminent replacement.

Main types in inventory
Fighter/attack: CF-18
Maritime patrol: CP-140 Aurora
Transports: C-130, A310, DHC-5, DHC-6, DHC-8, Challenger
Trainers: T-33, Challenger, CL-41 Tutor, DHC-8, T67 Fiirefly, King Air 90, Hawk, T-6 Texan II
Helicopters: Bell 206, Bell 412, Labrador (KV-107), S-61 Sea King

Ground forces are supported by six tactical helicopter squadrons, universally equipped with the Bell 412 Griffon.

Canada became the first nation to completely privatise its training requirements. Basic/advanced training is provided by the NATO Flying Training Centre, which uses the Raytheon T-6 and Hawk. All CAF Canadair Tutors have been retired except for those flown by the 'Snowbirds' aerobatic team. Primary training is performed on civilian-operated Fireflies, while King Airs are used for multi-engine training.

Chile

Until it decides on a new fighter, Chile remains dependent on the F-5, Mirage 5 Elkan and Mirage 50 Pantera for its main combat element. All of these types have been considerably upgraded. The CASA 101 is assembled in-country as the T-36/A-36 Halcón for use in the trainer and light attack roles. The air force is large and operates a wide number of types. There is also a patrol-dedicated naval air wing, and army air wing with mainly helicopters.

Main types in inventory
Fighter/attack: F-5, Mirage 5,
  Mirage 50, A-36
Transports/reconnaissance:
  C-130, Boeing 707, IAI
  Phalcon, P-3, EMB-111, Beech
  99, King Air 200, DHC-6
Trainers: T-36, T-35 Pillán
Helicopters: AS 332, SA 315 Lama, UH-1, BO 105

China

Massive in size, the People's Liberation Army Air Force is largely equipped with obsolete types such as the J-6 and J-7. China has embarked on a major programme to update the quality of the PLAAF's equipment through procurement of the Su-27 for fighter duties and Su-30MKK for attack tasks. The latter may include nuclear strike, for which the elderly H-6 and MiG-19-based Q-5 are currently employed. At the same time, China is developing new types (with foreign assistance). The large J-8 interceptor has been in service for some time, while the JH-7 maritime attack fighter has recently been deployed. A modern tactical fighter, the J-10, is being built, although had not, by 2000, been seen in the West.

The PLA Navy Air Force (PLANAF) is a major air arm in its own right, equipped with long-range bombers (H-5 and H-6), patrollers (SH-5 flying-boat and Y-8), fighters and fighter-bombers (including J-8s and JH-7s), and ASW helicopters. Like that of the PLA Army Aviation Corps, the PLANAF rotary-wing fleet is largely dependent on French

Main types in inventory
Bombers: H-5 (Il-28),
  H-6 (Tu-16)
Fighter/attack: J-5
  (MiG-17), J-6 (MiG-19), J-7 (MiG-21), J-8, J-11
  (Su-27), Q-5, JH-7
Patrol/recce: SH-5, Y-8 (An-12), A-50
Transports: Y-8 (An-12), Y-7 (An-24), An-26, Il-76,
  Y-5 (An-2), Y-11, Trident
Trainers: CJ-5/6 (Yak-18), JJ-5, JJ-6, JJ-7
Helicopters: Z-5/6 (Mi-4), Z-8 (SA 321), Z-9 (SA
  365), Z-11 (AS 355), S-70C, Bell 214, AS 332

helicopters (Frelon, Dauphin, Ecureuil) built under licence in China. The army, in addition, operates a large number of Russian-built helicopters, and has also received US equipment in recent years in the form of S-70C Black Hawks and Bell 214s. As well as the J-10/J-11, priority procurement programmes include an attack helicopter and an AEW platform.

Colombia

Apart from the jet fighter force, Colombia's air forces (air force, navy, army and police) are preoccupied with fighting the drug cartels which operate private armies through much of the nation. Much of the equipment has been donated or provided cheaply by the United States. Colombia makes use of Basler Turbo 67 (re-engined C-47) gunships, armed helicopters and a range of counter-insurgency types in the ongoing fight.

Main types in inventory
Fighter/attack: Kfir, Mirage 5,
  Basler Turbo 67, A/OA-37,
  OV-10, EMB-312
Transports: C-130, CN-235,
  Arava, Boeing 707
Trainers: Cessna T-41, Beech
  T-34, Cessna T-37
Helicopters: UH-60, UH-1, MD 500

Croatia

Following the collapse of the Yugoslav federation, Croatia established its own air arm, initially with light aircraft. These were used in combat roles during the bloody war which led to full independence. MiG-21s and Mi-24s were acquired from the Ukraine as the main combat element of the new force, along with Mi-8 assault helicopters. The MiGs are split between two bases: at Zagreb and Pula, while the Mi-24s are at Zagreb. New-build PC-9s were

Main types in inventory
Fighter: MiG-21
Transports: An-2, An-24,
  Challenger
Trainers: PC-9, UTVA-75
Helicopters: Mi-24, Mi-8, MD
  500, Bell 206
bought from Pilatus to establish a training syllabus, and to be used for light attack missions.

Cuba

Cuba's *Defensa Anti-Aérea u Fuerza Aérea Revolucionaria* (Revolutionary Air Defence and Air Force) is by a considerable margin the most capable air arm in the Caribbean/Central American region, although it is, of course, overshadowed by the US forces to the north. The backbone of the inventory is the MiG-21, which serves with nine squadrons. The spearhead of the air defence force, however, are single squadrons of MiG-29s and MiG-23MFs at San Julian, while the attack force is led by two squadrons of MiG-23BNs, one at Guines and the other at Santa Clara. The only other significant offensive force is a single squadron equipped with Mi-25 'Hinds'. Supporting this force is a large number of fixed- and rotary-wing transports, mostly Antonov products and

Main types in inventory
Fighter/attack: MiG-21, MiG-23, MiG-29
Transports: An-2, An-24, An-26, An-32, Il-76, Yak-40
Trainers: Zlin 526, L-29, L-39, MiG-17
Helicopters: Mi-8/17, Mi-14, Mi-25

Mi-8/17s. The Mi-14 is used for ASW patrols around the Cuban coast. The DAAFAR's training organisation is based at San Julian, employing Zlin 526s for primary training, L-29 Delfins for basic instruction, the L-39 Albatros for advanced training, and a handful of MiG-17s for weapons/combat instruction.

Czech Republic

Rationalisation after the end of Communism and the split from Slovakia has resulted in the Czech air force operating the MiG-21 as its primary fighter. The fleet of MiG-23s was retired, while even the MiG-29s inherited from the old Czechoslovak air force were swapped for new W-3 helicopters with Poland. The attack force, based on Su-22s, Su-25s and Mi-24s, remains strong, however. Although a new fighter is sought from Western sources, the Czech air force has begun the task of replacing the MiG-21 with the L-159, a radar-equipped and more powerful development of the L-39 Albatros trainer. The first entered service in 2000. The transport helicopter fleet, based largely on the Mi-8/17, includes a handful of

Main types in inventory
Fighter/attack: MiG-21, Su-22, Su-25, L-39, L-159
Transports: An-24, An-26, LET 410, LET 610, Tu-134, Tu-154
Trainers: Zlin 142, L-29, L-39
Helicopters: Mi-2, Mi-8/9/17, Mi-24, W-3

aircraft modified for electronic warfare purposes. Similarly, one of the three An-26s on strength is an EW jamming aircraft. Training is conducted on the Zlin 142 and L-29/L-39. Other indigenous products in service include the LET 410 and LET 610 transports.

Denmark

The *Flyvevåbnet* (Danish air force) operates only one combat type in the shape of the Lockheed Martin F-16. Four squadrons fly the fighter, from Ålborg and Skrydstrup. A small contingent took part in Operation Allied Force over Yugoslavia in 1999. A single transport squadron provides support with C-130 Hercules, while Challengers are employed in patrol and transport duties. A SAR squadron uses the Sikorsky S-61.

The small Navy flying service (*Søvaernets Flyvetjeneste*) operates the Westland Lynx, recently upgraded to Super Lynx standard. These are used on shipboard ASW duties, and for coastal patrols.

The *Haerens Flyvetjeneste* (army flying service) is also equipped solely with helicopters, based on the Hughes 500M for spotting duties and the Eurocopter AS 550C Fennec for armed attack using the HeliTOW system. The fleet is arranged in two anti-tank helicopter companies based at Vandel, each with 12 AS 550s and four Hughes 500s.

Main types in inventory
Fighter: F-16
Transports: C-130, Challenger, Gulfstream III
Helicopters: S-61 (air force), Lynx (navy), Hughes 500 and AS550 (army)
Trainer: Saab MFI-17

Ecuador

Continuing tension with Peru has dominated Ecuadorian defence policy in recent years, resulting in the strong fighter force. Kfirs and Jaguars have been recently upgraded in lieu of procurement of new types. The rest of the force has a counter-insurgency/anti-drug tasking. The army has a large air element, which includes several fixed-wing transports, while the navy operates helicopters and light patrol aircraft.

Main types in inventory
Fighter/attack: Jaguar, Mirage F1, Kfir, A-37, Strikemaster
Transports: C-130, DHC-5, DHC-6, HS748, Boeing 727, F28, Sabreliner, CN-235, Arava
Trainers: Cessna 150, T-34, T-41
Helicopters: Alouette III, Bell 212, Bell 222, AS 332, AS 350, Bell 412

Egypt

Occupying a strategic position in North Africa, Egypt has assembled a large air force, with elements dating from before the 1979 Camp David agreement which allowed a flood of US materiel into the country. Elderly Soviet-supplied aircraft still serve in large numbers, alongside Chinese-built equivalents. However, the cutting edge of the *Al Quwwat Al Jawwiya Il Misriya* (Egyptian air force) is provided by the F-16 and Mirage 2000, assisted by F-4E Phantoms and controlled by E-2 Hawkeyes. In the anti-armour role Egypt boasts the AH-64 Apache.

Electronic warfare is an important part of Egypt's operations, with modified versions of Beech 1900, Westland Commando, C-130 and a few Il-28s performing reconnaissance and jamming functions. The training syllabus is based on the Gomhouria (a locally-built version of the Bücker Bestmann used for primary training), Tucano (for basic training), and L-29/39/59s (for advanced training). Alpha Jets fly on weapons training tasks, and also serve alongside L-29 Delfins and Su-20s in a close

Main types in inventory
Fighter/attack: F-16, F-4, MiG-21, Chengdu F-7, Mirage 2000, Mirage 5, Shenyang F-6, Alpha Jet, Su-20, L-29
Recce/EW/AEW: E-2, Il-28, EC-130, Beech 1900, Commando
Transports: C-130, Boeing 707, Falcon 20, Gulfstream III/IV, DHC-5, PZL-104 Wilga, An-2
Trainers: Gomhouria, EMB-312 Tucano, Alpha Jet, MiG-15UTI, L-29, L-39, L-59
Helicopters: Gazelle, Commando, AH-64, S-70A, UH-12, AS-61, SH-2, Sea King

air support function. The navy air element is equipped with Sea Kings for shore-based ASW and Gazelles which have a limited anti-ship capability. For shipborne operations from frigates leased from the US Navy, the Egyptian navy recently acquired SH-2 Seasprites.

Finland

Limited to 60 combat aircraft by the 1947 Treaty of Paris, and initially obliged to procure aircraft from both Russia and the West, the *Suomen Ilmavoimat* (Finnish air force) operated the Draken and MiG-21 until the last of these was retired in 2000. Freed from its procurement constraints, the Ilmavoimat opted for the F/A-18 Hornet to replace both types within six squadrons dedicated to air defence. The Hornet was felt to offer excellent capability combined with twin-engined safety over the frozen north of the country. The Hornets are ably augmented by the Hawk, used as both a trainer and as a light attack platform. Finnish Hawks are wired for the carriage of AAMs for use as emergency air defenders. The small transport fleet is based on two F27s and a handful of light types. Another F27 is configured for Sigint-gathering, while the Learjets perform survey, EW training and target-towing tasks, as well as transport. The training organisation uses two local products, the Vinka and Redigo lightplanes, as well as the Hawk.

Main types in inventory
Fighter/attack: F/A-18C/D, Hawk
Transports: F27, Learjet, PA-31 Navajo
Trainers: Vinka, Redigo, Hawk, PA-28R Arrow
Helicopters: Mi-8, Hughes 500

France

The French air arms are in the throes of a major re-equipment and reorganisation. The most important new aircraft is the Dassault Rafale multi-role fighter, which is currently replacing the now-retired Crusader in *Aéronavale* (French naval aviation) use, and will ultimately replace the Super Etendard. The air wing of the new carrier *Charles de Gaulle* is completed by newly acquired Hawkeye AEW platforms. The *Armée de l'Air* (air force) will receive Rafales to replace the Jaguar, Mirage F1CT and some Mirage 2000s. In the meantime, the AdA has upgraded some of its Mirage 2000 fighters to 2000-5 standard, and has received a large fleet of Mirage 2000D/Ns to fulfil its strike/attack requirements, ably assisted by Mirage F1CTs. The attack fleet can all carry laser designators for autonomous delivery of laser-guided weapons. A nuclear role is retained through employment of the ASMP missile on the Mirage 2000N. The fighter force is augmented by tankers, Elint and AWACS aircraft.

The *Aviation Légère de l'Armée de Terre* (army aviation) is undergoing a major reorganisation with the emphasis placed on rapid reaction. Its offensive capability is due to be considerably enhanced by the adoption of the Tigre helicopter, while large numbers of Cougars have improved the assault transport force. France is a regular participant

Main types in AdA inventory
Fighter/attack: Mirage 2000C, Mirage 2000D/N, Mirage F1CT, Jaguar
Reconnaissance/AWACS: Mirage IVP, Mirage F1CR, E-3F, C.160, DC-8
Tanker/transports: C-135FR, C-130, C.160, A310, DC-8, CN-235, Falcon 20/50/900, Nord 262, DHC-6, TBM 700
Trainers: Alpha Jet, Epsilon, Tucano
Helicopters: SA 330, AS 332, AS 532, AS 355/555

Main types in *Aéronavale* inventory
Fighter/attack: Rafale, Super Etendard
Patrol: E-2, Atlantique, N.262, Falcon 10/20/50
Helicopters: SA 321, AS 365/565, Lynx, Alouette III

Main types in ALAT inventory
Gazelle, SA 330, AS 532, AS 555, PC-6, Cessna F406

in international peacekeeping efforts, and its fighters have seen action in the Gulf and over former Yugoslavia. The Transall/Hercules transport fleet has also been heavily tasked on international operations, as have army helicopters.

Germany

The 1990s were a notable period for the German armed forces, dominated by the reunification of the two Germanys and the large-scale withdrawal of UK and US forces from German soil. Of the former East German aircraft, only a squadron of MiG-29s and a few transports were retained. The MiG-29s, along with the Phantoms which fly on air defence missions, are due for replacement by the Eurofighter EF 2000. The large Tornado force, which includes the ECR defence suppression variant, will continue to fly the attack mission for some years, although more EF 2000s may be purchased to replace some of them. Another new venture for the Luftwaffe was its first post-war participation in combat, an act of parliament clearing the way for Tornados to join the UN/NATO efforts over former Yugoslavia and Kosovo. Germany's growing international commitments have led to the purchase of a sizeable fleet of Airbus A310s for strategic transport, and the nation is a lead partner in the A400M transport project.

The *Marineflieger* (naval aviation) uses the Tornado for maritime attack and reconnaissance duties, but is largely an ASW/patrol force with Atlantics, Sea Kings and recently upgraded Lynxes. The *Heeresflieger* (army aviation) is solely equipped with helicopters. It is due to introduce the Tiger attack helicopter later in the decade, greatly

Main types in *Luftwaffe* inventory
Fighter/attack/recce: Tornado IDS, F-4E, MiG-29
Transports: C-160, A310, Challenger, Let 410
Trainers (all in US): Beech F33, T-37, T-38
Helicopters: UH-1D, AS 532

Main types in *Marine Flieger* inventory
Fighter/attack/recce: Tornado IDS
Patrol: Atlantic
Helicopters: Lynx, Sea King

Main types in *Heer* inventory
UH-1D, BO 105, CH-53, EC 135

increasing its anti-armour capability by replacing the BO 105 in this role. EC 135s are entering service for training.

Greece

Although relations between Greece and Turkey have thawed considerably in recent times, Greece continues to build a powerful air force of modern aircraft. Large orders have been placed for more F-16s and Mirage 2000s, and for up to 70 Eurofighter EF 2000s. These will replace now-elderly F-4s, Mirage F1s and A-7s currently in *Elliniki Polimiki Aeroporia* (Greek air force) service. Other elderly types now out of service include the Lockheed T-33, which was retired in 2000, and the Grumman Albatross. Along with fighter equipment, Greece has also chosen the EMBRAER EMB-145/Erieye combination to provide an AEW capability. The *Elliniko Polimiko Naftikon* (Greek naval aviation) is helicopter-based, but also provides the mission crew and tasking for the air force's P-3 Orions. The *Elliniki Aeroporia Stratou* (Greek army aviation) is a growing

Main types in EPA inventory
Fighter/attack: F-16, F-4, F-5,
Mirage 2000, Mirage F1, A-7
Recce/patrol: RF-4, P-3
Transports: C-130, EMB-135,
C-47, CL-215, Do 28, YS-11
Trainers: T-37, T-2
Helicopters: AB 205, AB 206, AB 212

Main types in EPN inventory
Alouette III, AB 212, S-70B

Main types in EAS inventory
AH-64, UH-1, AB 205, AB 206, AB 212, CH-47, NH-300, U-17, C-12

force, flying AH-64A Apaches and CH-47D Chinooks alongside AB 205/UH-1 assault transports.

Hungary

Emerging in the 1990s from its Communist past, Hungary is now turning to the West for new fighter equipment. However, until a decision is made (and funded), the air force relies on the MiG-21 and MiG-29 for its tactical needs (the Su-22 and MiG-23 were retired in 1997).

Main types in inventory
Fighter/attack: MiG-29, MiG-21
Transports: An-26, LET 410
Trainers: L-39, Zlin 43
Helicopters: Mi-2, Mi-8/17,
Mi-24

India

The massive Indian Air Force faces procurement problems in the early 21st century, as the bulk of its equipment is old and unreliable. Numerically the most important types are the MiG-21, MiG-23 and MiG-27, which are in sore need of replacement or upgrading. Projects are under way to maintain the combat viability of the MiG-21 and MiG-27 through avionics upgrades. The attrition rate is high, a fact attributable to the poor level of training aircraft. A new advanced trainer is desperately needed, the Hawk having been chosen.

MiG-29s and Mirage 2000s represented the cutting edge of the IAF in the 1990s, to which has been added the Su-30MKI, a two-seat multi-role version of the well-known 'Flanker'. At some considerable cost India is developing its own LCA combat aircraft, although this project may yet founder. Helicopter forces of both the IAF and the INA (Indian Naval Aviation) will be enhanced by deliveries of the locally-developed ALH design.

India's navy presently operates Sea Harriers from a small carrier, but ambitions to develop a true blue-water capability may be realised by the potential purchase of an ex-Russian aircraft-carrier, complete with MiG-29K fighters to equip its air wing. Ka-31 helicopters will provide an AEW component. As part of the same deal with Russia, India is expected to acquire Tu-22M 'Backfire' long-range maritime strike aircraft.

Main types in IAF inventory
Fighter/attack: Mirage 2000,
Jaguar, MiG-21, MiG-23,
MiG-23BN, MiG-27, MiG-29,
Su-30MKI
Reconnaissance etc: MiG-25,
Canberra, Gulfstream III
Transports: An-32, Il-76, Boeing 737,
HS748, Do 228
Trainers: TS-11, Kiran I/II, Deepak
Helicopters: Mi-8, Mi-17, Mi-25, Mi-26, Chetak
(Alouette III), Cheetah (Lama)

Main types in INA inventory
Fighter: Sea Harrier
Patrol: Tu-142, Il-38, Do 228
Transport: BN-2, HS748
Trainers: Deepak, Kiran
Helicopters: Chetak, Ka-25, Ka-28, Sea King

Indonesia

Indonesia's air force has suffered recently from economic troubles, and arms embargoes associated with the breakaway of East Timor. An order for Su-30s was cancelled, leaving the F-16 as the most capable combat equipment, augmented by F-5s. A large number of Hawks fly on both training and combat duties, partnering A-4 Skyhawks in the attack role. The naval aviation service flies a number of light aircraft, its main fixed-wing equipment being the Nomad Searchmaster for coastal patrols. The only seagoing helicopter is the venerable Westland Wasp.

Main types in inventory

Fighter/attack: F-16, A-4, F-5, Hawk 100/200
Patrol: Boeing 737, OV-10, Nomad
Transports: CN-235, F27, C-130, Boeing 707, F28, CASA 212, DHC-5, Nomad
Trainers: Hawk 53, AS 202 Bravo, T-41, T-34
Helicopters: S-58, BO 105, NAS 330, AS 332, MD500, Bell 412, Wasp

Iran

Since the Islamic Revolution in 1979, Iran has struggled to keep its large US-supplied fleet of aircraft airworthy, although the local industry has achieved considerable success in this area, as well as producing new types, or developments of existing aircraft. The most capable of these is the Azaraksh, a fighter based on the F-5. In parallel, Iran has received Russian equipment, notably the MiG-29 and Su-24, as well as some aircraft which defected from Iraq. There are four air arms: the Islamic Republic of Iran Air Force (IRIAF), IRI Naval Aviation, IRI Army Aviation and the IRI Guards Aviation. The latter is a distinct air arm of the hard-line Revolutionary Guards

Main types in inventory

Fighter/attack: MiG-29, F-4, F-5, F-14, Chengdu F-7, Su-24
Transports: C-130, Boeing 707, Boeing 747, Il-76, An-72
Patrol: P-3 Orion
Trainers: PC-7, T-33, F33 Bonanza
Helicopters: AB 212, Bell 214, CH-47, Bell 206, AH-1, Mi-8/17, Sikorsky RH-53

organisation. It is believed to operate the Chengdu F-7 point-defence interceptors.

Iraq

Decimated during the 1991 Gulf War, the *Al Quwwat Al Jawwiya Al Iraqiya* (Iraqi air force) nevertheless maintains a sizeable force, although its operations are restricted by UN-enforced No-Fly Zones in the north and south of the country. Arguably the most potent aircraft are the Mirage F1EQs which were used to devastating effect during the 1980-88 war with Iran. Supporting them are an unknown number of MiG-21s, -25s and -29s which occasionally challenge UN aircraft during routine operations. Only about eight MiG-29s are thought to have survived Desert Storm. The Iraqi army also has an organic aviation

Main types in inventory

Fighter/attack: Chengdu F-7, Mirage F1, MiG-21, MiG-23, MiG-25, MiG-29, Su-22, Su-25
Transports: An-12, An-24/26, Il-76
Helicopters: SA 330, Bell 214, MD 500, Mi-6, Mi-8/17, Gazelle, Mi-24, Alouette III
Trainers: L-29, L-39, Tucano, AS 202 Bravo, Zlin 326

component, which operates around 110 helicopters, including Mi-24 'Hinds'.

Israel

The IDF/AF (Israeli Defence Force/Air Force) was fighting even before the creation of the nation itself, and it has been on a war footing throughout its existence. Having earlier relied on French equipment, the IDF/AF now buys its combat aircraft almost exclusively from the US, which has been willing to provide the latest hardware. Consequently, the large fighter fleet is concentrated on the F-15 (in both F-15A/B/C/D fighter and F-15I attack versions) and the F-16. Many of the latter have been tailored to defence suppression missions. Augmenting this

Main types in inventory

Fighter/attack: F-15A/C, F-15I, F-16, F-4E, Kfir, A-4
Transport/recon: C-130, Boeing 707, Arava, Westwind, Seascan, RF-4E, Beech King Air 200
Helicopters: AH-64, AH-1, CH-53, UH-60, Bell 212, Hughes 500, Bell 206
Trainers: Super Cub, Tzukit (Magister)

combat force are electronic intelligence and jamming aircraft, based on the Boeing 707, and 707 and KC-130 tankers. A few Phantoms remain in service, including RF-4E reconnaissance platforms. The anti-armour element is strong, with a large force of Apaches and Cobras, and a sizeable fleet of assault helicopters allows rapid mobility. A large reserve force is maintained, equipped with Kfirs, Skyhawks, Phantoms and early F-16 variants.

Italy

The *Aeronautica Militare Italiana* (Italian air force) operates a sizeable force of modern attack/reconnaissance/anti-ship aircraft (Tornado IDS and AMX) which have seen action over Yugoslavia in recent years. However, the air defence force is based on the elderly F-104 Starfighter, albeit upgraded, pending delivery of the Eurofighter EF 2000. To cover the shortfall in capability, the AMI leased 24 Tornado ADVs from the RAF, and in 2000 seemed likely to lease F-16ADFs from the US. Further procurement is concerned primarily with the transport fleet, which has received its first C-130Js, while the C-27J (upgraded G222) is also on order. The air force is also tasked with SAR/combat rescue, for which the AB 212 and HH-3 helicopters are used. A small fleet of Piaggio PD.808s provides EW training, while P.166s are used in the survey role. Special versions of the G222 are used for navaid calibration and Sigint-gathering.

The *Marina Militare Italiana* (Italian navy) has one carrier (*Giuseppe Garibaldi*) from which it flies AV-8B Harrier IIs. The navy provides mission crew for the Atlantic

Main types in AMI inventory
Fighter/attack: Tornado ADV,
  Tornado IDS, F-104, AMX
Transports: C-130, G222,
  Boeing 707, Falcon 50, P.180
Maritime patrol/recce/EW:
  Atlantic, P.166, G222, PD.808
Trainers: SF.260, S.208, MB-339
Helicopters: HH-3, AB 212, NH 500
Main types in MMI inventory
AV-8B, SH-3, AB 212
Main types in AvES inventory
A.109, A.129, AB 205, AB 206, AB 412, CH-47,
  Do 228, P.180

maritime patrollers, although they are operated by the AMI. The *Aviazione dell'Esercito* (army aviation) has a large rotary-wing fleet spearheaded by the A.129 Mangusta attack helicopter. The AB 412 is the main assault transport, while CH-47s provide a tactical heavylift capability.

Japan

Japan's desire for greater military self-sufficiency has resulted in licence production of US types and local development proceeding in parallel. Mitsubishi has built F-4s and F-15s for the fighter force, and its own F-1 design for attack duties. It is now flying prototypes of the F-2 (based on the F-16) which will replace the F-1 and some F-4s in what the Japanese call the Fighter Support role. Mitsubishi also builds the Sikorsky S-70 in the UH-60 version for the JASDF SAR role, and SH-60 version for the Japan Maritime Self Defence Force ASW role. Kawasaki is another manufacturer, supplying P-3s for the JMSDF, CH-47s and OH-6s. It, too, is developing a new type in the form of the OH-1, an indigenous scout helicopter design. An armed version may be developed to form the successor to the Fuji-built AH-1s which are the main weapon of the Japan Ground Self Defence Force. Many of the trainer/transport types are of local origin, notably the NAMC YS-11 and Kawasaki C-1 transports, Fuji T-5 primary trainer, Mitsubishi T-2 and Kawasaki T-4 jet

Main types in JASDF inventory
Fighter/attack: F-15, F-4, F-1
Reconnaissance/AEW: RF-4,
  E-2, E-767, YS-11, U-125
Transports: C-130, C-1, YS-11,
  Boeing 747, U-4, MU-2
Trainers: T-2, T-3, T-4, T-400
Helicopters: UH-60, CH-47, KV-107
Main types in JMSDF inventory
Patrol/EW: P-3, US-1, U-36, YS-11
Trainers: TC-90, T-5
Helicopters: UH-60, SH-60, S-61
Main types in JGSDF inventory
Fixed-wing: LR-1, LR-2
Rotary-wing: CH-47, AH-1, UH-1, OH-6, AS 332

trainers, and the Mitsubishi MU-2/LR-1 general-purpose twin. Perhaps the most remarkable type in Japan's inventory is the ShinMaywa US-1, a large amphibian used for patrol and SAR work.

Jordan

Sandwiched between Iraq and Israel, Jordan maintains a strong defensive air arm centred around five fighter squadrons. The force was recently bolstered by the arrival of 16 F-16As for No. 2 Squadron. Two squadrons of Cobras provide an anti-armour capability. A C-130 squadron provides the main transport element, although there is also a Royal Flight. The 'Falcons' national aerobatic team flies the Extra 300.

Main types in inventory
Fighter: F-16, F-5, Mirage F1
Transports: C-130, CASA 212,
  Islander, TriStar 500,
  Gulfstream III,
Trainers: Bulldog, CASA 101,
  Extra 300
Rotary-wing: AH-1, UH-1,
  AS 332, MD 500, S-70A

Kenya

The small Kenyan Air Force has the F-5 as its primary combat type, assisted by Hawk attack/trainers. A transport force employs a selection of STOL types which can be used on rough-field operations. The Kenyan Army Flight is the main user of the Hughes 500/MD 500 Defender, many of which are armed.

Main types in inventory
Fighter/attack: F-5, Hawk
Transports: DHC-5, DHC-8,
  Do 28, Fokker 70
Trainers: Bulldog, Tucano
Helicopters: SA 330, BO 105,
  Hughes 500, MD 500

Korea (North)

The Korean People's Army Air Force comprises mostly obsolete Soviet and Chinese types, its most modern equipment being the MiG-29, of which around 30 are in service. The front-line force numbers around 500 aircraft, with the Shenyang F-5 (MiG-17), Shenyang F-6 (MiG-19) and MiG-21 being the most numerous. The transport fleet relies heavily on the An-2 (and Chinese-built Shijiazhuang Y-5s), with the larger types operating in airline colours.

Main types in inventory
Fighter/attack: Harbin H-5,
  MiG-21, MiG-23, MiG-29,
  Nanchang Q-5, Shenyang J-5,
  Shenyang J-6, Su-7, Su-25
Transports: An-2, An-24, Il-18,
  Il-62, Il-76, Tu-154
Trainers: L-39, MiG-15UTI, Nanchang CJ-5
Helicopters: MD 500, Mi-2, Mi-8/17, Mi-14, Mi-24

Korea (South)

Despite a recent slight thawing in relations, South Korea remains on full alert against intervention by its northern neighbour. A large air force with modern equipment is augmented by a sizeable USAF presence. The F-16 has been procured in large numbers, although older F-4s and F-5s remain in use. Korea is developing the T/A-50 supersonic trainer/light attacker to swell its attack/trainer fleet, while the KTX-1 turboprop trainer is due to replace the T-37. An air superiority fighter is on the 'wants' list, for which the Eurofighter, Rafale and upgraded F-15 are likely contenders. The naval air arm is concerned primarily with ASW, operating Orions from land and Lynxes from ships.

Main types in inventory
Fighter/attack/recce/patrol:
  F-4, F-5, F-16, A-37, O-1,
  O-2, OV-10, P-3, Hawker
  800
Transports: C-130, CN-235,
  Boeing 737
Trainers: Hawk, T-41, T-37, T-38
Helicopters: UH-60, CH-47, AH-1, Hughes 500,
  Lynx, Alouette III, Bell 212, Bell 214, UH-1

Korean army aviation is based on the US Army, with UH-60s, UH-1s, AH-1s and CH-47s as the principal types.

Kuwait

The cornerstone of the Kuwaiti Air Force are the 40 Hornets ordered prior to the 1991 Gulf War, delivered from 1992. They perform air defence, ground attack and anti-ship duties. The Hawk advanced trainers can also be used for light attack, while the Cougars are Exocet-capable for anti-ship duties.

Main types in inventory
Fighter/attack: F/A-18 Hornet,
Transports: L100 Hercules,
  DC-9, MD-83
Trainers: Hawk, Tucano
Helicopters: Puma, Gazelle,
  Cougar

Libya

Libya's air forces are modelled along Soviet lines, and consist of a separate air defence force equipped with MiG-23s, MiG-25s and Mirage F1Es, and a tactical air force which flies Mirage F1As, MiG-21/23s, Su-22/24s and a few Tu-22 bombers as its main equipment. The Mirage 5, L-39 and Jastreb fleets are believed to be in storage. Naval and army aviation elements are mainly equipped with helicopters, the principal naval type being the Mi-14.

Main types in inventory
Fighter/attack: MiG-21, MiG-23, MiG-25, Mirage F1, Mirage 5, Su-22, Su-24, Tu-22, L-39, J-1 Jastreb
Transports: Il-76, An-26, G222, C-130
Trainers: SF.260, G-2 Galeb
Helicopters: Mi-24, Mi-8, Mi-2, Mi-14, Super Frelon, CH-47, Alouette III, AB 206, Gazelle

Malaysia

Until the Far East economic crisis hit Malaysia hard in the late 1990s, the nation was building up its air forces with two-seat Hornets and MiG-29s. Further procurement is on hold, but the aircraft already delivered represent one of the more powerful forces in the volatile region. Much of the build-up is due to a rise in Chinese activity, and tension over sovereignty of the Spratly Islands. Malaysian Hawks have fired on Philippine aircraft in the region at least once. Economic problems have forestalled plans to replace two veteran types: the DHC-4 Caribou and the S-61 Nuri transport helicopter. The dispersed nature of Malaysia's territory makes maritime patrol a key role, radar-equipped and armed King Airs being the main patrol

Main types in inventory
Fighter/attack: F/A-18D, F-5, MiG-29, Hawk 100/200
Maritime patrol: King Air 200, C-130
Transports: C-130, DHC-4, CN-235, Challenger
Trainers: MD3-160 Aerotiga, PC-7, MB-339, Hawk 100, Cessna 402
Helicopters: S-61, Alouette III, S-70A, Wasp

vehicle, backed by specially modified C-130s. A small navy contingent flies elderly Wasps (until replacement by Lynxes) and an army unit flies Alouette IIIs.

Mexico

With little to fear from outside, Mexico maintains only a token air defence force in the form of a single squadron of F-5s. Much of the air force is concerned with internal security affairs, notably in the south of the country where PC-7s and Aravas have been widely used against rebels in Chiapas province. Anti-drug work also occupies much of the fleet, which is composed of a plethora of light utility types. For larger helicopters, Mexico has recently turned to Russia, which has supplied Mi-8s, -17s and even the heavylift Mi-26. The US supplied 73 Cessna 182s to equip light patrol units mainly concerned with anti-drug duties.

Main types in inventory
Fighter/attack: F-5, PC-7, T-33
Transports: C-130, Boeing 727, 737, 757, Arava, C-47, Cessna 182, CASA 212
Trainers: Maule MX-7, SF.260, PC-7
Helicopters: Mi-8/17, Mi-26, Bell 212, MD 530, BO 105

The naval aviation element is equipped with a collection of light transports and Mi-8 helicopters.

Morocco

The Royal Moroccan Air Force is totally Westernised, having been equipped from mostly French and US sources. Two large bases at Meknes and Sidi Slimane house the fighter/attack force, which includes Broncos, Magisters and Alpha Jets used for counter-insurgency work. Two 707s and two KC-130s provide inflight refuelling, while two EC-130s are fitted with side-looking radar for reconnaissance. Another EC-130 has a Sigint fit. The Royal Gendarmerie also operates aircraft, including S-70 Black Hawks.

Main types in inventory
Fighter/attack: Mirage F1, F-5, Alpha Jet, Magister, OV-10
Transports: C/KC-130, Boeing 707, CN-235, Falcon 20, Gulfstream II/III
Patrol/recce: Do 28, EC-130
Trainers: CAP 10/230, AS 202 Bravo, T-34, Magister, Alpha Jet, King Air
Helicopters: SA 330, Gazelle, CH-47, Bell 205, Bell 206

Netherlands

The *Koninklijke Luchtmacht* (Royal Netherlands Air Force) has settled on the F-16 as its only combat jet. Four squadrons operate in air defence/ground attack roles, while another squadron has an air defence/reconnaissance tasking. Single units support the fleet as the training squadron and as a trials unit. The fleet is undergoing the MLU programme. Dutch F-16s were active over Kosovo during Allied Force, scoring one confirmed kill against a Serbian MiG-29. The transport fleet includes two KDC-10 tanker/transports, which support overseas fighter deployments. Fokker 60s and C-130Hs are used for tactical transport. The Fokker 50 and Gulfstream IV are used for staff transport. Army support is provided by the Tactical Helicopter Group, equipped with CH-47Ds and Cougars for assault transport, BO 105s for scouting and AH-64D Apaches for attack. The *Marineluchtvaartdienst* uses the Lynx for shipboard ASW and SAR operations, and the P-3 Orion for land-based patrols. An Orion detachment is maintained in Curaçao in the Caribbean.

Main types in inventory
Fighter/attack/recce: F-16
Tanker/transport: KDC-10,
 C-130, F50/60, Gulfstream IV
Maritime patrol: P-3 Orion
Trainers: PC-7
Helicopters: AB 412, BO 105,
 AH-64, CH-47, Alouette III, AS 532, Lynx

New Zealand

Crippling defence budgets have reduced the Royal New Zealand Air Force to a tiny, yet still professional, air arm. The elderly Skyhawks have been upgraded under the Kahu programme with F-16 radar, but a deal to replace them with F-16s was cancelled in 2000. A sensor update for the P-3s has also been recently shelved.

Main types in inventory
Fighter/attack: A-4K, MB-339
Maritime patrol: P-3 Orion
Transports: Boeing 727,
 C-130, King Air 200
Trainer: CT-4E Airtrainer
Helicopters: UH-1, Bell 47, SH-2

Nigeria

Successive military coups, corruption and related embargoes have hampered Nigerian Air Force procurement, and also rendered much of the fleet unserviceable through lack of spares. Particularly affected is the fast-jet fleet of MiG-21s and Jaguars. Transport, trainer and helicopter fleets have been affected less, although procurement of Slingsby T67s was halted in favour of the indigenous Air Beetle design.

Main types in inventory
Fighter/attack: MiG-21, Jaguar
Transports: G222, Do 28/128,
 C-130
Maritime patrol: F27MPA
Trainers: MB-339, L-39, Alpha
 Jet, PC-7; AIEP Air Beetle
Helicopters: SA 330, AS 332,
 BO 105, Schweizer 300, Lynx

Norway

The *Luftforsvaret* (air force) operates four squadrons of F-16A/B MLUs as its principal equipment. Although most training is conducted in the US, students return to fly with an F-5 unit before joining the F-16 force. A stated requirement for a new fighter, with Eurofighter EF 2000 and F-16 Block 60 being the contenders, had not resulted in any decision, or funding, by the end of 2000. Other Norwegian forces are assigned to maritime duties, including Sea King SAR helicopters, Lynxes for ASW and Orions for long-range patrol. The Orions have undergone a

Main types in inventory
Fighter/lead-in trainer: F-16, F-5
Transport/EW trainer: C-130,
 DHC-6, Falcon 20
Maritime patrol: P-3C, P-3N
Trainers: MFI-15, MFI-17
Helicopters: Bell 412, Sea King,
 Lynx

wide-ranging sensor update. A small transport force includes Hercules and Bell 412 helicopters.

Oman

With strong ties with the UK, the RAFO (Royal Air Force of Oman) predominantly uses UK equipment. The Jaguar remains the most potent combat aircraft, these having recently been updated with precision attack capability. The Hawk 100/200 mix provides Oman with an advanced trainer and light multi-role fighter. There is a Royal Flight which operates the Boeing 747SP, Gulfstream IV and AS 332 Super Puma.

Main types in inventory
Fighters: Jaguar, Hawk 200
Transports: BAe One-Eleven, Skyvan, C-130
Trainers: Hawk 100, PC-9, Mushshak, Falke
Helicopters: AB 205, AB 212, Bell 214, Bell 206

Pakistan

Pakistan's defence posture is concerned primarily with its neighbour, India, with which it has fought two full-scale wars and numerous border skirmishes. Recent events have triggered a nuclear arms race between the two nations, developments which have seen an arms embargo imposed on Pakistan by the US, its main supplier. To circumvent this, Pakistan has looked elsewhere for arms, notably striking up a strong accord with China, resulting in a steady influx of Chinese equipment, and joint development in certain areas. However, the most potent aircraft fielded by the Pakistan Air Force (PAF) is the F-16, which has proved itself in combat along the border with Afghanistan. Augmenting this small force are a large number of Mirage variants, which have been acquired from a variety of sources and updated. Chinese aircraft in service are the A-5, F-6 (largely relegated to training) and the F-7, the latter representing a useful, cheap point defence capability.

The Pakistan Army Aviation Corps (PAAC) is a large organisation, spearheaded by the AH-1 Cobra attack helicopter. Assault transport is provided by the Mi-8/17

Main types in PAF inventory
Fighter/attack: F-16, Mirage III/5, Chengdu F-7, Shenyang F-6, Nanchang A-5
Transports: C-130, Y-12, F27, Falcon 20, Boeing 707
Trainers: Mushshak, T-37, Hongdu K-8
Helicopters: Alouette III

Main types in PNA inventory
Fixed-wing: F27, P-3 Orion, Atlantic, BN-2
Helicopters: Sea King, Lynx, Alouette III

Main types in PAAC inventory
Fixed-wing: Cessna O-1, Mushshak
Helicopters: UH-1, Alouette III, SA 330, AH-1S, Mi-8/17, Bell 206

bought from Russia. The PAAC still uses fixed-wing observation types. Pakistan Naval Aviation (PNA) at Karachi has a mixed fleet of Atlantics, Orions and F27s for maritime patrol, Lynxes for shipboard ASW and Exocet-armed Sea Kings for anti-ship attack.

Peru

Peru has one of the largest air forces in South America, split between the air force, navy, army, coast guard and police. Border tensions with Ecuador have led to an increase in capability with the arrival of Russian types such as the Mi-24/25, Mi-26, MiG-29 and Su-25. Peru, nevertheless, also sources material from the West, and its Mirage 2000s are arguably the most capable fighters in the region. A sizeable attack component is based on the Su-20/22 (and newer Su-25s), and includes the world's last operational Canberra bombers. Counter-insurgency and anti-drug patrols are also important tasks, for which A-37s and armed Tucanos are employed, alongside Mi-24 helicopter gunships.

The naval air arm operates shipborne AB 212s and AS-61s, while army aviation uses the Mi-8/17 and Mi-24/25 as its primary types, with Agusta A.109s employed on scout duties.

Main types in inventory
Fighter/attack: Mirage 2000, Mirage 5, Su-20/22, Su-25, MiG-29, A-37, Canberra
Transports: C-130, An-32, An-74, DHC-5, DHC-6, Y-12, PC-6
Trainers: T-41, EMB-312, MB-339
Helicopters: Mi-8/17, Mi-24/25, Mi-26, UH-1, Bell 212, Bell 214, AS-61, A.109, Enstrom F28

Philippines

In recent times the Philippines have suffered from natural disaster, political unrest, corruption and the Asian economic crisis. The result is an air force struggling to find cash to meet its urgent equipment needs. The F-5 fighter fleet is in need of replacement, but the procurement process has been long, with no end in sight. Used F-16s or more modern F-5s appear the most likely outcome. Much of the air force's inventory is concerned with internal security, and has seen considerable action in the ongoing fight against guerrillas. Armed helicopters include the MD520 and AUH-76, the latter being a unique armed variant of the S-76. OV-10s also fly on counter-insurgency

Main types in inventory
Fighter/attack: F-5, OV-10
Transports: C-130, BN-2,
  Nomad, F27, F28
Trainers: S.211, T-41, SF.260
Helicopters: MD520, AUH-76, Bell 205, UH-1,
  Bell 214, BO 105, S-76, SA 330, S-70A

duties. The seas around the Philippines are patrolled by F27s and Nomad Searchmasters. The Philippine navy operates a small air element with BO 105 helicopters for SAR and BN-2 Islanders for transport, but has an outstanding requirement for a new shipboard helicopter.

Poland

Emerging from Communism, Poland has turned to NATO in its military alignment, and although funding has not yet been forthcoming to procure Western types, a new fighter remains a national priority. Until funding becomes available, the *Wojska Lotnicze I Obrony Powietrznej* (Air and Air Defence Forces of Poland) have adopted a policy of modernising existing equipment to become NATO-compatible, while engaging in exercises with western European nations when possible. The strong fighter force is spearheaded by the MiG-29, of which 12 were bought initially. To these were added another nine from the Czech Republic, in return for W-3 helicopters. Poland has a competent aviation industry which has produced helicopters (Mi-2, W-3), trainers (TS-11 and PZL-130 Orlik) and light transports (An-2 and An-28).

Main types in inventory
Fighter/attack: MiG-29,
  MiG-23, MiG-21, Su-22
Transports: An-2, An-26,
  An-28, Tu-154, Yak-40
Trainers: PZL-130, TS-11
Helicopters: Mi-2, Mi-8/17,
  Mi-14, Mi-24, W-3, Bell 412

The *Lotnictwo Marynarki Wojennej* (Polish naval aviation) uses helicopters such as the W-3 and Mi-14, and the fixed-wing An-28, to patrol the Baltic coast. It also operates fighter/attack types (MiG-21, TS-11). The *Lotnictwo Wojsk Lodowych* (army aviation) is a rotary-wing operator, the Mi-24 'Hind' gunship being its main asset, backed by Mi-8/17 assault transports.

Portugal

The delivery of a second batch of ex-USAF F-16s has allowed the *Força Aérea Portuguesa* to retire its A-7 Corsairs. Two squadrons of F-16s fly from Monte Real, and in 1999 took part in Operation Allied Force. With a large maritime responsibility (which includes the Azores and Madeira), the Orion fleet is an important one, ably assisted by CASA 212s in a variety of survey roles. The trainer fleet received a major boost with the delivery of 50 ex-Luftwaffe Alpha Jets in 1993, which are also used operationally in the light attack role. The small naval

Main types in inventory
Fighter/attack: F-16, Alpha Jet
Transport/patrol: P-3, CASA
  212, C-130, Falcon 20/50
Trainers: Epsilon, Cessna 337,
  Alpha Jet
Helicopters: SA 330, Alouette III,
  Lynx

aviation component has five Super Lynxes for ASW duties from three frigates.

Qatar

This Gulf state has turned to France for combat equipment in recent years, its current fighter squadron flying the Mirage 2000-9, backed up by Alpha Jets in the training/light combat role. The Commando is the main helicopter type, used for assault transport and in the maritime role, for which it can carry Exocet anti-ship

Main types in inventory
Fighter: Mirage 2000
Trainer: Alpha Jet
Helicopters: Gazelle, Commando

missiles. There is also a sizeable Royal Flight equipped with VIP types.

Romania

Romania was only ever a half-hearted member of the Warsaw Pact, and although it received much of the standard Soviet-supplied equipment, its strong indigenous aviation industry also provided additional types in association with non-WarPac nations. The Alouette III and Puma helicopters have been built under licence, while IAR and SOKO of Yugoslavia jointly developed the IAR-93 Orao attack aircraft. An ambitious plan to build a version of the Bell AH-1 Cobra, to be known as the AH-1RO Dracula, foundered in the late 1990s. Nevertheless, the state industry has proceeded with two major upgrade programmes in association with Israeli suppliers to create the MiG-21 Lancer (available in air defence or multi-role variants) and the new MiG-29 Sniper upgrade, which also involves DASA of Germany. The IAR-330 Puma has also been updated with Israeli equipment. Of totally indigenous

Main types in inventory
Fighter/attack/recon: MiG-29, MiG-23, MiG-21 Lancer, IAR-93, IAR-99, Harbin H-5, An-30
Transports: An-24, An-26, Boeing 707, C-130, Tu-154, An-2
Trainers: L-29, L-39, Iak-52
Helicopters: IAR-316 (Alouette III), IAR-330 (Puma), Mi-14 (navy)

design, although available with a high Israeli avionics content, is the IAR-99 Soim, an advanced trainer and light attacker. These programmes aim to 'Westernise' the force without the expensive procurement of new types. At the other end of the spectrum, Romania continues to operate a handful of Harbin H-5s (Ilyushin Il-28s), relics of the early Cold War days.

Russia

Following the dissolution of the Soviet Union, the Russian federation was formally established on 7 May 1992. Through the 1990s, as the huge nation struggled to come to terms with a new, capitalist economy, the defence forces could scarcely find the funds to keep operating, and procurement took a back seat. Although the sophisticated arms industry continued to develop new types, the forces themselves were cut back dramatically, and looked to improve, rather than replace, their equipment. However, by 2000, increased funding had been promised, no doubt fuelled by the bloody war fought against Chechen rebels in 1999.

The previously separate air force (VVS) was merged with the IA-PVO air defence organisation and their assets integrated into a new VVS. While the numbers of combat aircraft are sharply down on pre-1990 levels, it is mostly the older types such as the MiG-21/23 and Su-17 that have been retired, leaving a force dominated by the MiG-29 and Su-27 fighters, and Su-24/25 attackers. The strategic bomber force of Tu-22M, Tu-95 and Tu-160 remains intact, although operational levels are affected by lack of spares and crew training time.

New equipment is being worked on, in the shape of a new air superiority fighter (for which Mikoyan and Sukhoi have produced technology demonstrators – the 1.44 and S-37), a Tu-22M replacement (Sukhoi T-60), a lightweight fighter, advanced trainer (MiG-AT and Yak-130) and other projects. However, progress on these programmes has been slow, more effort being expended in the upgrade and development of the MiG-29 (as the MiG-29SMT and MiG-29UBT) and Su-27, the latter having spawned a large family of variants. The Su-34 with side-by-side seating is set to replace the Su-24 as a strike/attack platform.

Main types in VVS inventory
Bombers: Tu-22M, Tu-95, Tu-160
Fighter/attack: MiG-23, MiG-25, MiG-27, MiG-29, MiG-31, Su-17, Su-24, Su-25, Su-27, Su-30
Patrol/recce/EW etc: A-50, Tu-22, Su-24MR, MiG-25R, Il-18/20/22
Transports: An-2, An-12, An-22, An-24, An-26, An-32, An-72, An-124, Il-62, Il-76/78, Il-86, Tu-134, Tu-154, LET 410
Trainers: L-29, L-39, Yak-18, Yak-52
Helicopters: Mi-2, Mi-8/17
Main types in AVMF inventory
Bombers/fighters: Su-33, Su-17, Su-24, Su-25, Su-27, Tu-22M
Patrol/EW etc: Il-38, Tu-142, Be-12
Transports: An-12, An-24, An-26, An-72
Helicopters: Ka-25, Ka-27, Ka-29, Mi-8, Mi-14
Main types in SV-AA inventory
Mi-2, Mi-6/22, Mi-8/17, Mi-24, Mi-26, Ka-50, An-2

The AVMF (naval aviation) has received more attention, now fielding a full-size carrier with an air wing built around the Su-33 naval 'Flanker'. It retains a large land-based patrol fleet with Il-38s and Tu-142s and land-based fighter/attack regiments with Su-24s, -25s and -27s.

The SV-AA (ground forces - army aviation) is a massive organisation equipped almost exclusively with Mil helicopters. Many of these are near or at the end of their lives, and new equipment is urgently needed. The Ka-50 and Mi-28 gunships are under trial for the attack mission, while the Ka-60 and Mi-38 are being considered as Mi-8 replacements.

Saudi Arabia

Major procurement programmes have seen the Royal Saudi Air Force grow to become one of the largest in the region, although recent economic setbacks have curtailed purchases, including around 150 F-16s to replace the F-5. The fighter force consists of five squadrons of F-15C/Ds and a single unit operating the Tornado ADV, while the attack capability comes from three Tornado IDS units and a single F-15S squadron. F-5s augment this main force, and are supported by E-3 Sentries in the AWACS role and KC-130 tankers. The training fleet was provided by British Aerospace in the form of the Pilatus PC-9 and Hawk Mk 65. Transport is the province of the C-130, the fleet including several special-mission aircraft. Of the rotary-wing fleet, the most notable aircraft are the AS 532 Cougars recently acquired for the combat rescue role.

The Royal Saudi Navy Force has a small but potent helicopter unit equipped with Exocet-carrying Cougars and AS 15-armed Panthers, while the Royal Saudi Land

Main types in RSAF inventory
Fighter/attack: F-15C/D, F-15S,
  Tornado ADV, Tornado IDS, F-5
Reconnaissance/AEW: RF-5,
  Tornado IDS, E-3A
Tanker/transport: KE-3A,
  C/KC-130, Boeing 707, CN.235
Trainers: Cessna 182, PC-9, Hawk, Jetstream
Helicopters: AB 205, AB 206, AB 212, KV-107, AS 532
Main types in RSLF inventory
Bell 406, AS 365 Dauphin, AH-64, UH-60
Main types in RSNF inventory
AS 565 Panther, AS 532 Cougar

Forces have a growing helicopter fleet based on US Army lines, primarily equipped with the Bell 406 Combat Scout for observation/light attack, the UH-60 for assault and the AH-64 for heavy attack. The government also maintains a large fleet of transports, including many airliner variants.

Serbia (Yugoslavia)

Following the 1999 NATO air campaign over Serbia and Montenegro, the state of the RViPVO (air force and air defence force) is difficult to assess. In 2000, some aircraft were shown to the world, including G-4s and MiG-21s. It is likely that some numbers of all types survived the war, even a few MiG-29s, despite NATO claims that they had all been destroyed. A number of helicopters were transferred to the police (MUP), including Mi-24 'Hinds' which were noted in action in Kosovo prior to the NATO intervention.

Main types in inventory
Fighter/attack: MiG-29, MiG-21,
  J-22 Orao
Transports: An-2, An-26, Yak-40
Trainers: G-2 Galeb, G-4 Super
  Galeb, UTVA-75
Helicopters: Mi-8, Mi-24, Gazelle

The small naval air component, with Ka-25s and Mi-14s, is believed to have ceased operations in 1998.

Singapore

Tiny in size but huge in wealth, the island state of Singapore spends a vast amount of money on defence. Its size and proximity to other nations creates a unique set of defence problems, requiring that it maintains a technological advantage over its neighbours. The fighter force consists primarily of F-16s, recent orders having swollen the fleet considerably. Among the aircraft are F-16D two-seaters with additional avionics in the spine, which are believed to have a defence suppression role. F-5s and A-4s augment the F-16s in the fighter and attack roles. Early warning of attack is vital to Singapore's defence, making the E-2 Hawkeyes of 111 Squadron among the nation's most important assets.

Owing to the lack of available airspace, most training is 'exported', being conducted in Australia (Cougar and advanced training on S.211s), France (tactical combat training on A-4s) and the United States (KC-135, F-16 and CH-47). A new fighter in the class of Rafale or Eurofighter is being sought.

Main types in inventory
Fighter/attack: F-16, F-5, A-4
AEW/patrol: Fokker 50, E-2
Tanker/transports: KC-135,
  KC-130, C-130, Fokker 50
Trainer: S.211
Helicopters: AH-64, AS 332,
  AS 550, UH-1, CH-47

Slovakia

The Slovak air force was created when the Czech and Slovak Republics dissolved their union on 1 January 1993. The former Czechoslovak air force was divided between the two new nations along a roughly 2:1 split in favour of the Czech Republic. However, Slovakia received none of the MiG-23s, but took half (10) of the MiG-29s. To these were added another 14 aircraft from Russia as part of a debt repayment scheme. These equip two fighter squadrons at Sliac. The other main tactical base is

Main types in inventory
Fighter/attack: MiG-29, MiG-21,
 Su-22, Su-25
Transports: An-24, An-26,
 LET 410, Tu-154, Yak-40
Trainers: L-29, L-39
Helicopters: Mi-2, Mi-8/17, Mi-24

Malacky, home to the ground attack element which flies Su-22s and Su-25s.

Slovenia

On 25 June 1991 Slovenia became the first ex-Yugoslav republic to declare its independence. The first military aircraft of the 15 Brigade, Territorial Defence Force, was a Gazelle which defected from the main Yugoslav forces. The fleet has now standardised on the Bell 412 as its primary transport/rescue helicopter, assisted by the Bell 206. Fighter equipment is sought, the F-16 being the most likely candidate, but until they arrive the fixed-wing fleet

Main types in inventory
Fixed-wing: PC-9, Zlin 142, Zlin
 242, PC-6', LET 410
Helicopters: Bell 412, Bell 206

relies on the PC-9. These aircraft have been upgraded by Radom of Israel to offer a comprehensive light attack/weapons training facility, allowing pilots to maintain currency.

South Africa

Despite a considerable contraction in size in recent years, and the retirement of the Mirage F1 fleet, the South African Air Force remains the most powerful in southern Africa. The fighter force relies on the Atlas Cheetah, a radically improved Mirage III. These are to be replaced by the Saab Gripen, South Africa becoming the first export customer for the multi-role state-of-the-art fighter. Boeing 707s are used for Sigint and tanking, as well as long-range transport. The other main combat element of the SAAF is the Rooivalk gunship helicopter, which was developed by Denel. Another local product is the Oryx, a

Main types in inventory
Fighter/attack: Cheetah
Transports: Boeing 707, C-
 130, BAe 125, C-47, King Air
 200, CASA 212, CN-235,
 Cessna 185, Cessna 208.
 Falcon 50/900, PC-12
Trainers: PC-7, Impala
Helicopters: Rooivalk, Oryx, Alouette III, BK 117

helicopter based on the Super Puma. Maritime patrol is accomplished using turboprop-powered Douglas C-47s

Spain

The combat force of the *Ejército del Aire* (air force) is built around the F-18 Hornet and Mirage F1, with reconnaissance support provided by RF-4E Phantoms and EW support from a modified 707. The Boeing transport is also available for tanking, as are KC-130s. The fighter fleet is eagerly awaiting the arrival of the Eurofighter EF 2000. Northrop F-5s have been retired from front-line duties and now serve as lead-in fighter trainers. The *Arma Aérea de la Armada Española* (Spanish naval air arm) operates EAV-8Bs from a single carrier, and ASW helicopters from Spanish navy vessels. The *Fuerzas Aeromoviles del Ejército de Tierra* (army aviation) is an entirely rotary-wing force, using the Super Puma/Cougar for assault, CH-47 for heavylift and the BO 105 for both the scouting and attack roles, employing HOT missiles in the latter.

Main types in EdA inventory
Fighter/attack: F-18, Mirage F1
Patrol/EW/recce: P-3, F27MPA,
 Boeing 707, RF-4
Tanker/transport: Boeing 707,
 KC/C-130, C.212, CN-235,
 Falcon 20/50/900, CL-215,
 Citation, Do 27
Trainers: F-5B, C-101, T-35 Pillán, F33 Bonanza,
 B55 Baron
Helicopters: AS 332, AS 532, S-76, Hughes 269
Main types in AAAE inventory
Fixed-wing: EAV-8B, Citation
Helicopters: AB 212, SH-3, S-70B, Hughes 500
Main types in FAMET inventory
BO 105, UH-1, AS 532, CH-47, OH-58

Sri Lanka

The Sri Lanka Air Force is actively engaged in the long struggle with the LTTE (Liberation Tigers of Tamil Eelam), and its inventory has been built up considerably in recent years, from a variety of sources. Israel supplied Kfirs, while China provided F-7s. The Mi-24 gunships, acquired from the Ukraine, have born the brunt of the fighting, although even trainers like the SF.260 have been used. Four Pucarás arrived from Argentina, and were heavily used, although two were written off and one grounded.

Main types in inventory

Fighter/attack: Chengdu F-7, Kfir, Pucará
Maritime patrol: King Air 200, Cessna 337
Transports: HS748, Y-8 (An-12), An-32, An-24, Cessna 421, Y-12
Trainers: SF.260, Cessna 150, Guizhou FT-7
Helicopters: Bell 206, Bell 212, Bell 412, Mi-24, Mi-17

Sudan

In recent times Sudan's political alignments have varied widely, with the result that its air force has been assembled from many sources, beginning with Soviet aid, before the US and Saudi Arabia became the main suppliers. Libya followed, as did Iraq, before equipment arrived from China and Iran. Many of the aircraft have been lost in the many civil wars.

Main types in inventory

Fighter/attack: F-7, MiG-21, MiG-23BN, Shenyang F-5/FT-5, Shenyang F-6/FT-6
Transports: An-24, An-32, DHC-5, DHC-6, C-130, Y-8
Helicopters: AB 212, BO 105, IAR-330, Mi-8, Mi-24

Sweden

For Sweden's *Flygvapnet* (air force), the future is Gripen. The JAS 39 will replace all Viggens in the next few years, having already displaced the last Drakens. For the time being, Viggens remain in the fighter (JA 37) and attack/reconnaissance (AJS/AJSF 37) roles. A few two-seaters have recently been converted to SK 37E standard to perform the EW training/escort jamming role. Sweden has adopted a high-technology approach to its airpower, the highly capable Gripen being a prime example of this small nation's technical prowess. Equally impressive is the development of the Erieye AEW system, which is carried by Saab 340s (as S 100Bs). Another important system is the S 102B Korpen, a much-modified Gulfstream IV used for electronic reconnaissance. Gripen, Argus and Korpen are integrated into a total defensive system which includes ground stations and dispersed off-base operating locations.

Main types in inventory

Fighter/attack: JAS 39, JA 37, AJS 37
Reconnaissance/AEW/EW:
S 100B Argus (Saab 340), S 102B Korpen (Gulfstream IV), AJSF 37 Viggen, SK37E Viggen, SH 89 (CASA 212)
Transports: TP 84 (C-130), TP 100 (Saab 340), TP 101 (King Air), TP 102 (Gulfstream IV)
Trainer: SK 60 (Saab 105)
Helicopters: HKP 4 (KV-107), HKP 5 (Hughes 300), HKP 6 (AB 206), HKP 9 (BO 105), HKP 10 (Super Puma), HKP 11 (AB 412)

Swedish helicopter operations (SAR, army support, anti-armour and ASW/coastal patrol) are now administered by a single joint-service command.

Switzerland

Fiercely neutral, Switzerland maintains a capable defensive force and a large reservist force with a high state of readiness. After a protracted national debate, Switzerland ordered 34 F-18 Hornets to be its principal fighter, these being armed with AMRAAM missiles. Their delivery allowed the retirement of the Mirage IIIS interceptors, although a few IIIRS reconnaissance aircraft remain. The second fighter type is the F-5E. Swiss aircraft practice operating from bare-base locations hidden in deep mountain valleys, even using motorways as

Main types in inventory

Fighter/attack/reconnaissance:
F-18, F-5, Mirage IIIRS
Transport: PC-6, Learjet, Falcon 50
Trainers: PC-7, PC-9, Hawk
Helicopters: AS 332, Alouette III

runways. Some bases have cave hangars carved out of mountains. A requirement now stands for a small number of transports to support overseas detachments.

Syria

Almost exclusively equipped with Soviet equipment, the *Al Quwwat Al Jawwiya Al Arabiya As'Souriya* (Syrian air force) suffered badly at the hands of the Israelis in the 1982 war. Apart from recent deliveries such as the Su-24/27 fleet, equipment is in generally poor condition. Transport is usually performed by aircraft wearing Syrianair colours, types including the An-26 and Il-76

Main types in inventory
Fighter/attack: MiG-21, MiG-23, MiG-25, MiG-29, Su-20, Su-22, Su-24, Su-27
Trainers: L-29, L-39, SIAT 223, MiG-15UTI, Mushshak
Helicopters: Gazelle, Mi-2, Mi-6, Mi-8/17, Mi-24, Ka-25, Mi-14

Taiwan

Facing the might of Communist China across the Formosa Strait, the Republic of China Air Force is organised along USAF lines. Massive procurement in the 1990s saw the RoCAF acquire a large fleet of modern fighters, allowing it to maintain a qualitative, if not quantitative edge over its giant neighbour and rival. AIDC designed and developed the Ching-kuo fighter, of which 130 have been procured. This indigenous project (together with locally developed Sky Sword 1/2 missiles) has not been without difficulty, but the result is a competent fighter of which more would have been built had not Taiwan had the chance to purchase a huge batch of F-16s. Altogether, 150 F-16A/Bs were bought, along with AIM-7 Sparrow missiles and ECM pods. The F-16s are to Block 20 standard, with many features of the USAF's latest standard Block 50. Shortly after the F-16 deal, Taiwan also ordered a batch of 48 Mirage 2000-5 fighters, complete with MICA and Magic missiles, and advanced RDY multi-target radar. A number of the once-predominant F-5E are being upgraded by AIDC to act as lead-in trainers and emergency fighters.

Main types in RoCAF inventory
Fighter/attack: Ching-kuo, F-16, F-5, Mirage 2000, AT-3,
Recce/AEW/EW: RF-5, E-2, C-130
Transports: C-130, Boeing 727, Beech 1900, Fokker 50
Trainers: AT-3, T-34
Helicopter: S-70C

Main types in RoCNA inventory
S-2 Tracker, MD500, S-70C

Main types in RoCAA inventory
AH-1, OH-58, UH-1, CH-47, TH-55, TH-57, O-1

The Republic of China Naval Aviation is a small shipborne ASW helicopter force employing Hughes 500s, unusually fitted with MAD equipment, and the S-70C(M)-1 Thunderhawk, similar to the US Navy's SH-60.

The Republic of China Army Aviation is organised along US Army lines, and has similar equipment (except for Apaches), including OH-58D scout helicopters.

Thailand

The Royal Thai Air Force's procurement plans, which had included an order for eight F/A-18C/D, were hit hard by the Asian economic crisis, resulting in the cancellation of the Hornet order. The F-16 and F-5 remain the principal fighters, with ex-USAF F-16s now being supplied to bolster the original batches. One of the two F-5 squadrons is an air combat training unit. Ex-*Luftwaffe* Alpha Jets have also been acquired from 2000 to bolster the close support/weapons training fleet, which also includes L-39s.

The Royal Thai Naval Air Division operates a single carrier with ex-Spanish navy Harriers, while A-7 Corsairs form a powerful shore-based attack force. The seas around Thailand are patrolled by Orions, F27s and Do 228s. The Royal Thai Army Air Division is largely helicopter-equipped, although a fleet of fixed-wing transports provides support. The AH-1 is the most potent weapon in its inventory. In addition to the three regular services, there is a border police air wing and an agricultural air division.

Main types in RTAF inventory
Fighter/attack: F-16, F-5, AU-23, OV-10, L-39, Alpha Jet
Transports: C-130, Basler Turbo 67, HS748, G222, A310, Boeing 737, Merlin, Learjet, Arava, Nomad
Trainers: T-41, SF.260, Airtrainer, T-37, PC-9
Helicopters: S-58, UH-1, AS 332, Bell 412

Main types in RTNAD inventory
Fighter/attack: AV-8, A-7
Patrol/transport: P-3, F27MPA, Do 228, Cessna 337, N-24 Nomad, CL-215
Helicopters: S-70B, UH-1, Bell 212, Bell 214

Main types in RTAAD inventory
Fixed-wing: Maule M-7, O-1, T-41, U-17, Cessna U-27, Shorts 330, CASA 212, Jetstream 41, Beech 1900, King Air 200
Rotary-wing: AH-1, CH-47, Hughes 300, Bell 206, Bell 212, UH-1

Tunisia

Arguably the most stable of the North African states, Tunisia nevertheless is facing growing internal security problems. The US and France are the principal arms suppliers, although when Tunisia required a new advanced trainer/light attacker it turned to the Czech L-59. The elderly MB.326K single-seat attacker is still in use.

Main types in inventory
Fighter/attack: F-5, MB.326K
Transports: C-130, LET 410
Trainers: MB.326, L-59, SF.260
Helicopters: AB 205, Alouette II,
    Alouette III, AS 350, Bell 205,
    UH-1

Turkey

Traditional enmity with Greece showed signs of receding in 2000, following mutual earthquake assistance after natural disasters in the region. However, Turkey maintains a strong air arm (the *Türk Hava Kuvvetleri*) which, like that of Greece, is shaking off the label of being Europe's dumping ground for obsolete aircraft in favour of modern equipment. Cornerstone of the rebuilding is the F-16, which is being built under licence by TAI. A total of 240 has been procured, allowing the formation of 10 squadrons and the retirement of the elderly F-104 Starfighter. Six squadrons still fly the F-4E Phantom, although the fleet is being upgraded in association with Israeli contractors, and the F-5A clings on to service. Tactical reconnaissance is performed by two squadrons flying the RF-4E, including aircraft delivered from Germany.

As well as the Greek dimension, Turkey also faces continuing internal unrest from Kurdish separatists in its eastern region. Helicopter use is intense, resulting in the purchase of AS 532s for several Turkish services. The army aviation (*Türk Kara Kuvvetleri*) employs the new Cougars, along with a force built mainly of UH-1

Main types in THK inventory
Fighter/attack/recce: F-16, F-4,
    RF-4, F-5
Tanker/transports: KC-135,
    C-130, C-160, CN-235,
    Citation, Gulfstream
Trainers: T-37, T-38, T-41, SF.260
Helicopters: UH-1, AS 532
Main types in TDH inventory
CN.235, AB 204, AB 212, TB 20 Trinad
Main types in TKK inventory
Fixed-wing: T-41, Citabria, U-17, King Air 200
Rotary-wing: AH-1, UH-1, S-70A, AS 532, Bell
    206, AB 212

derivatives and S-70A Black Hawks. Cessna U-17s are used for liaison. The small naval aviation element (*Türk Donama Havaciligi*) has recently acquired CN.235MPAs with which it can resume the patrol work temporarily abandoned when its S-2 Trackers were grounded. The Turkish coast guard and police force also operate aircraft, the latter including the S-70A and Mi-17 in its inventory.

Ukraine

Following the dissolution of the Soviet Union, the Ukraine was declared independent on 24 August 1991. Its armed forces assumed control of the former Soviet forces stationed on its territory, which consisted of three Frontal Aviation air armies, two Strategic Air Armies, two Air Defence air armies, two Military Transport divisions, army units of three Military Districts and part of the Black Sea Fleet. The organisation follows that employed previously, although the frontal and air defence forces were merged to become the *Viys'kovo-Povitryani Syly*. The MiG-25 and Su-15 were retired, while the strategic bomber fleet of 19 Tu-160 'Blackjacks' and Tu-95MS 'Bear-Hs' was either scrapped (with US funding) or returned to Russia. The Ukraine retains the Tu-22 and Tu-22M long-range bombers, although the serviceability of the former is questionable. Augmenting them is a large force of Su-24 'Fencers', including reconnaissance and EW variants, while air defence is the province of the MiG-23, MiG-29 and Su-27. Much of the transport force (especially the

Main types in inventory
Bombers: Tu-22, Tu-22M
Fighter/attack: MiG-23, MiG-29,
    Su-17, Su-24, Su-25, Su-27
Patrol/recce/EW etc: An-30,
    Be-12, Il-22, Su-17M4R,
    Su-24MP, Su-24MR
Transports: An-12, An-24, An-26, Il-76/78, Tu-134
Trainers: L-39, Yak-52, Yak-55, PZL-104 Wilga
Helicopters: Ka-25, Ka-27, Ka-29, Mi-2, Mi-6/22,
    Mi-8/17, Mi-14, Mi-24, Mi-26

Il-76s) operates in quasi-civil colours, undertaking commercial charters. The army is well-equipped with a range of Mil products, including command post and EW variants. The small naval aviation element has a few coastal patrol helicopters, and still uses the Be-12 amphibian. In addition to these forces, there is a National Guard (with Mi-6s, -8s and -24s) and a government aero club organisation (TSOU).

United Arab Emirates

Of the seven Gulf states which form the United Arab Emirates, only Abu Dhabi and Dubai provide an air component to the UAE Air Force, of which Abu Dhabi is by far the senior. With large oil revenues, and faced with tension with both Iran and Iraq, the UAE has adopted a high-tech approach to its air force, resulting in several major purchases. The most recent of these is the decision to acquire 80 F-16 Block 60 aircraft and state-of-the-art weapons, this coming on the heels of an order for Dassault Mirage 2000-5 Mk II fighters and the decision to upgrade the existing Mirage 2000s to the same standard. These are ably backed by Hawk trainers which, in the Hawk 102 version, can also be used for ground attack. Potent attack helicopters are available in the form of the AH-64 Apache. The UAE is anxious to become more internationally involved, and Apaches were sent to operate alongside US Army aircraft with the Kosovo peacekeeping force. As well as the air force, the UAE has a small naval aviation component employing Eurocopter AS 565 Panthers and AS 532 Cougars.

Main types in inventory
Fighter/attack: Mirage 2000,
  Mirage 5, Hawk 102
Transports: C-130, Skyvan,
  CN.235
Trainers: Hawk 61/63, PC-7,
  Grob G115, MB 326, SF.260
Helicopters: AH-64, AS 532, SA 330,
  SA 342, BO 105, AS 350, AS 365/565,
  Bell 206, Bell 214

United Kingdom

A dramatic downsizing after the end of the Cold War has left the Royal Air Force as a much leaner organisation than before, yet it is committed to major procurement programmes for its future equipment. The most important of these is the Eurofighter, of which 232 are on order to replace the Tornado F.3 and Jaguar. The Tornado GR.1 fleet is undergoing an update programme to GR.4 standard which will see it serve until replaced by the outcome of the current FOAS studies. Other important current programmes are the modernisation of the Hercules transport fleet with the C-130J (Hercules C.Mk 4/5), the introduction of the Merlin to replace the Wessex and Puma in the support helicopter fleet, and the leasing of four C-17s from 2001 to augment the strategic airlift fleet. For the future, in addition to FOAS, the UK is eyeing two new carriers to replace the Navy's current 'Invincible'-class 'Harrier-carriers'. These will carry new fighter equipment, for which the JSF is the main candidate, and a new AEW platform, possibly based on the V-22 Osprey. The UK is a full partner in the JSF programme, this type having also been viewed as a possible replacement for the Harrier fleet.

The UK has fully embraced the ideas of 'jointness' and privatisation in an attempt to stretch the defence budget further. The RAF's Harriers and Royal Navy's Sea Harriers now operate as a joint command, reflecting the mixed carrier air wings fielded for peacekeeping operations, while the battlefield helicopters of the RAF, RN and Army Air Corps are administered by a Joint Helicopter Command,

Main types in RAF inventory
Fighter/attack: Tornado F.3,
  Tornado GR.1/4, Jaguar, Harrier
Patrol/recce etc: Nimrod MR.2,
  Nimrod R.1, Sentry, Canberra,
  Tornado GR.4A
Tanker/transports: Hercules,
  TriStar, VC10, BAe 146, Islander, BAe 125
Trainers: Hawk, Tucano, Jetstream, Dominie, Firefly,
  Grob 115, Bulldog
Helicopters: Chinook, Puma, Wessex, Sea King,
  Merlin, Griffin, Squirrel
Main types in RN inventory
Fixed-wing: Sea Harrier, Hawk, Jetstream, Grob G 115
Rotary-wing: Lynx, Sea King, Merlin, Dauphin
Main types in AAC inventory
Fixed-wing: Islander
Rotary-wing: Apache, Lynx, Gazelle, Bell 212, A.109

with rapid mobility as its watchword. The AAC is in the process of introducing the WAH-64 Longbow Apache, which significantly enhances the JHC's striking power.

Privatisation, a controversial issue, has made large inroads into the training organisation, with joint-service primary and rotary-wing training already being undertaken by private consortia. Planning for further training contracts is being undertaken. Another area being examined for privatised operation is the strategic airlift and refuelling mission, for which a requirement to replace the VC10 and TriStar has been identified.

United States

The US Air Force is the world's most powerful air arm, and maintains this position by following a course of procuring cutting-edge technology. Today's fighter force, largely composed of F-15 fighters, F-15E dual-role fighter-bombers and multi-role F-16s (including night attack F-16CGs and defence suppression F-16CJs), will under current plans be replaced by the F-22 Raptor and Joint Strike Fighter. The main striking force remains the large bomber fleet, with the B-2 Spirit 'stealth' bomber at the tip of the spear, augmented by Rockwell B-1B Lancers in the conventional bombing role, and the elderly yet still awesome B-52H, which can either be used as a launch platform for cruise missiles or as a free-fall bomber in benign air defence environments.

The 'high-tech' approach is very noticeable in the recce/EW arena, where the USAF operates RQ-1 Predator drones, the E-8 J-STARS ground surveillance platform, and RC-135 Rivet Joint electronic reconnaissance aircraft. The trainer fleet is undergoing an overhaul as the Raytheon T-6 is delivered to replace the Cessna T-37.

US Naval Aviation has three principal components, the embarked carrier force, ship-based ASW force and land-based maritime patrol force. Small ship operations are handled by the SH-60 Seahawk, while land-based patrols are the province of the large P-3 Orion fleet. On board the carriers the F/A-18 Hornet is the dominant type, although each carrier maintains at least one squadron of Tomcat fighters. These will slowly be ousted by the F/A-18E/F Super Hornet, which began to enter service in 2000. A naval version of the JSF is expected to be the Hornet's successor.

Marine Corps aviation is dedicated to the support of Marine troops during assaults. Hornets provide the main 'muscle', although the AV-8B Harrier can operate from assault carriers or makeshift beachhead bases to provide timely close support. The large helicopter fleet is being overhauled, the AH-1 Cobras and UH-1Ns being upgraded with new equipment, while the CH-46 Sea Knight force is to be replaced by the revolutionary tilt-wing V-22 Osprey.

The US Coast Guard is a full military service, with aviation detachments provided around the coast equipped

Main types in USAF inventory
Bombers: B-1, B-2, B-52
Fighter/attack: F-15,
  F-15E, F-16, F-117,
  A-10, AC-130
Recce/EW/AEW etc: E-3,
  E-4, E-8, E-9, U-2, EC-130, RC-135, RQ-1
Transports: C-5, C-9, C-12, C-17, C-20, C-21,
  C-25, C-26, C-32, C-37, C-130, C-141
Tankers: KC-10, KC-135, HC/MC-130
Trainers: T-1, T-6, T-37, T-38, T-43
Helicopters: HH-60, MH-53, UH-1
Main types in USN inventory
Fighter/attack: F-14, F/A-18, A-4, F-5
Patrol/AEW/EW etc: P-3C, EP-3, E-2, E-6, EA-6B,
  S-3B, RC-12
Transports: C-2, C-9, C-20, C-130, UC-12
Trainers: T-2, T-34, T-39, T-44, T-45
Helicopters: TH-57, HH-60, SH-60, H-46, MH-53
Main types in USMC inventory
Fighter/attack: F/A-18, AV-8B
EW: EA-6B
Transports: C/KC-130, C-20, C-9, UC-12, CT-39
Helicopters: CH-46, UH-1, CH-53, AH-1
Main types in USCG inventory
Fixed-wing: HC-130, HU-25, C-20
Rotary-wing: HH-60, HH-65
Main types in US Army inventory
Fixed-wing: C-12, C-23, RC-7, UC-35
Rotary-wing: AH-64, AH-1, UH-1, A/MH-6, UH-60,
  CH/MH-47, OH-58, TH-67

with Hercules and Guardians for patrol/survey, and HH-60 Jayhawks and HH-65 Dolphins for rescue duties. The USCG is also active, along with other agencies such as the Customs Service and DEA, in the continual war against drug-runners, a conflict which consumes a large portion of the defence budget.

Army Aviation is huge in terms of numbers of aircraft, with thousands of helicopters on charge. The AH-64 is the principal attack weapon, to be joined by the RAH-66 Comanche armed scout at some point in the future. The Army is also embarking on a major battlefield reconnaissance programme dubbed Airborne Common Sensor, which will place radar, Elint, Comint and other sensors on board a single airframe type which has yet to be chosen.

In keeping with their traditions, the US armed forces are constantly studying and developing new technologies. They lead the way in UCAV (uninhabited combat air vehicle) technology which may one day remove pilots from cockpits, and continue to develop the low-observables ('stealth') theme.

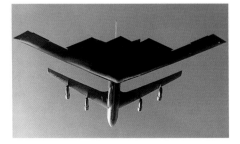

Venezuela

Venezuela has four separate military aircraft-operating agencies, the largest of which is the *Fuerza Aérea Venezolana* (Venezuelan air force). This air arm is unique in being the only force in Latin America to operate the F-16. Augmenting these aircraft are upgraded F-5s and Mirage 50s. A portion of the FAV fleet is assigned to COIN duties, using the OV-10 Bronco and UH-1. A large transport fleet encompasses a variety of types, of which the 707 and C-130 are the largest.

The naval air arm is divided between shore-based patrol aircraft, of which the CASA 212 is the most important, and shipborne ASW helicopters in the form of the AB 212. Agusta-built products also dominate the army's line-up, with four AS-61s providing assault transport alongside assorted UH-1s and Bell 412s. The *Fuerzas Armadas de Cooperación* are a group of quasi-military organisations which operate numbers of light transport aircraft and helicopters.

Main types in inventory
Fighter/attack: F-16, F-5, Mirage 50, OV-10
Transports: G222, C-130, Boeing 707, King Air 200, CASA 212, DHC-7, PZL M-28, Arava
Trainers: T-2 Buckeye, T-34, EMB-312
Helicopters: AS 332, UH-1, Bell 206, Bell 214, Bell 412, AB 212, AB 412, AS-61, A.109, AS 355

Vietnam

After the reunification of Vietnam in 1975, the Vietnamese People's Air Force was rebuilt using the North's MiG force combined with US types left over from the war. Since then the force has bought new aircraft from Russia, the most notable being the mighty 'Flanker'. In 2000 the fleet numbered 12, split between seven Su-27SK single-seaters and five Su-27UBK/Su-30K two-seaters. Another 24 are on order. This potent fighter is augmented in the air defence role by a considerable number of MiG-21s, while Su-22s undertake the main attack duties. A large rotary-

Main types in inventory
Fighter/attack: Su-27, MiG-21, Su-22
Transports: An-2, An-26
Trainer: L-39
Helicopters: Mi-6, Mi-8/17, Mi-24, Ka-25, Ka-28/32

wing force undertakes attack and assault duties on behalf of the army, and coastal patrol/SAR work. Transport tasks are undertaken by two units, one based in the north near Hanoi and another in the south near Ho Chi Minh City.

Zambia

Zambia's combat fleet has been assembled from Soviet and Chinese sources. Unconfirmed reports suggest that MiG-29s and Mi-24s have been acquired, these being used in neighbouring Congo. The MiG-21 force may also have been upgraded, possibly by Aerostar in Romania. The trainer inventory is made up of Chinese and Yugoslav types, while the helicopter force has been acquired from Agusta in Italy and the Soviet Union.

Main types in inventory
Fighter/attack: MiG-21, Shenyang F-6, Soko J-1 Jastreb
Transports: An-26, DHC-5, Do 28, Y-12, Yak-40
Trainers: Hongdu K-8, MB.326, Nanchang BT-6, SF.260, G-2 Galeb
Helicopters: AB 47, AB 205, AB 206, AB 212, Mi-8

Zimbabwe

Zimbabwe's small but effective air force relies on a single squadron of Chengdu F-7s for air defence, and a handful of elderly Hunters for ground attack. Relics of the Rhodesian bush war are the Cessna FTB337s, SF.260s and Alouette IIIs which were widely used in the attack role. The Hawks are used for training, but can also be fitted for light attack if required.

Main types in inventory
Fighter/attack: Hunter, Chengdu F-7, Cessna FTB337, SF.260
Transports: CASA 212, BN-2
Trainers: Hawk, Guizhou FT-7, SF.260
Helicopters: Alouette III, AS 532, AB 412

INDEX

GLOSSARY

AAM	Air-to-Air Missile	IAF	Indian Air Force	Sigint	Signals intelligence
AB	Air Base	IDF/AF	Israeli Defence Force/Air Force	SLAM	Stand-off Land Attack Missile
ABCCC	Airborne Battlefield Command and Control Center	IFF	Identification, Friend or Foe	SLAM-ER	Stand-off Land Attack Missile-Extended Range
ACC	Air Combat Command	IFR	In-Flight Refuelling	SLAR	Side-Looking Airborne Radar
ACM	Air Combat Manoeuvring	IIR	Imaging Infra-Red	SMD	Stand-off Munitions Dispenser
AEW	Airborne Early Warning	INAS	Inertial Navigation and Attack	SOA	Special Operations Aviation
AFB	Air Force Base	INAS	Indian Naval Air Station	SOM	Stand-Off Munitions
AFRC	Air Force Reserve Command	INS	Inertial Navigation System	SRAM	Short-Range Attack Missile
AFRES	Air Force REServe	IOC	Initial Operating Capability	SSN	Nucelar attack submarine
AFSOC	Air Force Special Operations Command	IR	Infra-Red	STO	Short Take-Off
AGM	Air-to-Ground Missile	IRADS	Infra-red acquisition and designation system	STOL	Short Take-Off and Landing
ALAT	Aviation Légère de l'Armée de Terre	IRIAF	Islamic Republic of Iran Air Force	STOVL	Short Take-Off and Vertical Landing
ALCM	Air-Launched Cruise Missile	IRST	Infra-Red Search and Track	TAC	Tactical Air Command
AMC	Air Mobility Command	ISAR	Imaging Synthetic Aperture Radar	TARPS	Tactical Airborne Reconnaissance Podded System
AMI	Aeronautica Militare Italiana	J-STARS	Joint Surveillance Target Attack		
AMRAAM	Advanced Medium-Range Air-to-Air Missile	JASDF	Japan Air Self-Defence Force	TBAP	Tyazhelyy Bombardirovochnyy Aviatsionnyy Polk: heavy bomber aviation regimen
ANG	Air National Guard	JASSM	Joint air-to-surface stand-off missile		
APACHE	Arme Propulsée A Charges Ejectables	JDAM	Joint Directed Air Munition	TERPROM	TERrain PROfile Matching
APU	Auxiliary Power Unit	JGSDF	Japan Ground Self-Defence Force	TFR	Terrain-Following Radar
ARM	Anti-Radiation Missile	JMSDF	Japan Maritime Self-Defence Force	TFW	Tactical Fighter Wing
ARNG	ARmy National Guard	JSF	Joint Strike Fighter	TIALD	Thermal Imaging Airborne Laser Designator
ASARS	Advanced Synthetic Aperture Radar System	JSOW	Joint Stand-Off Weapon	TINS	Tactical Inertial Navigation System
AShM	Anti-Ship Missile	JTIDS	Joint Tactical Information	TOW	Tube-launched, Optically-sighted, Wire-guided
ASM	Air-to-Surface Missile	LAMPS	Light Airborne Multi-Purpose System		
ASMP	Air-Sol Moyenne Portée	LANTIRN	Low-Altitude, Navigation and Targeting by Infra-red at Night	UAE	United Arab Emirates
ASRAAM	Advanced Short-Range Air-to-Air Missile	LASTE	Low-Altitude Safety and Targeting	UK	United Kingdom
ASV/AsuV	Anti Surface Vessel	LCD	Liquid Crystal Display	UN	United Nations
ASW	Anti-Submarine Warfare	LERX	Leading-Edge Root eXtensions	USAF	US Air Force
ATGM	Anti-Tank Guided Missile	LGB	Laser-Guided Bomb	USCG	US Coast Guard
ATM	Anti-Tank Missile	LII	Gromov Flight Institute	USMC	US Marine Corps
AWACS	Airborne Warning and Control System	LLLTV	Low-Light-Level TeleVision	USN	US Navy
BERP	British Experimental Rotor Programme	LOCAAS	Low-cost anti-armour submunition	USNR	US Naval Reserve
BVR	Beyond Visual Range	LOROP	LOng-Range Oblique Photography	USSR	Union of Soviet Socialist Republics
C²W	Command and Control Warfare	MAD	Magnetic Anomaly Detection	VHF	Very High Frequency
C³I	Command, Control, Communications, Intelligence	MFD	Multi-Function Display	VIP	Very Important Person
		MFI	mnogofunktseeonahl'nyy frontovoy istrebeetel: multi-role tactical fighter	VLF	Very Low Frequency
CAF	Canadian Armed Forces			VTA	Voenno-Transportnaya Aviatsiya
CAG	Commander, Carrier Air Wing	MICA	Missile d'Interception et de Combat Aérien: combat and air-intercept missile	VTO	Vertical Take-Off
CAP	Combat Air Patrol			VVS	Voenno-Vozdushnye Sili
CAS	Close Air Support	MLU	Mid-Life Update	WCMD	Wind Corrected Munitions Dispenser
CASEVAC	CASualty EVACuation	MSIP	Multi-Stage Improvement	WVR	Within Visual Range
CBU	Cluster Bomb Unit	MTOW	Maximum Take-Off Weight		
CEM	Combined Effects Munition	NACES	Naval Aircrew Common Ejection		
CIS	Commonwealth of Independent	NAS	Naval Air Station		
COIN	COunter-INsurgency	NATO	North Atlantic Treaty Organisation		
COMINT	COMmunications INTelligence	NBC	Nuclear, Biological, Chemical		
CONUS	CONtinental United States	NOE	Nap Of the Earth		
CRT	Cathode Ray Tube	NOTAR	NO Tail Rotor		
CTOL	Conventional Take-Off and Landing	NVG	Night Vision Goggles		
DLIR	Downward-Looking Infra-Red	OCU	Operational Conversion Unit		
EAP	Experimental Aircraft Programme	OCU	Operational Capability Upgrade		
ECCM	Electronic Counter-Counter Measures	OSF	Optronique Secteur Frontale		
ECM	Electronic CounterMeasures	OTH	Over The Horizon		
ECR	Electronic Combat Reconnaissance	PDLCT	Day/night (TV/thermal imaging) laser-designation pod produced by Thomson-CSF		
EFIS	Electronic Flight Instrumentation System				
Elint	Electronic intelligence	PGM	Precision-Guided Munitions		
EO	Electro-optical	PLA	People's Liberation Army		
ESM	Electronic Surveillance Measures	PLAAF	People's Liberation Army Air Force		
ESSS	External Stores Support System	PLANAF	People's Liberation Army Naval Air Force		
EW	Electronic Warfare	PLSS	Precision Location Strike System		
FAA	Fleet Air Arm	PVO	Protivovosduzhnaya Oborona –		
FAC	Forward Air Control	RAF	Royal Air Force		
FAV	Fuerza Aérea Venezolana	RAM	Radar Absorbent Material		
FBW	Fly-By-Wire	RHAW	Radar Homing And Warning		
FCS	Flight Control System	RMAF	Royal Malaysian Air Force		
FLIR	Forward-Looking Infra-Red	RNS	Russian Naval Ship		
FMRAAM	Future Medium-Range Air-to-Air Missile	RS	Reconnaissance Squadron		
FMS	Flight Management System	RWR	Radar Warning Receiver		
FOAS	Follow-On	SAC	Strategic Air Command		
GPS	Global Positioning System	SALT/START	Strategic Arms Limitation Talks/STrategic Arms Reduction Talks		
GvTBAP	Gvardeyskyy Tyazhelyy Bombardirovochnyy Aviatsionnyy Polk: Guards heavy bomber aviation regiment	SAM	Surface-to-Air Missile		
		SAR	Search And Rescue		
HARM	High-speed Anti-Radiation Missile	SARH	Semi-Active Radar Homing		
HDD	Head-Down Display	SATCOM	Satellite Communications		
HDU	Hose-Drum Unit	SCALP	Système de croisière conventional autonome à longue portée de précision: long-range precision cruise missile system		
HMMWV	High-Mobility Multi-purpose Wheeled Vehicle				
HOT	Haut subsonique Optiquement Téléguidé tiré d'un Tube	SEAD	Suppression of Enemy Air Defences		
HOTAS	Hands On Throttle And Stick	SFW	Sensor-Fuzed Weapon		
HUD	Head-Up Display				